The Path Through
GRIEF

The Path Through GRIEF

Marguerite Bouvard, Ph.D.
with Evelyn Gladu

Foreword by Sandra L. Bertman, Ph.D.
American Academy of Hospice and Palliative Medicine

A COMPASSIONATE GUIDE

Prometheus Books
59 John Glenn Drive
Amherst, New York 14228-2197

Published 1998 by Prometheus Books

Inquiries should be addressed to
Prometheus Books, 59 John Glenn Drive, Amherst, New York 14228–2197.
VOICE: 716–691–0133, ext. 207.
FAX: 716–564–2711.
WWW.PROMETHEUSBOOKS.COM

04 03 02 01 00   6 5 4 3

Library of Congress Cataloging-in-Publication Data

Bouvard, Marguerite Guzman, 1937–
    The path through grief : a compassionate guide / Marguerite Bouvard with Evelyn Gladu ; foreword by Sandra L. Bertman.
        p.   cm.
    Includes bibliographical references.
    ISBN 1–57392–189–0 (alk. paper)
    1. Grief. 2. Bereavement—Psychological aspects. 3. Death—Psychological aspects. I. Gladu, Evelyn. II. Title.
BF575.G7B674   1998
155.9′37—dc21   97–44051
                                                                      CIP

Printed in the United States of America on acid-free paper.

Contents

Part Two. When Someone Dies:
The Early Phases of Grief

Part Three. Losing a Loved One
Through Suicide or Homicide

Part Four. Losing a Loved One Through AIDS

Part Five. As Time Passes:
The Phase of Disorganization

Part Six. How We Can Help Ourselves

Part Seven. How Friends and Coworkers Can Help

Part Eight. Reaching the Other Side of Grief

Acknowledgments

The lines from "Of Grief" are reprinted from *Collected Poems, 1930–1973,* by May Sarton, by permission of the author and W. W. Norton, New York. Copyright © 1974 by May Sarton. "Visits" and "Flood" by Ruth Feldman from *The Ambition of Ghosts* by Ruth Feldman, Green River Press, University Center, Michigan, 1979. "When the Waters of Loss Rose" by Ruth Feldman, from *To Whom It May Concern,* William L. Bauhan, New Hampshire, 1986. "Grief" by Beatrice Hawley, from *Nothing Is Lost* by Beatrice Hawley, Applewood Press, Cambridge, Massachusetts, 1979, courtesy of John Jagel. "The Funeral" by David Citino, from *The Gift of Fire* by David Citino, University of Arkansas Press, Fayetteville, 1986. "Winter Rain" by Marguerite G. Bouvard, from *Of Light and Silence,* Zoland Books, Cambridge, Massachusetts, 1990. "Wanting a New Language" by Marguerite G. Bouvard, from *The Body's Burning Fields,* Wind Publications, Lexington, Kentucky, 1997.

With thanks to Jacques for his computer expertise and his support. With thanks to Bette for her encouragement.

With special gratitude to Michèle Cloonan and to my agent Mike Hamilburg for believing in this project.

With grateful acknowledgement to Mary Rosser, M.D.; Marilyn Ewer; Laurie Zwicky; Joanna J. Charnas, Group Program Coordinator of the AIDS Action Committee of Massachusetts Inc.; Elizabeth David of the AIDS Action Committee; Margaret Child; Tema Nason; Harriet and Dunlay McCord deButts; Chaplain Annie Lamuto; Fredda Zuckerman; and to all those who have shared their stories.

Foreword

"Remember only this one thing," said Badger. "The stories people tell have a way of taking care of them. If stories come to you, care for them. And learn to give them away where they are needed. Sometimes a person needs a story more than food to stay alive. That is why we put these stories in each other's memory. This is how people care for themselves.
B. Lopez, *Crow & Weasel*

Thirty years of teaching and training in the medical setting have convinced me that technology, pharmacology, and analytic theory are important, but that imagination, receptivity to the mysteries and meanings of a person's pain, and personal presence are the therapist's true resources. Poised on the brink of a new century we are moving toward a renewed appreciation of the early healing arts. In spite of scientific advances and groundbreaking technology, we are relearning that all of us need to be at the center of our own treatment.

The wisdom of Badger's remarks lies in the acknowledgment that stories and narratives are not only philosophically meaningful, they have a moral energy that is seductive and contagious. Seated in either chair of the therapist's office, we are invited by the tale told to become personally expressive, and in so doing, to relieve, perhaps, "relive" ourselves. What the therapist does is more a question of uncorking the creative potential that resides within us than providing a treatment. The marvelous bonus is that in so doing, the therapist is reflexively developing the creative possibilities latent in him- or herself.

For those of us in counseling, the personal accounts of so many different kinds of loss in *The Path Through Grief* tell us what to listen for. They tell us that truth cannot be taught, because in fact, for each pious message the exact opposite may be real for someone else. We must rid ourselves of preconceived judgments of the only "right" path a therapist can provide, instead listening for the ways our clients try to make sense of events, and reveal the meanings they attach to their experiences. Compassion, from the Latin, *com,* together and *pati,* to suffer, is the capacity to feel with another, to be able to enter another person's world and understand that experience from his or her perspective. When one of the persons in the narratives in *The Path Through Grief* hears "You're doing so well," he feels the question should have been rephrased to "What's wrong with you?"

I am delighted with the chapter on AIDS, in particular with Greg's narrative. I cannot wait to use this story with patients, support groups, and with medical and nursing professionals in hospital, hospice, and other therapeutic settings. Greg reminds us that it is not just the person living with AIDS, it is all of us—companion, family member, caregiver—who are living with AIDS and who are grieving throughout the course of this now long, chronic illness. This particular narrative is noteworthy because it is also about the bereavement that occurs before death. Furthermore, it is archetypal in the way it connects us to a distant past in our human consciousness. Is it coincidence that the one who died in Greg's story, "someone who loved me unconditionally and would have done the very same thing for me" was named Christian, that Greg's framework is so enlarged by the relationship, he has no intention of putting it behind him, that "it is a part of who[he is] and will always be" and finally that his quiet remembrance of Christian's birthday, for example, is a meaningful ritual.

The beauty of all the stories in this book is that they are presented to us firsthand. Can we believe Badger's words, that the stories told have a way of taking care of the tellers? Furthermore, can we appreciate, honor, and "care for them . . . learn[ing] to give them away where they are needed"?

Recovery from grief is a voyage in the dark; meandering detours, thickets, dead ends, cul-de-sacs, and occasional clearings. It is not straight and narrow, nor is the road well-traveled, because it is different for each of us. We would love a precise map, a template, a twelve-step-plan to a clear destination. In down-to-earth English, Bouvard and her collaborator have produced a practical guide, which includes such useful information as how to write letters to the bereaved, how to express one's own sorrow about someone else's loss, and how to demonstrate our concern and support to a friend, family member, or coworker. The narratives and the author's essays cover a wide spectrum of mortality whether or not anticipated, by illness, homicide, or suicide—the loss of a child, a lover, a friend. The narratives offered are "intended as mirrors in which we can see our stories, and which can diminish the feeling of loneliness so many of us face when we have lost someone," or, I would add, and as Greg's story qualifies, when we are losing or about to lose someone.

This book is valuable not only for those living in the depths of bereavement but also for the relatives, friends, coworkers, students, teachers for all of us who would benefit from a periodic review of the nature and dynamics of this kind of pain. We cannot be reminded too many times that anger, guilt, and sorrow are unpredictable and do not occur in an orderly sequence. They find their own ways of assaulting our hearts, in powerful and unexpected "sneak attacks." We need to be continually reminded that grief hits us at the very source of life; that "dosing oneself" with too much work, or turning to alcohol or sex is a way, albeit temporary, of numbing the pain. The firsthand accounts which punctuate this book remind us that grief breeds irrationality: like compulsions to tell a stranger "You look just like my wife who died," or being catapulted "from being a married woman to a time warp and the day before you got married—an adolescent" or refusing to change the bed in which a lover died.

All theories of recovery—stages, phases, circularities, or tasks— address the realities of adjusting to a changed life and a healing trajectory. This book makes no claim to offering an unalterable calendar for grief. What *The Path Through Grief* has given us are the tools to validate the pain of loss, to support others in the confusing relapses and stalemates of the process, and to trust that the process of grieving leads to greater psychological flexibility, resilience, and strength. The author's careful selection of narratives enriches our armamentariun by entrusting them to our memories so that we can more competently and confidently allow ourselves to join another on her or his pilgrimage, not as "guide" but as another, more seasoned, perhaps, pilgrim.

Sandra L. Bertman, Ph.D.—Professor of Humanities in Medicine University of Massachusetts Medical Center, Adjunct Professor, Graduate School of Nursing Faculty, New England AIDS Education & Training Center.

Introduction

Why This Book

Ihave always considered the most important aspect of my job as a college professor to be helping each student acknowledge and value his or her own experience and feelings. Therefore, I typically spend many hours talking to students in my office. It's in conjunction with these conversations with my students that I found them coming to me to discuss loss, the loss of parents, siblings, and friends. They came to my office to talk because the suffering they were experiencing seemed invisible to their friends and sometimes even to their families. Their feelings of anger, guilt, and despair seemed somehow unnatural to them. They had difficulty even admitting to themselves the intensity of their emotions. But I also discovered that this was a problem facing not only young adults. Many of my friends had experienced loss, and yet no one wanted to talk to them about their losses.

I decided to make a documentary film about grief based on the experience of a student of mine who had lost both parents and who was able to talk openly about her loss. I felt that seeing this young woman relate her experience would free others to express themselves and also minimize their sense of isolation. This film was the first step in a research project on grieving that I conducted over the past several years and which resulted in this book.

Part of my research was devoted to interviewing people who had expe-

17

rienced different kinds of loss. Some of these interviews are recorded as narratives within chapters of this book. Like the film, they are intended as mirrors in which we can see our own stories and which can diminish the loneliness so many of us face when we have lost someone. I wanted to be able to write a book that would not only help people who were experiencing grief, but would also put mourning in perspective, not as an aberration, but as part of our lives. I wanted to help not only those who were dealing directly with loss, but friends and acquaintances of the bereaved as well.

During my investigations of grief, I met Evelyn Gladu, director of the Omega Program in Somerville, Massachusetts, which provides emotional support services for the ill and bereaved. We found that we had similar outlooks and similar purposes and decided to collaborate on this book. I felt that her quiet understanding, her compassion, and her years of experience as counselor to the bereaved would bring a unique perspective to the project.

Why We Grieve Alone

While we have begun to admit the reality of death and dying in our culture, we have yet to publicly acknowledge the problems of the survivors and the importance of mourning. Recent films such as *Marvin's Room, Philadelphia,* and *It's My Party,* and plays such as *Angels in America,* have broken the taboo surrounding illness and created socially sanctioned images of illness and death, yet the plight of mourners remains invisible. After a death, we are left with disrupted lives and with months and often years of pain and suffering. We also suffer from loneliness, for in our contemporary society, we consider mourning to be morbid, something to be avoided at all costs. However, it is the denial of mourning that is unnatural and unprecedented in history.

The emotions associated with grief are very powerful and include anger, guilt, despair, and sadness. Imagine how they are heightened when society denies their very existence. Not only do we experience intense emotions when we grieve, but in addition, we are made to feel that somehow these emotions are inappropriate. Just when we are in need of social support, we find ourselves isolated, without a common ritual or even a language with which we can communicate our feelings to others.

When asked to list the major emotions we experience in our daily lives, very few people would include sadness or even consider it a powerful and enduring emotion. On the contrary, sadness is often regarded as an unacceptable sign of fragility or vulnerability. Therefore, the experience of sorrow may come as a great shock to us. We have not been prepared for its intensities by our education, by social ritual, or by the stream of publications and visual media that provide us with common experiences and fill so much of our lives.

Years ago when it was common to die at home, the close involvement of family members with the person's care and then the funeral and burial helped family members to view death as a natural part of the life cycle, not as something horrible to be avoided. The transformation of our view of death was part of the technological revolution, which ended a rural way of life and brought changes not only in lifestyle but also in ways of viewing illness. With the advances in modern medicine, death has come to be avoided at all costs as the enemy, the ultimate failure.

Not only death, but mourning as well was considered the province of the family and the community. In years past, a period of time was set aside for the purpose of mourning, and it was understood that during this period, the grieving person would be the object of special care and concern. The bereaved wore black to show that he or she was in mourning. A time of seclusion of the grieving was customary to allow the survivor to shelter his or her grief from the world and to wait until the pain diminished before returning to society. While no one would wish to return to wearing black, we still need to have others acknowledge our pain and to be with us during the difficult period of transition to a new life.

Today we still need to be able to communicate both the event of death and our own distress. It was common practice in the past to send announcements of the death of a loved one for those who lived far away and possibly to hang a bouquet of flowers on the front door to let neighbors know that a death had occurred. These served as social cues. Friends and neighbors would respond with various expressions of sympathy, letters, or visits. Today, the fact of death is communicated in the obituary column of newspapers, an impersonal though necessary gesture and one which may not elicit much response beyond attending the funeral. Although our social practices have changed, we still need a social acknowledgment of our sorrow and social rituals to accompany us as we traverse the phases of mourning.

It's as if our very consciousness of mourning has disappeared along with the rituals. In our contemporary society, we don't think about loss or grief. We prepare for happiness and success, not for personal catastrophe. The freedom and optimism which pervade our culture and which are so liberating are reinforced by our school curriculum. However, rarely is the other side of reality acknowledged, and it is only recently that colleges have begun to offer courses on death and dying. Usually these are included in psychology or sociology curricula and are intended for future health care providers. However, since everyone will experience the death of loved ones during his or her life, all students could benefit from learning about mourning. Even primary-school children could be introduced to loss and death in a way that corresponds to their special developmental needs. The fact is that the future we all dream of may hold loss and illness as well as joy and achievement. If these aspects of our life are introduced not as aberrations, but as part and parcel of the normal human journey, we will not be caught off guard and bewildered when we experience sorrow. Nor will we feel as if we have somehow failed.

In today's society, we all seem to believe that cheerfulness, a friendly face, a smile are socially necessary forms of behavior. Perhaps it's part of the Anglo-Saxon ethos to maintain a calm demeanor in all circumstances. While this style of behavior is certainly grounded in a deep courtesy for others, it can also be traced to uneasiness with deep-seated emotions. These deeper emotions can be less easily controlled and therefore are alarming. A doctor who had just emigrated from Russia once remarked that he found Americans phenomenally cheerful people. He was used to hearing melancholy complaints from his patients back home. However, in America, when he would ask even his gravely ill patients how they were doing, they always responded, "Just fine." So we often believe that we must answer, "I'm doing fine," when people query us after a loss or during an illness. However, we also need to learn how to acknowledge the profound pain that we all experience at certain times in our lives.

The range of emotions which are allowed social expression varies from culture to culture. In Latin societies, both sexes are allowed the release of tears in public. Greeks and Italians expect a very open show of emotions at funerals and are encouraged to express their grief during mourning. However, we tend to praise the person who shows control of his or her emotions. Perhaps anger or outrage are tolerable, but sadness embarrasses us. It reveals our fragility in a world in which we are always supposed to be in control.

We all try to draw a line between our private and our public lives. Certainly this is very necessary to protect the intimate details of our existence. However, this rule is difficult to apply to the very intense and disruptive emotions of grief, because these feelings may affect our working patterns and our sense of competence.

Another obstacle to learning about the emotions that will accompany us in our passage through the stages of life is the fact that death and illness occur in hospitals, out of sight. Science has not only reduced the mortality rate and alleviated the pain associated with illness, it has also brought us modern institutions of health care. We rarely learn about death and illness as part of family or community life because they occur apart from our daily routines and within institutions. Moreover, the influence of the family is minimal within these places.

Hospitals, where so many people die today, are places of cure, and hospital staff often have great difficulty communicating with dying patients and their families. They may be afraid of being caught up in emotional, dramatic situations with the patient or with his family and may prefer to carry on without acknowledging the fact of death. When my aunt was dying of cancer, my cousin, who is a doctor and who was treating her, made me promise not to tell her that she was dying. As she became permanently bedridden, she and I corresponded a few times a week, and her letters testified to the loneliness she felt during this period. She knew she was dying, yet because of the silence surrounding her, she felt compelled to keep silence herself and thus was unable to share her feelings and anxieties.

While the hospice movement is not a new phenomenon, the number of hospices in this country has risen to almost two thousand in the past few years. Hospices are unique institutions not only in providing palliative and spiritual care for the dying, but also in giving support to the family of the terminally ill person. Support groups working with families during the dying process can help them resolve unfinished issues of communication and in some instances plan funerals. Addressing family problems and conflicts before a death can ease the grieving process. While hospices vary in their practices, most of them sponsor bereavement support groups, some limited to a six- to eight-week period with the requirement that members attend each meeting, and others ongoing and less structured. Both provide grieving family members with a reassuring sense of continuity and support.

While this movement leads the way toward a more humane treatment of the dying and addresses the grief of family members, it is still limited to a relatively small population: there are too few hospices for the large population that could benefit from such services. Access to hospices is further limited by the requirements that an ill person have a physician-diagnosed six-month prognosis and a primary caregiver available. However, because our population is aging and particularly afflicted with terminal diseases, the hospice movement will have an important role not only in easing the passage toward death, but in healing the sorrow of survivors.

The culture of individualism and the weakening of social and extended family ties due to social mobility may have freed us to live, study, and work wherever we please without constraints. However, this freedom is not without costs. Religious ceremonies and many social rituals for bereavement have fallen into disuse. These rituals are part of the socialization process by which we learn about the roles we will assume in society. Without them, we must learn alone how to experience and incorporate sadness into our lives. It is an experience that will continually surprise us and add to the outrage we already feel in the face of death and its apparent injustice.

Given the great variety of religious practices in our society, mourning rituals as well as the whole question of the funeral service must frequently be decided on without the benefit of precedent. When my mother died, she was living in another city. The question arose of where to have the funeral, what type of service to have, and even what type of burial. I decided to have the funeral services in my town rather than in my mother's so that I could house family members who were coming from abroad. Many families are separated by long distances and practice different religions, so the location and type of service can be a difficult decision to make and might even become a source of conflict.

The ceremony of the funeral makes the reality of death a little more acceptable. It provides a safe and sheltering environment for those who were closest to the deceased. It is a time to express feelings and to receive support from others. Therefore, the type of service can have an important impact on the grieving family. The selection of eulogies and readings, the decisions of whether to have an open or closed casket, or whether to select cremation convey a very important sense of participation if all the family members are included. Depending on how it is handled, the funeral can be either an empty ceremony or a significant way of saying good-bye to the deceased. In the narratives that follow, we will find different types of funeral arrangements, and varying levels of comfort with them.

Today, it is becoming more common for the dying to express their wishes and actively participate in the preparation for their funeral service. In chapter 5, Eric discusses the funeral arrangements for his wife and how he honored her wishes. This is helpful not only to the dying, like Eric's wife, who receive acknowledgment from those who are close, but also to the family, who is given an opportunity to help carry out his or her wishes. In chapter 15, a young man dying of AIDS plans an elaborate memorial service with his friends. His family and friends regarded this as a gift because it gave them a sense of purpose after his death and helped them through their grief. But in another story, Greg's partner requested that no services be held after his death, and Greg suffered greatly from the lack of social support rituals provide.

Last spring I attended funeral services for a friend of mine who was a poet. She had arranged the service with her pastor, and he read several of her poems during the eulogy and shared significant moments of her life. Afterward, there was a receiving line of relatives which allowed all those who attended to express their condolences in person.

Most recently, unusual public memorials have helped link public and private expressions of grief, most particularly in the AIDS quilt project which travels throughout the country. Hanging from the heights of public buildings, the quilt recalls the agony of the loss of so many young people, and the dedication of each square within the quilt to a person who has died reminds us that epidemics are in effect the stories of countless suffering individuals. The survivors of family members who died of AIDS face unique problems in the planning of rituals and memorials, given the ambivalence of many religious organizations and the social stigma attached to this illness, and they have had to invent new ways of achieving public acknowledgment of their loss.

When TWA flight 800 mysteriously crashed into the ocean off New York City on July 17, 1996, a small group of friends and relatives created memorial sites on the World Wide Web. One such site was created by a town in memory of a couple who died on the flight, and it could be considered the equivalent of a statue in a town square. The parents of a young woman created a site with their daughter's photograph and a one-page account of her life. The Memorial Home Page also includes a moving essay written by a navy diver who spent five weeks on board the USS *Grasp* in support of the recovery operation. Rescue workers' grief often remains unacknowledged because of their lack of ties to the victims.

While new rites for funerals and unusual memorials are a way of reawakening community participation in the rituals surrounding death, we are still faced with major questions after the funeral of a loved one. The real process of separation begins after the funeral, yet there are no common practices to help us through the long period of adjustment and the re-forging of new roles.

Although bereavement rituals vary among societies, there are certain common threads running through them all. Most important, these rituals permit the public expression of private distress. Because there are no longer any commonly accepted ceremonies for mourning, the anguish of someone who has suffered loss is frequently endured in private. The suffering of the mourner may be increased by being ignored. When one of my colleagues lost her son, a few close friends sent her affectionate notes, but when she returned to work after the funeral, she was greeted by silence. No one mentioned the death of her son. She felt as if her pain were invisible, that it didn't matter to others at all. After the death of a loved one, we need more than ever to be accepted, to have our pain acknowledged.

But it wasn't necessarily a deliberate omission on the part of her co-workers as much as an absence of guidelines for facing the situation and perhaps an uneasiness at the reminder of their own mortality. Such an event generates conflicting feelings. While we may be relieved that our own families were spared, we may feel a deep sympathy as well as a frightening sense of our own vulnerability. Perhaps we think we are protecting our friends by not mentioning the deceased, but in reality, it is ourselves whom we are protecting. Or perhaps we want to do too much, feeling that we must make it all right. It may be difficult for us to acknowledge that in a world where there seems to be a solution to every problem, a cure for so many illness, there are things we cannot fix.

Those of us who are fortunate enough to have friends willing to share our sorrow may find a lack of understanding of the time needed to traverse our grief. We need time not only to heal, but to tell our stories, yet often our friends or coworkers are busy juggling jobs and family or are absorbed in problems of their own. Until we value listening as an important form of social connection and set aside space for such giving, those of us who are grieving will suffer from isolation and loneliness.

The powerful emotions we experience during grief are demanding and take a long time to abate. Yet many people expect those who are mourning the loss of a loved one to return to normal activities and behavior soon after the funeral. A leave of absence—usually a day or two—is normally granted for attending funerals, but a leave of absence for mourning would be considered strange and unnecessary. Yet the emotions we experience while grieving cause us great fatigue. It may feel as if we are recovering from a long and difficult illness. While work can be both absorbing and healing in the long run, it can be extremely burdensome immediately after a death, and we are generally less than effective in our jobs. If at all possible, taking time for the express purpose of mourning is extremely helpful to the grief-stricken person.

As we experience grief, we are truly in uncharted territory. We don't know just how long or how intensely we should feel the anger, pain, and guilt resulting from loss. Nor do we know how to behave toward others. Often we feel guilty because our emotions continue unabated and because we are afraid of imposing our sadness on others.

The father of one of my students was killed in an explosion while working inside a manhole. Because her mother "fell apart" during the year after the death, Joan took up the burden of household management. She told me that she felt nothing at the time. I asked her if she had discussed her feelings with anyone, and she replied that she didn't want to burden others. One of the outcomes of her postponing her grief was the development of an ulcer. It may be actually harmful to our health to deny our most powerful emotions. It is a paradox that by facing them, we eventually pass through them and reach the other side of grief where loss is no longer the center of our lives. Joan is now talking about the anger and sadness she feels about her father's death and realizing that it is all right to grieve. Just as the dying are made to feel that they have an obligation to keep silent and thus spare those around them, the grieving who are in need of comfort and support feel that they have to keep a "stiff upper lip" and not disturb family and friends. But maintaining a stoic silence may have serious consequences for our well-being.

Mourning is not an illness or an aberration. The pain of grief is an important part of our journey through life. Trying to control our feelings will not make them disappear. On the contrary, if we try to block or bury them, they will surface later in our lives and may cause us serious physical and emotional problems. If we acknowledge our grief and make room for the sorrow of loss in our lives, we can then put these emotions behind us. These extreme feelings of anguish are normal, and they also serve a very important purpose in our lives. Through the very hard work of grieving, we are actually healing ourselves.

We need a broad range of emotions and periods of intensity in our lives. If we cut off the profound sadness that wells up when we lose someone we love, we will also prevent ourselves from experiencing the greatest joy. We often undergo a variety of conflicting feelings at the same time. These are all functional. They help us to live as fully as possible and to change when necessary. If we allow these feelings to surface and find expression, we will be free to carry on our lives in the best way possible.

How to Use This Book

This book is intended to be a companion on your journey through grief. It is about the role of suffering and change in our lives and about the healing that change and suffering bring. It describes the common feelings, behaviors, and reactions that we experience when we lose a loved one.

The book is organized according to the phases of grief and different kinds of loss. Within each section you will find a chapter on the particular loss you are experiencing, whether the loss of a sibling, parent, child, or spouse.

Part one, "The Experience of Grief Today," presents an overview of the grief process and includes a chapter on losses other than death as well as a chapter on the crisis of meaning that may be precipitated by a significant loss.

Parts two, five, and eight deal with the stages of grief: part two, "When Someone Dies," describes the early phases of grief; part five, "As Time Passes," addresses the later phases of disruption and disorganization; and part eight, "Reaching the Other Side of Grief," describes the reorganization of our lives after the long process of grieving.

Part three, "Losing a Loved One Through Suicide or Homicide," presents some particularly difficult issues that deserve separate attention. Those who have suffered these types of losses may find the narratives and essays in parts two and five helpful as well.

The AIDS epidemic has simultaneously created a wave of fear and alienation that marginalizes significant sectors of our population. While public images of AIDS conjure up promiscuous lifestyles and drug addiction, the reality is much more complex and includes the heterosexual population, especially women and children. Like all epidemics, AIDS does not respect social distinctions, yet the survivors of AIDS-related deaths suffer the additional pain of social disdain. Part four, "Losing a Loved One Through Aids," explores the unique burdens of losing a partner or family member to this illness.

Part six, "How We Can Help Ourselves," comprises a practical guide on how we can help ourselves while we are traversing the phases of grief. Many of us who suffer grief feel that we must continue our professional and personal roles as if nothing had happened. We may be accustomed to taking care of others in a number of ways, but, it is extremely important to take care of ourselves while we are grieving. The chapters in this part will help with the problems of daily living and help us to express our feelings and find supports.

Part seven, "How Friends and Coworkers Can Help," is intended for friends and associates of the bereaved. Often friends and employers or coworkers are puzzled as how to deal with the bereaved. This part provides a guide which will help us understand the grieving person, and it provides some suggestions for things to say and things to do for the grieving person. Although mourning is an intensely personal and self-reflective phase of our lives, it occurs in a context of family, friends, work, and educational institutions. We can all benefit by learning about grief.

Part eight, "Reaching the Other Side of Grief," introduces us to the possibilities of creating a new and fulfilling life as a result of the long, painful years of our struggle through sorrow. This docs not necessarily mean cutting the ties with our deceased loved one, but rather incorporating that loss in new ways, for example, through involvement in social action, new careers, or the development of new perspectives. Ultimately we have learned how to mine the treasures within ourselves.

Although we grieve within social contexts, our grief is always intensely personal and has its own course. Each of us will find a chapter of this book that relates to our own loss and to our perception of our relationship with our loved one. If our friend who died was a like a sister to us, we may want to turn to the chapter on the loss of a sibling. If our grandparent or aunt was like a parent to us, we may find the chapter on the loss of a parent helpful. As time passes, we may be ready to read about the reactions to loss that our siblings, parents, spouses, or partners may be experiencing.

This book considers the loss of a partner in a heterosexual or homosexual relationship that is not formalized as the same as the loss of a spouse. The reference to loss of a spouse includes the loss of a partner in a committed relationship, and references to widow or widower are used in these contexts as well. While the responses of our family, friends, and associates may be different in these circumstances, our life partner is a chosen person, just as a married partner, and the grief we experience from such loss is the same.

The taboos surrounding grief are complicated by gender images that may further restrict the expression of feeling. Therefore, the narratives included thoughout the book detail the stories of both men and women on the premise that they may have had different socializations and could be expected to show different attitudes toward the expression of emotion.

The narratives are stories of ordinary people who have experienced different kinds of losses. Although they come from different backgrounds and family settings, and although they represent a broad range of religious backgrounds, they express feelings that all of us who have suffered loss have had at certain times in the grieving process. They are the accounts of people for whom the loss was not too recent and who have traversed all the phases of grief. Because a number of years had elapsed since their loss, they were able to bring the perspective of time to their experiences. Some of these stories will be similar to your own. Some will have their own unique character. We hope you will find that you are not alone and that this shared experience will help you on your own path through grief.

Part One
THE EXPERIENCE
OF GRIEF TODAY

It is the incomplete,
the unfulfilled, the torn
that haunts our nights and days
and keeps us hunger-born.
Grief spills from our eyes,
unwelcome, indiscreet,
as if sprung from a fault
as rivers seam a rock
and break through under shock.
We are shaken by guilt.

from "Of Grief," by May Sarton

Chapter One
GRIEF AS A
PERSONAL CRISIS

Grief and the Individual

Each one of us is unique in personality, family background, cultural heritage, and genetic makeup. Therefore, everyone's response to grief, how it is expressed and how it is coped with, will be different. Also, the nature of the relationship with the deceased is different for each person.

Only we can define the importance that a relationship has for us. We may grieve for a grandparent as intensely as for a parent, for an aunt as much as for a parent. To lose a child or a marriage partner is considered by many people to be the most painful kind of loss. However, sibling loss or the loss of an elderly parent can be just as painful. When a relationship is not recognized or legitimized, such as a lover, fiancé, or partner in a homosexual relationship, a loss does not elicit the same sympathy or may even be unrecognized.

Although each type of loss confronts us with its own issues of identity and with its own social problems, ultimately loss is painful regardless of age, sex, or relationship. For instance, some may pay little attention to the loss of elderly parents on the assumption that their parenting roles are no longer functional and that the primary focus of our caring has shifted to spouse, children, or lover. However, it is very difficult to lose elderly parents simply because we have had a long period of time in which to strengthen the bonds of love. While some people may comment that we had plenty of time with our parent, we regard our loss as untimely. We are never ready to lose a loved one.

31

We expect to grieve for someone with whom we have had a close and loving relationship. However, we also mourn for those we have lost in a troubled relationship, and our mourning may be complicated by the feelings of resentment and dislike we harbored for the dead person. A former student of mine had a very troubled relationship with her mother and still feels great anger years after her death. Given the nature of the relationship, she has been struggling with confusion and with the conflicting feelings of loss and relief. There is nothing wrong with feeling relief at being out of a problem-ridden situation, but feelings of guilt and self-blame may complicate and prolong the grieving process.

There are deaths that bear stigmas: suicides; homicides; deaths from AIDS, drug overdoses, and abusive behavior. Sometimes we may blame the victim of a violent death. It's almost as if by blaming them we mark them as somehow separate, distancing ourselves from the reality of the violence. In these cases, we frequently go over and over the details preceding the death. The senselessness of these deaths makes the circumstances seem so important, as if they could somehow bring us closer to the meaning that eludes us.

Sometimes the death of a loved one propels us into a new situation which leaves us little time or energy for grieving. If we are widowed and left with children, we need all of our energy to care for them. We may have to find work and face new financial problems, or we may find ourselves juggling the demands of work and child-rearing for the first time. If we are in the midst of working toward a college degree when our parent dies, we may still have to prepare for exams. Sometimes we are faced with important life tasks that claim our attention before we can face our grief.

There are other reasons for postponing our grieving. Maybe we have issues that we need to work through before we can give ourselves over to our sorrow. A woman I know spent years confronting the difficulties of having lived with alcoholic parents before being able to grieve for the sister she lost. She needed to address a difficult situation before she could begin the grieving process. It's not helpful to judge ourselves for postponing our sorrow while we face these tasks. On the contrary, once we have moved through these issues, we can allow ourselves to grieve more fully.

Once our new lifestyle as single parent, as student, or as someone who has addressed a difficult issue is established, our emotional demands arise and our grief surfaces. Sometimes that surfacing is triggered by an event such as another loss or the breakup of a relationship. Or we react intensely to a minor event, only to realize that it was a response to a loss we suffered years ago. Because each one of us faces such unique life situations, we all have our own calendar for beginning the process of grieving.

There are identifiable phases in the grieving process, but the duration of these phases and their sequence varies. Everyone has his or her own timetable, and while one person reconstructs his or her life within a year of a death, another person needs several years to complete the process of defining new roles and new identities. The most helpful remark someone made to me after my mother's death was that it generally takes three years to recover from a major loss. The emotions I was feeling at the time were so intense that I knew I could not work through them in a matter of months. Her comment relieved the pressure for a speedy return to "normalcy."

The Phases of Grief

Many researchers have studied the process of grieving and have identified common patterns. The model described in this chapter is similar to the one developed by John Bowlby and Colin Murray Parkes (see appendix B). Although the phases of the grieving process do not necessarily unfold in an orderly manner, we can nevertheless distinguish between the immediate reactions to loss and long-term responses. The immediate response to the death of someone we love is shock and protest or denial. This is followed by a period of disorganization during which the routines, habits, and roles we are accustomed to are disrupted. Ultimately we reach a period of recovery or the reorganization of a new life. It does not mean forgetting the person we have lost, but instead placing that relationship somewhere inside us where it's comfortable so we can carry on with our lives. The profound sadness is no longer the center of our attention.

When we know that a person is dying, or when a person has been suffering from a long illness, we may begin grieving before the event of death. During this anticipatory period, we do some of the work involved in grieving. We can resolve some of the issues in a relationship, gain perspective on that relationship, and say some of the necessary things. While we grieve the loss of who that person was before his or her illness, we still focus our attention on that person. During bereavement, we focus on ourselves.

SHOCK

The initial phase of bereavement is shock and disbelief. We are confused and disoriented by the death and keep hoping that we will wake up and discover that it was all just a mistake. We keep hoping that it is reversible, like a movie. This wish to deny the event of death may last for days or even weeks. We move as if in a dream, filled with a sense of unreality and distance. Sometimes these feelings persist even though we communicate with others about the death and arrange for the funeral and the disposal of the body. People frequently speak of a sense of unreality, of going about daily activities in a dreamlike state. This period of numbness actually gives us the time we need to mobilize our resources and cope with the impact of the loss when we are more able to.

Being present at a death or viewing the body helps acknowledge the reality for us. Though some people avoid this, the experience of seeing and saying good-bye to the dead person makes it possible to develop an image of that person as dead. When a friend of mine delivered a stillborn baby, the hospital staff encouraged her to hold it in order to be able to have an image of her child. When there is no body, as happens during a war, an airplane crash, or an accident at sea, feelings of unreality and denial are prolonged. We feel that somehow that person will return as if she or he had been on a trip. The funeral and the disposition of the body are occasions for private and public farewell. When we are denied this important ceremony, our grieving is made more difficult. This may help to explain the years of time and effort spent recovering the bodies of those who were reported missing during the Vietnam War.

After the funeral, the real work of grieving begins. We are confronted with a home that is full of painful reminders of the dead person. During these early weeks, we are preoccupied with the dead person, continuing to converse with him or her in our thoughts. Many people report that they can actually sense or feel the dead spouse, child, or sibling around them. This is not unusual and can actually be a source of comfort. There is nothing wrong with continuing this communication, with talking to or writing to the deceased. Visiting the cemetery or writing letters are ways of prolonging the leave-taking, of acknowledging the continued presence of that person in our lives.

During this period, we are experiencing the pain of separation. The sadness comes in waves, and we frequently feel the need to cry. Often we are seized with a desire to cry at the most inopportune and unexpected times. We may be driving to work, reading the newspaper, or sitting in a crowded cafeteria. It is very important to allow these moments of great sadness to surface. Crying is very cleansing and will relieve us. Any time thoughts of the deceased well up is a good time to cry. Tears cannot be postponed for a more convenient time, and trying to block them may cause us problems.

In our society, it is difficult for men to shed tears, especially in public. For some men, a close friend can help facilitate the flow, almost like granting permission. In Bill's narrative in chapter 22, he describes how he was helped to shed those tears by a woman friend. They were putting flowers on his wife's grave and she told him, "Go ahead and cry." His friend gave him permission to step outside of the image of male behavior. Although younger men are becoming more comfortable with expressing their emotions, this is still difficult for middle-aged and older men. However, both sexes are vulnerable to demands for being "brave" or "strong."

During the early weeks after a death we need to tell the story about those last hours, to go over the details of the illness, the accident, the last words spoken. It is as important to listen to these stories as it is to tell them. They are an attempt to find meaning in a very bewildering event. A friend of mine who lost his wife kept repeating the story of her death and the trip to the hospital. She died very suddenly at home, and though she had been very ill with cancer, he had blocked any thought of her death. He told me the story over and over. This was very helpful to him in leading him to accept both the reality of her death and the seriousness of her illness. The person telling the story is healing him- or herself. He or she is adjusting to a new and painful reality and exploring its meaning.

DISORGANIZATION

The period of numbness, which is the early phase of grief, shelters us until we are able to feel the very painful emotions which come with loss. After the shock wears off, the sadness wells up. Not only do we feel a profound sorrow, but other powerful emotions assail us, occurring in combinations. We simultaneously feel guilt and anger, sadness and depression. We experience abrupt changes in our daily routines, in our behavior, and in the way we see ourselves.

The death of a loved one also means the disruption of lifelong habits and patterns. Most of us who live with someone have developed habits for the most minute details of our lives. For instance, one of us may sleep on a certain side of the bed. One of us may wake up earlier and prepare the morning coffee. Each of us has certain preferences in food or music that the other complements in a number of ways. More importantly, family members, lovers, or trusted friends share each other's deepest thoughts, fears, and hopes. In losing a loved person, we also lose the roles of companion, confidant, lover. We therefore experience significant changes in status.

Our sleeping patterns are likely to be disrupted at this time, and many people have difficulty falling asleep or wake up feeling tense and uneasy in the middle of the night. Frequently we dream about the dead person, although the nature of these dreams changes over a period of time, as will their frequency. In the early period after a death, our loved one may appear in our dreams as if he or she were still alive. One of my students had a recurring dream about her mother in the months after her death. She dreamed they were having a picnic together, but when she reached out to hold her mother, she vanished. We may continue to dream of the deceased for years. In our later dreams, the fact of the person's death may be reflected in their lack of response to us.

We may neglect the need for nourishment just to avoid the loneliness at mealtimes, or overlook our own health by ignoring physical symptoms or missing an important checkup at the doctor. We need to be reminded by our friends or family to take care of ourselves.

Not only are we apt to be fatigued by the great demands of our emotions, but our self-esteem is very low at this time. In losing a loved one, we have received a heavy blow and feel a greatly diminished self-confidence. Our close friends may expect us to pull ourselves together and resume our normal pace, or former friends shy away and avoid us just when we need them the most.

Often in sudden deaths, and even in deaths resulting from a long illness, we tell ourselves, "If only . . ." We think that if only we had done things differently, we could have prevented the death. When my mother died of a heart attack, I kept thinking of the flu shot she had received and of all the studies which described them as dangerous to older people who were suffering from heart conditions. We feel responsible, as if somehow we should have prevented the death. Even under the best of circumstances we feel a powerful sense of guilt.

Our feelings of guilt are heightened after a suicide as we grapple with the meaning of the act, wondering if we could have done something to prevent it. This is especially true if the suicide comes as a complete surprise. Suddenly we are confronted with all the issues, stresses, and problems in the relationship, as well as rejection, for suicide is sometimes regarded as a rejection. While we move through the same phases of grief, the initial period is prolonged because of guilt. We feel that we failed as a friend, spouse, or parent. We go over and over past events. We must remember, however, that these feelings of guilt are normal and will be with us until we can see the relationship we had with our loved one from a clearer perspective.

During this period we go over our past behavior and wish it could have been different. A mother who lost an adult daughter remembered the times she had lost her temper with her daughter during her teenage years. She also told me that she had gone shopping with her daughter and found a very beautiful coat, which she decided not to buy because of the cost, an incident that kept haunting her after her daughter's death. As Maureen points out in chapter 8, siblings remember the times they quarreled and wonder whether the deceased brother or sister really knew that they loved him or her. As time passes we regain a sense of perspective and remember the good times as well as the difficult ones. But in the early months after a loss we are frequently troubled by scenes from the past.

Along with guilt, anger assails us. The targets of our rage vary, whether it is directed at the doctor or nurses for being insensitive, or at family members for not helping during an illness or during the funeral arrangements. If we have lost a spouse, we may be angry at other people who are still living with a partner. In the case of a homicide, we are filled with rage at the perpetrator. If we have lost a loved one through AIDS, we may be angry at the government for moving too slowly in making new drugs available. Anger is a very complex emotion, and we may experience a free-floating anger that erupts at the slightest provocation. Some of us may be angry with God for the injustice and senselessness of the death. Most of all, we are angry at the dead person for leaving us.

Sometimes we erect a shrine to the dead person, keeping our loved one's room in its original state or acting as if he or she were still present, not making any changes in our life. We may even expect our family members to adopt this behavior and believe that we are grieving the most. It is normal to be obsessed with the loved one in the early months after a death, but prolonging this behavior and erecting a shrine draws out the early phases of grief and prevents us from moving on.

Anger, guilt, and sorrow are unpredictable and do not necessarily occur in sequence. We feel very vulnerable because of the intensity and unpredictability of these feelings. However, wishing to control or deny them only means a postponement. Denying these early manifestations of mourning can even push us into extreme forms of behavior such as losing ourselves in work or turning to alcohol and drugs as a way of numbing our pain. Frequently, adolescents adopt antisocial types of behavior as a way of acting out anger. If we allow ourselves to express it, the terrible pain we feel moves and changes. It seems the same over a long period of time, but it is constantly transforming and ultimately will move to the margins of our lives.

Family dynamics are sometimes changed by the death of a family member. Death means not only a crisis in personal identity but also the loosening of family ties. The death of a family member affects us all differently, depending upon the nature of our relationship with that person, our involvement during the time of dying, and how close we were. Some of us experience grief in an anticipatory manner, while others display little grief. The variety of our responses can complicate communication among family members. When both parents die, for instance, an older child may find that he or she is relinquishing the sibling role and assuming that of parent. The other siblings may respond to this change in a number of ways, from adaptation to profound resentment. Couples may draw closer together after the death of a child or they may project their anger on each other and create bitter dissension. Sometimes the death of one parent means the loss of the key element keeping the family together.

It is not unusual for tension to rise in a family after a death because the enormity of the feelings aroused leave us little emotional strength for mutual support. Each one of us has a different rhythm in our grieving and entirely different coping styles. One of us wakes up one morning feeling energetic and ready for new activities, while another feels consumed by pain and fatigue. In such situations, it is helpful to seek out separate supports.

The reorientation of our habits and expectations occurs within the context of the family. During at this time of relative instability or of reordering of family relations, it is helpful to maintain stability in other areas. For instance, after the death of a parent, keeping a child in the same school or in the same living arrangements will give that child the security he or she needs and the assurance that life will go on without other major changes. If we are an adult, that sense of stability may come from keeping the same job or residence. This is not a time for major changes or decisions. We are spending a great deal of energy dealing with our emotions, and even the smallest chores may be burdensome. It is a time to be as gentle as possible with oneself while placing other demands in the background.

Holidays are especially difficult after we have suffered a loss. These are often occasions for family reunions, and we will feel a heightened sense of pain at this time. A mother who lost her son through AIDS found the first Thanksgiving with her family after his death very trying. She wanted to talk about her son and felt very alone as her other children were absorbed in the bustle of preparations or watching television. Even others' expectations that we share their joy are a heavy burden. It seems as if time were standing still, as if all the progress we accomplished during the year were evaporating. For some of us, the first holiday may be not as trying as we expected, but as the second one draws near we are surprised to find it even more difficult as we become aware of the long, lonely road ahead. We expect that we will feel better as time passes, only to be overwhelmed by the realization that *this is the way it's going to be.*

Anniversaries of the death and the birthday of our loved one are just as painful. Some people have found that the anticipation of holidays and anniversaries were more difficult to deal with than the actual events. It is normal to feel a renewed sense of loss during these periods. Many people have found unusual, nontraditional ways of observing holidays, forgoing their usual rituals. Some people observe a modified Christmas, focusing on the children rather than on the social practices of sending cards or entertaining friends and neighbors. In chapter 25, Anne tells us about her decision to take her children to Disneyworld over the Christmas holiday rather than staying home and putting up a tree. An older widower decided to take a trip to Italy to visit his relatives during this time. The important thing is to find a way to observe the holidays that is both comfortable and meaningful.

Painful as they are, the emotions we experience during this phase of grieving are part of the long process of healing. Because they are so absorbing, we need plenty of time to move through them. This varies with each individual. Some people pass through this phase in a few months, while others require many months or even years. Also, we may move back and forth between phases in an unpredictable manner. It is helpful to remind ourselves that this is a very necessary and normal part of grieving and that even though the signs of progress may not be readily apparent, we are doing some very important work. During these difficult months, we think over our relationship with our loved one and our own role in the world. Although it may seem like a period of turbulence and confusion, we are paving the way for the reconstruction of our lives.

REORGANIZATION

One morning we may wake up with a new sense of energy and a new interest in the world. We discovered new friends while we were in the most difficult period of our grief, and now we turn to them to share other interests. We changed our daily routine and now take more of our meals out with friends. We come to understand that the fabric of our lives has been disrupted and we have stopped anticipating the events of our former lives. As time passes we not only change our lifestyles, but actually enjoy these changes. We even look forward to being alone at home listening to music, curling up with a favorite book, and simply enjoying our own company. We begin to experience moments of contentment even though we thought we could never be happy again.

We see our whole network of relationships in a new light. At first we may have been disappointed in our friends, but ultimately these tensions and stresses help us to make the decisions we need in order to create a new life for ourselves. It is a long process that moves in fits and starts, but there are joyous as well as painful aspects to it. While we may have been hurt at the behavior of some of our old friends, we have discovered new friends and interests, the surprise and pleasure of being liked by different kinds of people. Or we discover new talents. A close friend of mine who lost her mother discovered a bent for writing. She even learned another language and became a well-known translator. Another friend who was widowed decided to go to graduate school in painting and design and is now showing her work at a number of galleries. In chapter 23, Eric describes his decision to enter the field of filmmaking. While we expended tremendous energy in the previous phase of grieving, now we discover a surge of talents and interests that will bring us a satisfaction we could not have predicted. We are changing as we move through the grieving process, even though the changes are slow and barely visible from week to week.

Perhaps we still feel married, or still miss that best friend, or feel that our life has lost its meaning without our child, but gradually our loved one is less and less in our thoughts. We continue to feel sadness, but the intensity has diminished. Our relationship with that person is no longer at the center of our lives. We have new energies to invest in other activities and persons. New relationships or the decision to have another child are not a sign of betrayal. They do not mean that we are "replacing" the deceased. Beginning a new relationship or a new lifestyle is a sign of recovery.

Chapter Two
LOSS AND CHANGE

We associate grief with loss through death, but we also experience grief as a consequence of some of the major changes and other kinds of loss in our lives. We experience the emotions and disruptions of grieving as a result of these losses just as if we had lost a loved one. This book deals primarily with loss through death, but the accounts of the phases of the grieving process and the coping styles for dealing with loss through a death help us to face other major losses.

As we move through our lives, we continually experience change, and while change is beneficial, it also involves loss. It's as if one hand were for receiving and the other hand for letting go. The important passages of life—marriage, the birth of a child, the change of residence or a job, the growth of one's children, and our own aging—fill us with a sense of fulfillment while also striking us with sadness. Each of these events sets in motion a whole series of changes in our roles and status, which involve considerable loss.

When we face change, such as moving to a new home or a new job, or sending our child off to college, we think of these changes in terms of practical tasks. For example, we expend great energy in preparing for our child's departure for college, gathering packing cartons, purchasing clothing and small appliances. We may even accompany our child to the college dormitory and spend an afternoon or a day moving boxes and arranging for telephone service. But after we have negotiated all the physical changes and returned to our home, we begin to feel uneasy. We now face the emotional toll of an empty nest and the changes in our roles. We feel a profound grief at our loss without necessarily acknowledging it.

When we change jobs or move to a new home, there are myriad practical tasks to accomplish, from packing to making new connections in a neighborhood or office. But while we are gaining a new working life or a new home, and even if we view these changes as improvements in our lives, we still feel disrupted. Because these changes are not recognized as involving loss, we may not allow ourselves to feel and to express the grief that comes with loss. But for many of us, both work and home are important parts of our identity, and though we are moving forward, we need to mourn the loss of the network of friends in our old neighborhood, the home where our family grew up, or the job which filled our life for a number of years.

In this age of rapid technological and economic changes, some of us will be fired or laid off. While some of us find new and rewarding jobs, others have difficulty finding the kind of work we feel we are suited for or that fulfills our needs for creativity or esteem. And some of us never find work again. It is not always possible to retrain for another field if we are in our forties or fifties. Because work represents such an important part of our identity, we grieve as though we had lost a loved one, and we experience all of the stages of the grieving process. Not only have we lost a career, but we have also lost our dreams and hopes for the future.

Our population is aging, and while there are numerous studies of the aging process and midlife changes, few of them acknowledge the attendant grief that accompanies aging. In the middle of our years, we may feel sadness and anger at the realization that we have not fulfilled our hopes in our work or in our personal relationships. We go through all the emotions associated with the grieving process. It is helpful to recognize these feelings and to give them room both because of their emotional impact and to help clear the path to changes that will address our needs.

The aging process is imperceptible to many of us. But one morning we look in the mirror and notice that our hair is thinning or that our waistline has expanded. Changes in our body cause us to feel a loss of self-esteem. We mourn the loss of our looks and our vitality. We also experience changes in our sexual responses and in our physical vigor, and we may suffer an impairment of vision or hearing. While we tend to think of these as "physical problems," they take an emotional toll on us as well. As in any other type of loss, we need to take time to express our anger, our sadness and the dips in our self-esteem. The changes we continually face are painful, but if we allow ourselves to experience grief, we will find ourselves growing in strength, resourcefulness, and compassion.

While there are many resources dealing with issues associated with key changes in our lives, the following sections will discuss some losses that are particularly traumatic and for which we may grieve as deeply as we would for the death of a loved one. Even though our own loss is unique, the coping styles for living through grief presented in this book may answer our individual needs.

Divorce or a Broken Relationship

The loss of a partner through divorce or through the breakup of a less formal though committed relationship involves all of the feelings and reactions we have after the death of a spouse. However, the person we lose nevertheless remains present in our lives in some way. In some cases we are able to maintain an amicable relationship with our former spouse or lover. A friend of mine who divorced nine years ago still has an abiding friendship with her former spouse, and the two of them cooperate in raising their daughter.

However, in many cases our former spouse remains an ever-present threat in our lives, especially if there are difficulties with custody of the children. If we have been given joint custody or we must share the children for holidays and summer vacations, we are continually faced with the pain of separating from our children and perhaps anxiety for the well-being of the child while he or she is with our former partner.

There are multiple losses involved in a divorce or separation when we have children. We grieve the loss of a family unit. We grieve what we had dreamed of and which proved unattainable, the creation of a family with our partner and the hope of being loved. A friend of mine who retained partial custody of her son after her divorce described feeling less whole after the divorce and feeling that she and her son were not a complete family.

If we do not have children, regardless of whether we were in a formal relationship or not, we lose our dream of building a life together. It is no comfort to be reminded by our friends and acquaintances that we can begin again or find a new relationship. We mourn a specific loss: the wish to have a life with our former partner.

We also experience a profound sense of guilt for the failure of our relationship, especially if we were the one to initiate the breakup. Both of us feel that we have failed in one of the most important relationships in our lives. We feel angry at the situation, at our partner, and also at ourselves.

The breakup of a marriage or a relationship has ramifications throughout our extended families. If the breakup was a bitter one, it may be difficult to keep up a relationship with our former in-laws, who are grandparents to our children. Each member of our family experiences loss in multiple ways. Our child will lose his or her siblings if the children do not remain together. He or she may lose grandparents, cousins, aunts, and uncles. Knowing that these people are there but are inaccessible to us is a continual source of pain.

There are so many losses involved in a broken relationship. For example, we may face the loss of our home and our possessions. Many women who divorce experience a significant drop in their standard of living. They find that in order to keep their home, they must take a new job or enter the work force for the first time. Frequently, women move to a smaller home or apartment. Both partners often face the stress of a new neighborhood and a new lifestyle just when their self-esteem may be particularly low.

For many of us, losing a partner also means losing our friendship group. Just as when we lose a spouse, we find that we are suddenly a single person in a world of couples and that we no longer feel comfortable with or even feel rejected by our former friends.

In many societies, the breakup of a relationship is taboo. If the members of our family had never undergone a divorce, we may experience diminished parental esteem. Perhaps our parents tried to dissuade us from initiating a divorce or breakup and we feel the pain of their judgment. This is especially true in an extended family with more traditional values regarding marriage.

There are particular issues that cause us pain if we have lost a partner from a less formal relationship. People feel that we should go out and find someone new right away rather than taking the time to integrate the loss in our lives. Many couples, homosexual and heterosexual, live together for years without marrying. They have invested the same hopes, dreams, and efforts as are in a marriage. Because these relationships were not formalized and there may be fewer material, visible results such as children or possessions, the importance of that bond tends to be invisible to society.

It's important to allow ourselves to feel all of the emotions of grief when a relationship ends. The importance we attach to a relationship is highly personal. Some of the chapters in this book that address specific losses will be relevant to our own situation.

The Serious Illness of a Loved One

When a loved one contracts a life-threatening illness or a serious illness like Alzheimer's, heart disease, cancer, or mental illness, it feels as if he has died even though his body is still there. Perhaps our loved one was in a serious accident and remains in a coma or a vegetative state. We have all the emotions, stresses, and strains resulting from a death, but we cannot carry on a new life. We must continue to care for and to visit our loved one even though others do not understand our continued attachment.

If our loved one has a life-threatening illness such as cancer, we live with all of the effects of treatments, like chemotherapy, which weakens and transforms that person. If our loved one is our parent, we may find ourselves in a new role as the provider of support, and we may both resent this change and feel guilty about our resentment. If we are young adults, we resent the fact that our parent needs constant care and is weak. If we are middle-aged, we are caught between the demands of caring for our own children and caring for our ill parent or relation. Or perhaps our children recently left home and we were looking forward to having some time for ourselves after the long years of nurturing them. When we are absorbed in the care of a loved one, it's easy to forget our own needs, both physical and emotional. We may even feel guilty about wishing for time to be with ourselves and to pursue our own interests. It is helpful to remember that we can care for others only if we ourselves are in good shape.

If our loved one has suffered for a long time from a serious and painful illness, we may find ourselves wishing for his or her death and then feeling guilty about that wish. We suffer a complex set of emotions in such a situation—guilt, anger, profound sadness. We are grieving for the person who can never be the same but who is still present in our lives.

If our child was born with a mental or physical disorder or becomes mentally ill, we grieve for the child we thought we had. We grieve for the wished-for child, and that grief continues throughout our lives. With each passage of life—the time for starting school, for becoming an adolescent—we feel a fresh surge of sadness and the pain of comparison with others whose children develop normally. A good friend wrote to me about her young son who is autistic, "So we keep on going, day to day, marveling at his growth, until we see a 'normal' four-year-old."

In addition, we have other children and other burdens in our lives. We may feel the stress of trying to divide our attention between the child who is ill and his or her siblings, and we wish we could do more for both. We feel guilty, as if somehow this illness were a judgment on us. We experience the lack of understanding from other people. There is also the ever-present worry about the care of our child or relative when we are no longer able to provide that care.

Some of us are able to confront our anger and guilt and come to an understanding of our disabled or ill child as a rare opportunity for loving. A woman whose young son had leukemia described how she felt a special closeness as they struggled together with his disease. A former student of mine had a brother with Down's Syndrome and always described the special love and support her brother had from his siblings. He brought out a rare tenderness in the whole family.

The Loss of Health Through Illness or Injury

Losing our health through illness or injury is a great blow to our self-esteem, and we are surprised at the intensity of our emotions as we grieve for the self we were. We are angry at our body for somehow "failing" us, and we may even try to punish ourselves by either undereating or overeating. If the onset of our illness or the loss of a bodily function such as vision or hearing is sudden, we feel as if we were projected into a new world with few guides to help us. While others see us as struggling with our new physical condition, the emotional struggle is even greater as we are pounded by waves of anger, despair, and sadness.

If we must be hospitalized we lose our autonomy as we become subject to hospital schedules and regulations. We feel like an object as we are wheeled from one test to another or to treatments such as chemotherapy.

If we are the breadwinner in the family, we lose income and the sense of identity that came with our work and our salary. For many of us it is humiliating to have meals brought to us or to have a nurse bathe us and take care of our most basic needs.

Some of us who have lost our health experience a loss of our sexuality. We no longer feel feminine or masculine. This is especially true if we undergo chemotherapy or radiation and suffer the side effects of water retention and hair loss. A friend of mine who became ill with bone-marrow cancer mourned the loss of her long, wavy hair. It was part of her distinctive beauty. We mourn our disfigurement and, just as if we had lost a loved one, wish we could go back to the time when we felt whole.

We may lose not only our looks, but our independence, our very mobility. Perhaps we suffer from a severe case of arthritis that makes it difficult to accomplish the simplest tasks. It may become very hard to hold on to our autonomy in face of our family and friends' well-intentioned desire to take care of us. A number of disabled people have confided to me that they had to struggle to keep their loved ones from "smothering" them with care, and that struggle is a daily one. When we go out, we have to confront the stares of passersby or some people's assumption that disabled persons are also mentally deficient.

When we lose a body part through surgery we experience profound grief. We are angry over the need for surgery and perhaps guilty about the role our own behavior had in bringing about this condition, such as smoking or postponing a medical checkup. We have difficulty sleeping or become extremely anxious or depressed, just as if we had lost a loved one.

It has been projected that one in ten women in the United States will develop some form of breast cancer. While not all of these cases will result in a mastectomy, and while new treatments for breast cancer such as lumpectomy and hormonal treatments are being developed, those who acquire this illness and undergo a mastectomy feel mutilated. We feel shocked and numb for weeks and even months after the procedure.

Losing a breast means losing our body image, our view of ourselves, and our perception of our attractiveness to others. We worry whether our husbands or partners will continue to love us. One woman contemplating prophylactic surgery remarked that if she were alone, she would have no hesitation, but she worried about her husband's reaction: "He loves me and he loves my body."

Such a disease involves a threat to our very life. A woman in her thirties who had cancer described changes in her fundamental sense of self, that she had lost her sense of eternal youth that one has in one's thirties and developed a phobia of being ill. Anyone who loses a limb, a part of the body, or a bodily function comes face to face with mortality. We need to be able to express our sadness, anger, guilt, and especially our anxieties about our altered self and its acceptability to others.

Finding a support group of people who have experienced similar losses helps us to express our sorrow and to receive affirmation for our feelings. Bereavement centers often include support groups for those with serious illness, and most hospitals have begun to sponsor such groups on their own premises.

We gradually come to accept our different body and develop a new sense of self. We gain a sense of pride and accomplishment for the battle we have fought. We also acquire a new perspective on life.

A Runaway or Missing Child

A close friend of mine whose child ran away when she was an adolescent kept telling me that there are some situations in life which have no redeeming sides to them. "What lesson could there possibly be in this terrible pain?" she asked. When our child runs away, we face the same welter of conflicting emotions as when a loved one is seriously ill. We mourn a loss, but the person is still alive. We are torn with anxiety, with hope for our loved one's survival, and with guilt. In the first months or years we devote all of our energy to finding our child. These efforts give structure and meaning to our life. We are also angry at our child for abandoning and rejecting us. The anger is so overwhelming at times that it masks our sorrow.

We blame ourselves for our child's disappearance and sift our past behavior relentlessly for clues to our "failure." As parents, we want to be omnipotent, to give our child the very best we are able. It is very difficult not to judge ourselves under these circumstances. We may have been the very best of parents to our child and still find fault with ourselves. Perhaps our child had difficulties and we went out of our way to do extra things for him or her, and yet we were unable to prevent that child's disappearance. It's helpful to be gentle with ourselves and to acknowledge our sadness. In time we will see ourselves in perspective and remember all we were able to do for our child during the years he or she was home.

The disappearance of a child places great strain on our marriage or relationship, in the same way as the tragedy of a child's death. Because we each grieve in our own ways and because we have built up a set of expectations for each other, we have difficulty communicating in the long, painful months and years after such a loss. Some families seek separate supports, or some turn to a counselor as a family. Counseling or support groups will help us not only through our grief as a family, but also in responding to unhelpful comments by friends and coworkers.

There is no calendar for moving toward an understanding of our child's separateness. We make progress, and then some incident sparks our memory and plunges us back into sadness. Some of us are ready to go on with our lives in a year, and some of us need more time. As years pass, we notice the changes in our appearance and in ourselves, but the image of our child is frozen in time. Although we will always wonder where our child is and what he or she is doing, we need to go on with our daily life. We harbor a hope deep within us for our child's return, but gradually we allow ourselves to let go and move on.

Chapter Three
THE CRISIS OF MEANING

A s we traverse the phases of the grieving process we experience the transformation of our lives and feelings. However, the quest for meaning is also a part of our journey through grief. As we struggle with our religious beliefs and our views of a just world, they change radically. When a loved one dies, our belief in a benevolent Creator is often shaken as we ask ourselves, "Why did this happen to my spouse or child; why did this happen to me? I've always been a good person." We wonder why good people are not spared illness, accidents, and untimely death. We question a divine plan in which we lose a child at an early age, a spouse when we have children, a lover, or a friend. We think, "Unjust, unfair, inexplicable," as we examine our shattered lives.

In the early period after the death of a loved one, we are thrown back on ourselves and the ground under our feet no longer seems solid. Some of us find our faith a source of support and experience a deepening of our beliefs. Others find emptiness in religious ceremonies and withdraw from religious observances for a while. Even those who turn to their religion with a renewed understanding may feel angry at a Creator who allowed the death of a loved one. Death causes us to examine not only our lives, but also our place within the universe.

The death of a loved one through suicide or homicide seems senseless and defies our structures of meaning, our very sense of justice. We feel deeply confused and fragile, as if we were adrift in a hostile universe. One of my daughter's close friends was brutally murdered. She and her friend were very similar physical types, petite and slender. "Does that mean I could also be a victim?" my daughter wondered.

While these questions do persist, we gain new insight into life as we progress through the grieving process. Many of us discover that we have developed a new sense of what is important. Things that used to be significant to us, whether success in our careers or material wealth, are now unimportant. We gain a keen sense of how much our relationships with family and friends matter, and we feel that we have come closer to ultimate reality. Along with a new scale of values comes a new understanding of life's fragility. If someone who is the center of our life can be snuffed out in minutes, everything else seems tenuous.

Ultimately we discover that we are survivors, and as survivors we have gained new strengths and new insights. We have incorporated sadness and pain in our lives and understand how these emotions transform us. Our own suffering has helped us to feel and express compassion for others and to discover just how precious life is.

Many of us who have endured of a loved one's violent death or agonizing illness have learned that it is possible to live without answers to our fundamental questions, and that some experiences have no redeeming sides to them. Having to live with this dichotomy is not unusual.

These insights into life's meaning can be expressed in so many different ways, ranging from working to helping others who have suffered similar tragedies to changing our line of work to the simple ability to appreciate the elements of our everyday lives and the facts of the human condition (chapter 14 describes how Margaret began to work with victim rights). The search for meaning was a terrifying journey, but along the way we discovered our own hidden resources and affirmations we never expected.

Part Two
WHEN SOMEONE DIES: THE EARLY PHASES OF GRIEF

One of our nephews drove me
to the cemetery.
You weren't there.

I stood in the temple
with the mourners.
You didn't hear.

I go to dinner
at friends' houses;
Their silence

pins you deeper underground
than the earth
heaped on your coffin . . .

from *Visits*, by Ruth Feldman

Chapter Four
WHEN A PARENT OF
YOUNG ADULTS DIES

Jeremy

Mom and I had gone to pick up a part at Sears and we were driving back. We drove up to the house and there was a police car at the next-door neighbor's, so I thought, "Uh oh, maybe our dog bothered them again." So we went inside the house and I was just sitting down when the doorbell rang. It was the police, and that's how we found out my father had a heart attack. I can still see everything there and I can feel that moment. My sister Anne said to me that she had changed, that she's a different person. And I said that I wasn't any different, but when I think about it, she's right. That day really made me change.

I haven't cried since the funeral. The funeral, I think, was very, very good for my family. We had Father Krauss come up and help with it. What we did is that each of us children picked a passage we wanted to read for a eulogy, so instead of just sitting in the pew and listening to someone read, we actually stood up and read to the friends and the family. It pulled my brother and me much closer than we have been in a long time, and it sort of helped me because I felt that I had something to do and I felt that I was part of it. It was hard.

The summer before he died I was at home, and my mother wanted me to go down with her and visit my father and I was thinking, "I don't want to go. Why should I have to go?" I felt very angry at my mother. I wanted to stay home and have a good time, but I went because my parents asked me. We spent four days down there, and it was great and we had a really nice time. We did a lot of nice things, just the three of us. At least I don't feel guilty about how I treated my father at the end. I feel unhappy that things were just starting to come together for my father. He had this new job that was going well.

The weekend before he died we went up to New Hampshire. We have a house up there that the whole family built together, and this was something that he put a lot of effort into. He just loved New Hampshire. (My family went up there again for the first time after he died, and that was really hard because a lot of him was up there.) Anyway, that was a nice weekend. He really enjoyed it. One of the reasons I feel guilty is because I didn't want to go up to New Hampshire. I didn't want to be there with them and I was forced to. I wasn't in a good mood that weekend. Everyone was saying how good my father was feeling and how well they connected with him, and I didn't feel that way at all. I remember that I had been rude or something like that. I thought he was being a jerk, really obnoxious to me. I thought, "I don't need this garbage from him." And then when I found out that he had died four days later, I thought like, "Gosh, I know it was really minor, but I felt bad that that had to happen."

Sue

I was twenty-three when my mother died. It'll be ten years this year. It's hard to believe it has been that long. It doesn't seem like it because she is still so alive for me.

It was her third bout with cancer. I was home when she had an operation to remove her bladder. It was right after I graduated from college. A year later she was diagnosed as having cancer again. I was [living] in Boston when she died. I had been planning to go home at Christmas and possibly stay longer if I was needed. I had seen her the previous September when I'd been home for my sister's wedding.

She died the day after Thanksgiving. I was on an island in Maine and I had a dream Thanksgiving night that I had gone to her bedside. It was a very strong dream. When I woke up, I felt very uneasy. When I got back from Maine that night my sister called to say she had died that morning. I had dreamed that when my mother pulled down the sheet, her body was transparent and I could see the cancer through her body.

I had many other dreams about her after she died. I would dream that

I would be somewhere and that I would run into my mother and she would say, "I'm not really dead. Why did you bury me?" Some of them were accusatory, and some of them were joyful reunions.

I went home for the funeral. My father had taken care of most everything. There were viewings in the mortuary, which I just hated. My two younger brothers refused to go. They were fifteen and nineteen. They didn't want to deal with it at all. They did not want to talk about it. My father got very closed up in a lot of ways. My mother had not wanted any extreme lifesaving measures. She had wanted to stay home and she did, although she went to the hospital the night before she died.

I took care of my mother's belongings because my father just couldn't do it. I must have cried nonstop for weeks. Then, when I came back to Boston, I didn't have any family. But I didn't feel that staying home would work either, though some relatives felt that it was my responsibility as the older daughter to stay home and take care of my brothers and father. He didn't put pressure on me to do that, though there were times I thought I probably should have done that.

My mother and I had been through a very long struggle and were just resolving it when she died. My whole breaking away from the family and the church when I went away to college was very difficult, and there were a lot of things I still felt very guilty about when she died. I know I caused her a lot of pain, and we really didn't talk very openly for several years. I didn't come home much during the college years. I was glad we had gotten to some point of resolution. We had some of the best times we ever had during the week I was home for my sister's wedding. Luckily, the last time I saw her we were on better terms than we had been for quite a while.

I was thirteen when my paternal grandmother died, I had been at loggerheads with her and so I had some worries about that. Then my maternal grandmother died. It seems as if there was this period when everyone died. I was very strong-willed and my grandmother and I had a lot of arguments. It wasn't the same with my mother, but there was a lot of guilt I felt along with the grief. If my mother had died a few years earlier in the midst of all that turmoil it would have been worse than it was, because I really feel that we had been working things out.

As young adults we experience a whole spectrum of initial reactions to loss such as shock, anger, and denial. Moreover, we are more vulnerable in general than the mature adult. During this period of our lives we are exploring new identities and our relationships with our parents are changing. We are forging new roles either as students or as new members of the work force. It is a time when we are keenly sensitive to the judgments of our friends and families.

Efforts to develop new roles often cause tensions within the family. Jeremy was in the process of a very normal separation from an intense dependency on his parents when his father died suddenly. On the surface, his conflicts with his parents over how to spend his time may have seemed contentious, but they were actually part of the normal process of trying to establish his own identity and seek his own separate destiny. Sue had disagreed with her mother about religion, and her decision to leave the church caused a great deal of misunderstanding between her and her family.

Such stresses cause us to feel an enormous guilt when a parent dies. We feel responsible for the tension and pain we believe we caused. On the other hand, both Sue and Jeremy had positive relationships with their parents. Also, for both, the quality of the relationship as well as the quality of the time spent together before the death were important in the successful unfolding of the grieving process. Sue had a period of warm companionship with her mother during her sister's wedding. Jeremy could look back at a harmonious and enjoyable summer visit with his father.

If, on the other hand, we had a bitter and contentious relationship with a deceased parent, we struggle for years with feelings of guilt and anger. We try to deny these feelings either by suppressing them or by idealizing the parent. This makes it difficult to move beyond the first reactions to grief. Counseling helps resolve some of the issues in such a relationship, freeing us to feel and express sadness.

Because we are still so dependent on our parents at this age, we often have fewer significant others to turn to when a parent dies. In fact, we might find ourselves isolated from our friends as we cope with new family responsibilities. Sue faced "not having a family" when she returned to graduate school, as her friends were absorbed by romantic ties or academic issues.

When we return to high school or college after a loss, we may not find anyone to talk to about our anger and turmoil. Because we are in shock, we continue attending classes and writing term papers as if nothing had happened, causing our friends and professors to conclude that we are feeling better. Our deep distress is not visible to those who could help us, thus increasing our sense of separation from the world. Sometimes we are conflicted about returning to college and leaving behind a parent and younger siblings. We think that we should have stayed at home to care for them, yet at the same time we want to get on with our lives. Many young adults plunge themselves into school work and manage not only to finish their studies, but to do very well. However, we are only postponing the grieving process, and our grief will surface again later on in our lives.

When older adults experience loss, they have a sense that others around them have had similar or even greater problems. Certainly they are more likely to have friends who have suffered loss. What we as young adults perceive instead are friends who have "normal" families or situations. The perspective an older person develops from a life of experience and of observing others is not available to us. What we see are friends who have "normal" lives. It is difficult to talk about sadness or despair to others who are dealing with what may suddenly seem to be minor issues such as grades or dates. Therefore, it is particularly difficult for us to reach out. Not only are we suffering from what seems like an unusual situation, but because we want people to like us and worry about being accepted by others at this stage in lives, we hesitate to make demands on others just when we need to.

Religious explanations may not have much meaning when we are faced with the terrible injustice of a parent's untimely death. Jeremy felt very keenly that his father died just when his job and life circumstances were improving. We may not have had any prior experience of death, or perhaps if we have, it was an elderly person with whom we had little contact. It's important to turn to a close friend whom we trust. Just talking about our feelings will be a great relief. It will help us to realize that we are not "abnormal" or "crazy" but that others have similar responses to loss. A real friend won't misjudge us.

Sue refers to her younger brothers' apparent detachment during the wake and funeral. They were feeling the shock of mortality—their own vulnerability to death—and were therefore unable to acknowledge their mother's death. Maybe they were afraid of losing control of their emotions or experiencing others' negative reactions to their responses. Fear that our emotions might be unacceptable to our friends and family causes many of us to suppress our anger, guilt, and insecurity. The college-age son of a friend of mine reacted to his mother's death by plunging himself into social activities with his friends, suppressing his initial shock and bewilderment at his terrible loss.

There are many difficulties complicating the grieving process during this period of our lives. We are facing crucial choices: a major in college, a new job, whether to continue a romantic relationship. We have anxieties about our performance in school, about money, about our appearance. There is so much to challenge our self-confidence that makes the death of a parent even more overwhelming.

The demands of our families coupled with social pressures can cause us to bury the troubling emotions that assail us after a death. Watching the terrible sorrow of our surviving parent, we feel that we don't have a right to grieve, or we don't want others to know how we feel because they might criticize us for those feelings. It is important to remember that everyone feels profound emotional turmoil after a death and should feel free to express anger and sadness. Our real friends will want to listen.

When a parent dies we are engulfed not only by waves of powerful feelings, but also by a host of new worries. We wonder if the illness or even the accident that caused the death will happen to us. We are suddenly brought face to face with our own fragility. It is normal to think we might develop cancer or a heart condition because our parent died from that disease. We should discuss these fears with others.

My students have suggested that when a friend loses a parent or loved one, it is sometimes necessary to remind that person of his or her importance. Friends need to tell each other to take care of themselves, to get plenty of sleep, or to eat properly. After a death we sometimes feel that our own well-being no longer matters. At a time like this we need to take special care of ourselves, not only of our physical well-being, but also of our emotional well-being.

Chapter Five
WHEN A SPOUSE DIES

Anne

He died on January 14th. The previous Thanksgiving, he did not feel that well. His stomach was bothering him. Finally, it was bothering him so much that we decided he might as well go and see a doctor and get it over with. December 11th he went to see our doctor. We go from stomach ache on Thanksgiving to dead in January. It turned out to be cancer of the pancreas and they operated on December 23rd. I found out before he did because they were doing tests. It looked like it might be jaundice. They had to do CAT scans. We were assuming that it was gallstones. Then they said at the hospital that they were going to look at the pancreas. I went home and got a book about adult diseases from Better Homes and Gardens. *So I looked up cancer of the pancreas, and when I saw it I said, "I'm going to be a widow." I knew it right then. Thank God I knew it before he did. The next day, after he was operated on, the doctor was back in half an hour. I wouldn't have been so ready if I hadn't read that book. So then I told him. He knew or he was afraid of it underneath. So I said, "It's not very good news. They say it's cancer and your time will be numbered in months." Months! You think ten months. Meanwhile I am coming in twice a day, taking care of kids, working.*

The kids were in school, and as each one came home, I told them he was going to die. I could have waited, but I didn't. They asked, "How's Daddy?" and I said, "Well, he came through the operation and it wasn't good. The doctors said they were going to do the best that they could, but they say he has cancer of the pancreas, and you don't get better from that. They say he has months." That was hard, but I knew it was the right thing to do. Good news you can surprise people with. But not bad news.

Every day I would wake up and think it wasn't true. It's as if you had an automobile accident and thought if you could just go back for three hours, like on a movie tape, it wouldn't have happened. So you have that feeling. The children cried, but they were pretty good. They went in on Christmas and we brought presents. I was strong at that time. I had the initial strength you have from adrenalin. I had people over and I thought I'll do this and I'll have insurance money. It was a little macabre because he was going to die, but he wasn't dead yet. Then he would say to me, "Well, you'd better sell the car." We always thought we had more time than we did, and that was merciful during that period of time.

You say a person is dying, but they are alive. When they are dead you can go back and say, "He was dying." When they are dead. We would talk about the fact that we hoped he would be home. It turned out that he developed phlebitis of the leg, which kept him in the hospital. It was fortunate because they don't want dying people in the hospital. Hospitals are for sick people who are going to be better, so they wanted him out as soon as he was dying. The only reason that he could stay was because he needed an IV. It's merciful that he didn't come home because the children would have had to see ambulances and stuff. He never came home. That was it. He was on morphine and cocaine mixtures. I was very pleased that everyone was respectful to him. He wasn't a casual person. They called him Mr. Ross. And we talked frankly. It was good.

Bill

My wife, Ginny, had breast cancer and she was on chemotherapy and had been on radiation. Apparently she knew that she was dying but she had never told me. I suppose I should have known it, but I didn't really want to know it. We went away to Maine on the Fourth of July, and she obviously knew something was wrong then, because she was very insistent that our daughter and son-in-law come down. My daughter had planned to go somewhere else. Normally she would have said, "Okay, go somewhere else," but she was very insistent that Patty go with us, which tells me that she had an omen. The whole family went and we had a wonderful weekend.

When the weekend was over, she was in the kitchen cooking and I was in the dining room eating and she walked by me and said, "I can't get my breath." That's not an unusual thing to happen to people, but there was something that told me I should go in the bedroom and check. When I got in the bedroom, she was sitting on the bed, and I sat next to her and put my arm around her. As soon as I did that, she lay down on the bed and died without saying another word. I didn't know that she was dead and I didn't check her pulse or anything. We struggled her into the car and my daughter Patty drove. We took her to the hospital. It took about twenty minutes. She was lying in my arms in the back seat. I still thought she was alive but unconscious. When we got to the hospital, Patty ran in to get the doctors. At that point I gave her mouth-to-mouth resuscitation. At that moment one of the interns came out, took one look at her, rolled her eyes back and said, "She's gone." I answered, "Of course she's not gone." He was just a young intern so he pounded on her chest to get her breathing, and then they rushed her into the emergency ward.

My daughter and I went into the office to fill out the forms, assuming that in a few minutes everything would be all right. The doctor came in and told us that she was dead.

I was just numb. I had heard something that didn't seem possible. We got up and left, drove down to the cottage. I just was in a numb state as if it couldn't be. I had lived with this lady for thirty-three years, known her for thirty-five, and suddenly she couldn't be dead. The rest of that day all the friends and relatives started to accumulate. I still had no sadness. I was still in a state of shock.

I still don't remember when I first had the feeling of sadness, but I think it wasn't until after the funeral. Even during the funeral I had this numbness.

When I came home and everything was over with, I was alone. I can remember cooking and crying. Men don't cry, of course. So many times the doorbell would ring and I would run around and get a towel and dry my eyes, stalling until I let that person in. This is the way I went on. In five or six months I started to date women, and that got my mind off it. But every now and then I would think of it. Of course you can't help it. You think of the things you did together.

A difficult thing was when little by little I had to get rid of her clothes. I still find some of her personal belongings. Even today, if I come across those things, that gives me bad memories.

Eric

Diane died in April 1983 of melanoma, which is a form of skin cancer. She had first been diagnosed when she was twenty-one and died when she was thirty. When she was about twenty-nine she found some tumors in her stomach, so that was the first indication that the melanoma had gone anywhere else besides her skin. That was when it became very frightening, but even then it had stabilized and we thought she would really beat it. She had always been a very spirited, very energetic person, incredibly positive, full of life and energy. She didn't seem like a cancer victim. She also took a very strong hand once she realized that the melanoma would not go away. She became very active in searching out ways of dealing with cancer. She found a program at the Beth Israel Hospital called the program of behavioral medicine where they teach people how to meditate and try to reduce stress. Diane worked with a woman there and became a pretty disciplined meditator.

When we returned from our honeymoon she didn't feel well, and it turned out that she had a very large tumor in her abdomen. She had surgery, but she never quite recovered. She decided to stay home, although it turned out that she was in very bad pain the last two weeks. They kept giving us stronger and stronger painkillers. It wasn't working. It seemed like the only thing that would work would be intravenous morphine, which they couldn't give us at home.

That process of preparing for death was really good in some ways. Diane's younger sister is a nurse, so she came to stay with us and brought all these books on death and dying. Diane and I read a lot of books, and we were great researchers. We had researched melanoma, but it had never occurred to us to research death.

Diane was a real stoic. She had always been very brave, and it was hard for her to admit that the pills weren't working, that she was in such pain. But we had this time to talk, and we did talk a lot. I had started to see a therapist and she saw a therapist too. I started to see a therapist about a month before Diane died because it was clear that I just had to have someone to talk to. Both our therapists kept telling us that the thing to do was to talk to each other about it. It was our last chance. Also, if you don't talk, it becomes this great unmentionable that just snowballs. When there is no future, it becomes very superficial if you don't talk about that, because you can't talk about anything else. I mean, you can't make plans.

Everything becomes heightened, takes on this emotional meaning. You really lose touch with other things. There is only one thing that is important, and then this person dies. She had been my whole reason for living, my whole huge effort for the past few months. Not only had I lost, but it was a double whammy because I failed. I felt that there's nothing left, that there's nothing to do. You feel you failed because this person died and you didn't prevent it. There's still a sense that you failed the person, that there are things you didn't say that you should have. It comes and goes. There's a great sense of letdown when someone dies after a long illness; it has been your whole life, then there's nothing.

Her whole family came, her parents, her brothers and sisters. They're a very close family. But then they left. There's a new life. There's a sense of adjustment, really different and foreign, unwanted and unknown.

It's hard to believe that all that energy disappears. Diane. I mean, it has to be channeled. I don't have any religious beliefs, and she didn't either. She had this kind of pantheistic view, nothing really to do with God. She had a sense of spirituality. She wanted her memorial service in a church done by a clergyperson. She didn't care where. Also she didn't want God mentioned or Jesus Christ.

She was very specific about the kind of music she wanted. She wanted people to talk about her, to say what they wanted. It was actually very moving. Three hundred people came, including her first-grade teacher, an old woman who said, "She made a lasting impression on me." All our friends came. When I said that Diane had asked anybody that wanted to get up and say whatever they wanted, there was this pause. Then there was this woman who works with me who stood up. She had never met Diane in her life, and she got up, went to the microphone, and said what it was like to work with me for the past couple of weeks. It was just beautiful and very touching. It turned out to be the perfect way to break the ice. The last one to speak was a woman leaning over the railing in a white dress. She had been in a BBC film with Diane, a documentary about mind, body, and healing. Diane was doing very well in the meditation exercises, and this woman who couldn't meditate and relieve herself of stress was getting better. She said she had been in the film with Diane and why should it have been Diane who died and not her.

She was cremated. She didn't want her body there or in a casket. In a way that's hard for people. Seeing a body makes you realize that it's the end. When there is no body, it's harder. It helped to have these people talking about her.

I remember she died at the end of April. You get so absorbed in the funeral arrangements and the mail and the people who come, all the details, which is good. But it has to end, and it does end. And there you are. I was still in shock, still not all there.

I went to get my hair cut one day, and this young girl asked me, "What do you do?" I answered, "Oh, I don't do anything because my wife just died." This was a few days after she died. Then I was running at Fresh Pond and I saw this girl who looked like Diane. I mean, there was probably a very vague resemblance to her. I went running up to her and said, "You look just like my wife who died." This poor woman. She must have thought I was crazy. You do things like that and they're irrational. It is a sense of shock and numbness.

The death of a husband or wife is devastating, one of the most stressful events we face in our lives. There are as many different kinds of marriages as there are couples, and though the intensity and strength of ties vary, all marriages contain powerful emotional bonds. Some consist only of sharing household management and daily routines. Companionship and sharing intimate lives characterize other marriages. But in all types of marriages, loving or troubled, the partners function as one. Losing a partner leaves us feeling incomplete.

Couples who are living together in a committed relationship, whether heterosexual or homosexual, also experience these powerful emotional bonds, as do elderly couples who may have already been widowed and who have chosen to live together rather than to remarry and lose their Social Security. Their relationship is functionally a marital one, yet these relationships do not have social status. This complicates the grieving process, because while the sadness and pain of loss may be as intense as the pain of losing an "official" spouse, these feelings elicit no response from others, and we may believe that somehow we are not entitled to feel so strongly. Because of this we may want to hide our emotions. However, it is important for all of us to realize that the loss of a life shared with another is just as overwhelming to those who have not had their living arrangements acknowledged by society.

When we lose a spouse after years of marriage, we lose the years of growth in intimacy and companionship. The dreams we shared for the future become memories. Even if the relationship was a troubled one, we miss the presence of our spouse. If there were difficulties, the opportunity to try to solve the problems and strengthen the bonds is lost. We are burdened by regret as well as guilt.

If we are young when we lose a spouse, we are robbed of a life of sharing, with its joys and difficulties. We will never have the children we dreamed of bringing up together. We have not only lost a life in common, but have been robbed of our future. Some people try to console us by saying that since we are still young, we will find another partner, but this is hardly a consolation. The future we are cheated of is a future with our loved one, and it cannot be replaced.

Many people are not used to encountering widows or widowers in their twenties or thirties and don't know how to respond. These are years of building, of beginning new relationships, of bearing children. People feel uneasy when meeting the newly widowed because it reminds them of their own mortality and also because they may lack experience with this happening at an early age. This can make us wary of burdening others with our feelings. However, as Eric's narrative in chapter 26 shows us, expressing our feelings when we are with our friends is actually helpful to them. It not only relieves us but also teaches them. It's important not to worry about burdening others at this time. We are carrying enough of a burden ourselves without adding additional guilt. A real friend will treasure our openness and will learn from our experience.

The way our spouse died will have an important effect on our immediate response to the death. In the case of a sudden death such as an accident or a heart attack, the initial shock is much greater and can be overpowering. We are seized with a sense of unreality. How can a person be with us in the morning and not in the afternoon or evening? We expect him or her to return, keep thinking that he or she will eventually come back. In the narratives we can see that Bill experienced a feeling of numbness for a longer period of time than Eric did. Although Bill's wife was also ill with cancer, he either did not admit to himself or was unaware that she was not going to recover.

If our spouse has a terminal illness and we know that he or she will die in the near future, we might have begun to prepare ourselves for this event. Often, however, we have hopes that our spouse will survive or that a cure will become available. Our expectations change throughout the illness, bringing sharp mood swings in their wake. Sometimes we entertain unrealistic hopes that cause us to resist thoughts of death. This adds to the pain of adjustment after death.

We usually have mixed feelings as our spouse is dying. Imperceptibly, we begin to think about our future alone and start to plan for it. However, as Anne's narrative points out, it is troubling to think of preparations for our future when our loved one is not dead. We feel it is a betrayal. How does one deal with a spouse who has no future? We may want to talk about these arrangements with our spouse and to share our thoughts with him or her. The dying person might have some wishes and concerns to share at this moment, and we may wish to have their own thoughts on our plans.

Watching a loved one suffer and feeling powerless to help that person is emotionally draining. We become angry at our helplessness or at the demands placed on us. We are afraid of losing our spouse while wishing that his or her suffering will end. We are assailed by a whirl of conflicting emotions. These are all normal reactions, and we should not burden ourselves by feeling guilty about our responses. These emotions are the rafts that will carry us through the stormy times.

How to deal with children and relatives is a very important issue. As Anne's narrative points out, it's best to be open with children and tell them exactly what is happening and what to expect. Sooner or later children will find out that a parent is dying, and they will feel betrayed if we keep that information from them. The mother of one of my students died of cancer when my student was ten years old. Her father didn't tell her how seriously ill her mother was, and when she was finally hospitalized, he brought her to the hospital only at the very end. By then her mother was comatose and swollen with cortisone. She felt she should have been prepared for this and was shocked and terrified at the sight of her mother and the very sudden revelation of her impending death. Children need our guidance in preparing for death. Our silence can be interpreted by them as helplessness or as a sign of more dire things to come.

After the shock of the death wears off, we are confused by the storm of emotions that assail us. Many people speak of waking up in a panic during the night and especially of feeling terribly lonely. Our spouse may have provided us not only with a sense of identity, but also with a reason for living, and therefore we feel an anguishing emptiness and a loss of meaning. We wonder why we should get up in the morning, why we should work or carry on our daily routines.

In fact our daily routines have changed dramatically. We don't know what to do with the loneliness in the house. An empty house can be particularly difficult for men, and they may respond by working longer hours or by taking their meals out. The pain might be so intense that we wish to make changes in our life, perhaps move to a new location or take a new job; but this is not a good time to make an important decision that will profoundly affect our lives. Rather, we should concentrate on taking care of ourselves, trying to get as much rest as possible, eating properly and communicating our needs to those who are close to us and to other members of our family.

Many practical problems and tasks must be tackled, such as arranging for the funeral and informing friends and relatives. We must fill out the death certificate and deal with wills and financial issues. These tasks can actually provide an order to our otherwise disrupted life, but for someone unfamiliar with financial and legal matters, this is a very difficult period. This is a good time to seek appropriate help in dealing with these matters. For example, a retired woman who was suddenly widowed turned to the association of retired people in her town to help her file her tax return.

Most marriages are characterized by a division of labor. When a spouse dies, we acquire a whole new set of chores in addition to accustomed ones. A woman will have to deal with repair people, lawyers, and bank personnel without the input of her husband. Women frequently experience sudden changes in status with respect to credit and financial situations. These are not small burdens, considering the depth of our distress. In more traditional marriages, a widower is faced with learning to shop or cook, especially learning how to be in an empty house. Organizing a household may seem as complex and difficult to a widower as learning to deal with tax forms and bank statements is to a widow. In addition to learning how to function emotionally without our partner, we are tackling new tasks every day.

Besides the allocation of chores, spouses collaborate in making important decisions about household and child-rearing. A widow or widower might be left with the sole responsibility for earning a living and also bringing up children. If our marriage was conflict-ridden, we may find rueful gratification at being able to make certain decisions alone. However, we all feel the difficulties of having to shoulder responsibilities ourselves. We become angry at the sudden increase in responsibility for decisions and the number of tasks we have to handle. We ask ourselves, "Why me?" We are angry at everyone else who still enjoys being a couple and at a world in which everyone seems to have a partner.

If we have children, we are faced with being both father and mother to them, acting as provider and a source of emotional support. It is difficult enough to accomplish this when one is feeling well, but such a great responsibility when we have just experienced the death of a spouse is even harder and will often lead us to postpone our own grief.

After our spouse dies, we step out into the world with a different identity. As a widow, we may be perceived as a "sad" person, reminding others of the fragility of life. We may also be considered a threatening sexual rival. The social supports we enjoyed while still married may no longer be available. People whom we considered friends sometimes avoid us, intensifying our feelings of loneliness and confusion. On the other hand, we may be surprised by gestures of friendship from members of our family or acquaintances who have suffered from loss themselves and are sensitive to our needs.

While a woman experiences special difficulties in facing the world after her husband has died, a man experiences problems with living in an empty house. He might take his meals out or go out every night just to avoid being in the house alone. He may even avoid spending time with old friends, knowing that after a round of golf or a drink, the friends will be returning to their wives. This is especially true for men whose children have grown up. Children may not understand their father's need for company and new friends and might regard their father's behavior as a betrayal of their mother's memory.

However, although it is just as stressful for a man to "reenter" society as a single man, he is not likely to be perceived as a threat. It seems to be easier for men to establish new relationships a few months after the death of a spouse than for women. However, our family and friends can misunderstand our efforts to develop new ties as a betrayal of the former marriage, while we may see no conflict between a new relationship and a commitment to our deceased spouse.

After our spouse's death we feel empty and incomplete. Perhaps it is not possible to reach out immediately for comfort or for new friendships. However, added to our deep pain is the stress of adjusting to changed social roles and status. Our standing within the family may have changed drastically; maybe we find our role changed from that of giver of advice to recipient. Perhaps we used to host family dinners during the holidays, and now this ceremony is taken over by an adult child or another member of the family. We are already experiencing low self-esteem from the blow of the death, and these additional changes diminish our self-confidence.

When our partner in a lesbian or gay relationship dies, we are often suddenly cut off from our partner's immediate family or are denied access to the extended family. Often we are so affected by society's reaction to our situation that we hesitate to seek outside help. But one woman who lost her partner in a lesbian relationship joined a support group of widows and found both help and acceptance. Just because society minimizes a relationship doesn't mean that we have no right to our grief or outside support.

The weeks after the death of our spouse are not only very lonely and confusing, but are also a time of gathering in. We feel very private at this time, not ready to reach out. During this period we should be very kind to ourselves and avoid taking on any unnecessary burdens. Even if we are responsible for others, we must take special care of ourselves, making sure that we have periods of rest and times of privacy for the tears to flow. We need to think about the deceased and continue our communication with our spouse in our thoughts or by wrapping up his or her affairs.

Chapter Six
WHEN A CHILD DIES

Phil

When I first heard about it, I was in the classroom. I got a phone call from my best friend, who told me that there had been an accident. I jumped in the car and drove I-don't-know-at-what speed. In the next few days when my daughter was in the hospital, I learned what really happened. An elderly man not attending to his driving caused the loss of life of my daughter Jenny. She was walking her bicycle across the street. She had stopped at the crosswalk just like she had been taught to do. This is a quiet little town where we lived. It was in the fall. It was the afternoon, three o'clock a nice clear day. She was waved across by another person. Then she saw this man who wasn't looking while he was driving. He stepped on the gas instead of on the brakes. What happened after that wasn't very nice.

That has always been difficult for us, the injustice of it all. Afterward he didn't behave in a manly, human way. The legal proceedings were terrible. The worst thing is that he continues to drive his car. That's always been a thorn in our sides. In addition to the loss, we've always had to deal with that other aspect of it, the conduct of that person. As a Christian you don't want to harbor hard feelings, but I have those feelings because it was an injustice. This man is in his late seventies and does not belong behind the wheel. It causes my wife a tremendous discomfort. Society doesn't have a resolution for the victim.

For three years we've had constant news bulletins about the case.

And each time we have to relive this thing. It opens those wounds again. It also opens up that feeling about how unnecessary it all was.

Jenny was one of our three children. She was the middle child. For us, Jenny was the catalyst in the family, the source of energy for us. For me, she was my ever-present shadow. My older daughter and I had a wonderful relationship. But when I would come home from meetings, Jenny would always be waiting for me. I would run late after work and she would always go with me. When I went to the ball park, she always wanted to go. She was a big baseball fan. She went to about nine or ten games with me, and every time the Red Sox won. The last time we had a lot of difficulty in getting in and finally got some standing room tickets. We were standing way in the back. We could hardly see. Then this gentleman walked up to me, looked at me and at Jenny and said, "I've got some great seats. You know, I have to go back to work. Stay right where you are and I'll come get you." She was just enthralled. I can remember seeing her expression, and I have just memorized the whole thing. She had a very magnetic personality. She was a tremendously alive person and had a great deal of hopefulness about her. It's not a case of making someone bigger than they are. When your daughter and your companion and your friend goes, that's very difficult. We didn't know how to deal with that.

A friend of mine was a member of the Resistance to the Nazis during World War II. She was caught and spent the war years in concentration camps. Who can imagine a worse fate? Yet years later, her son Peter was killed in an automobile accident. In the epilogue to her book on the Holocaust she wrote about her son, "The wound is deeper than Auschwitz." No one anticipates such a loss. We expect to lose our parents through old age or illness, but no one expects to survive one's own child. It seems contrary to nature, a blow which is barely comprehensible in its cruelty.

Although there are differences in the grief we feel for the death of an infant, the death of a child, or of a young adult, as parents our role is to protect, nurture, and love. We want to be omnipotent, to arrange our child's circumstances so that he or she will be as happy and healthy as possible. When our child dies, we feel as if we have failed in our role as parents. Our helplessness in face of illness or an accident compounds our guilt.

If our child died of an illness, we may have had to watch the child suffer for a long period of time and undergo the pain of his or her progressive decline. After such a death we go over and over this period, reviewing it. We wonder if we should have done things differently, whether we could have done just a little bit more. Even those of us who spent all of our time in the hospital at the bedside of our child agonize over the care we provided while our child was ill.

Many deaths of children are due to cancer. This may mean that the child had to endure chemotherapy or radiation treatments with all the painful side effects. One of my neighbor's children died of a brain tumor when she was eighteen. The chemotherapy and cortisone caused Julie's hair to fall out, and her face swelled and puckered like a newborn's. Eventually she became partially paralyzed. Looking back, we wonder whether we were sufficiently loving and reassuring at these times. Children worry about how their peers and others will react to them, whether they will still be accepted, and how, finally, they themselves can accept this transformed self.

When we look back on this period, we sometimes think that we were so caught up in the physical side of our child's care or in our own sadness that we wonder whether we were sensitive enough to our child's reactions to his or her illness. Children respond differently to these disfigurements. Because of her age, Julie felt more comfortable being bathed by a visiting nurse than by her mother. However, this was difficult for her mother, who was already grief-stricken over the impending end of her parenting role.

As Julie's condition worsened, she stayed home. Although the family made every effort to organize their life so that she would be as comfortable as possible, family activities continued. Her mother's friends stopped by once a week for a game of bridge, and her sister continued to pursue her own activities at school. Trying to keep home life as normal as possible is helpful both for the parents and for the dying child.

Children of any age have anxieties about dying. Parents who are already suffering the difficulties of facing a child's death may not find it easy to address the questions and fears of the child. The child may want to know whether he is going to get better or not. Pretending or side-stepping these questions leave children feeling confused. Trying to maintain a stoic attitude before a terminally ill child can make that child feel that he must behave in the same way. Children are very sensitive to our behavior. They know when we are lying. When we are trying to cover something up, they can read our body language with great acuity and are bewildered when our words and nonverbal signals conflict. They take their cues from us, so if we express our sadness and pain, they will be able to share their own grief with us.

Children grieve not only for their impending death, but for the separation from family and friends. A child's age, personality, and coping styles determine how he grieves. His way will not be our own way of grieving, and we might have a hard time reading his cues. A child may express regret over not being able to attend graduation, a school dance, or a basketball game. We don't always see his mourning in these regrets. When we are burdened with the care of a terminally ill child, it's not always possible to have the perspective that time and distance bring. We shouldn't blame ourselves for not having the wisdom that comes only with hindsight.

When a child suffers from an illness, we seek out superior care, try to do everything humanly possible to assure the child's recovery. We often become absorbed in the physical care of the child, and when we are not actually caring for her we are thinking and worrying about her. After the death, we are suddenly cut adrift. It's as if we had lost a large part of our life, the very meaning of our life. Even if we have other children, each child is unique. Each child has his or her own place in our hearts and lives. Even if our days are filled with other responsibilities and concerns, the emptiness after such a death often makes us feel as if we were living a nightmare.

Because our role is that of caregiver, we parents have great difficulty not only with the brutal termination of our parental role, but with our own need for nurture and support. It is confusing and disorienting to find ourselves suddenly in the grip of overwhelming anger, guilt, and sadness. It's as if we were propelled out of our nurturing role and into our deepest selves.

Living together as a family is especially difficult after the loss of a child. For instance, a wife may not want to go out to a movie or dinner with her husband because she is having a bad day, but that doesn't mean she doesn't want to be with him. If a mother is sitting on the living-room sofa crying when a child comes home, the child may feel that he or she is not important to her. It's very difficult to be a parent after the death of a child because we are so caught up in our emotions that we have little to give. But we need to level with our children, let them know where we are. We can tell our children that we are feeling bad that afternoon but that we still love them and that they are still very important to us. Surviving children need to know and to be constantly reassured about where they stand, even though our parenting energy is drained and we need to be nurtured ourselves. They are often able to understand our needs better than we imagine.

We might think that not talking about the death will protect our children, but they may respond by withdrawing and engaging in antisocial behavior. If we show our own tears and sadness, while assuring the surviving children that they are very important to us, they will feel free to express their sorrow. The tears we shed do not necessarily cause others to cry. When our crying sparks tears in others, it is only because we have tapped the tears that were already inside them. Think of it as liberating those tears. We may not realize how deeply children grieve or that silence or withdrawal do not indicate the absence of sadness.

When a child dies, everyone in the family is affected and everyone grieves in his or her own way. This places a tremendous burden on the nuclear family. Perhaps we have built up expectations over the years and are now not able to live up to them, to be the strong, supporting, nurturing parent or the well-behaved child. It is extremely helpful to seek outside supports at this time, not only for our own relief and but also for the health of the family. Phil started going out with an old friend and both he and his wife saw a counselor.

Our family does not expect us to be strong or invulnerable at all times, but they do expect that we communicate with them. It's important to recognize that we can't control each other's feelings. Grief is so powerful and unpredictable that it is difficult to communicate clearly after a loss. However, if we can be patient and tolerant with each other and not expect too much, that in itself will help our family life.

While we may have had a chance to prepare ourselves for the death of a child during an illness, losing a child by accidental death is more difficult. The shock is more intense and lasts longer and the guilt is apt to be stronger. As parents, we feel that we should have prevented the accident. We go over and over the details as if we were replaying a film. Phil's daughter was killed as she was crossing the street. She had wanted to come to work with him that day, but his schedule was too crowded. After the accident, he thought that if he had not been so busy, his daughter would still be alive. We blame ourselves for not being able to prevent accidents, for failing as protectors.

Often our anger is as intense as our shock and guilt and is directed at the driver of the car if the child died in an automobile accident, at the policeman who informed us, or at the hospital personnel who had to give us the news of our child's death. Most of all we are angry at the sheer injustice of such a death. In addition, we will have the added anguish of dealing with courts and lawyers and having our distress prolonged as the legal battles drag on.

As parents we believe that the worst thing that could ever happen to us would be if one of our children were killed. We want to die on the spot ourselves. We don't see how we can possibly continue. We wish it had been us and are stunned at the senseless way a precious life can be snuffed out in just a few minutes. Losing an adult child by accident has its own particular difficulties. The married daughter of a middle-aged couple decided to sail across the English Channel with her husband. The parents felt this would be taking a risk given the poor condition of the boat. Nevertheless, the young couple decided to go ahead with their plans. The boat did capsize and the young woman, who was pregnant at the time, drowned. This family lost not only a daughter who showed great promise, but also a grandchild. It's as if their future had been canceled. When we lose adult children, we are robbed not only of future generations, but also of watching a young person unfold and develop a new identity. It is a terrible waste of a life.

My great aunt was eighty-five when her only daughter was killed in a head-on automobile collision at the age of sixty. "Why couldn't it have been me?" she wept. "My life is over." Frequently, and this was certainly true in my aunt's case, there is a role reversal as mature adults assume the parenting role for an elderly mother or father. It is difficult not only to deal with such a shock physically and emotionally, but also to comprehend the enormity of such an event. Friends kept telling my great aunt that she had grandchildren, but grandchildren, no matter how much one loves them, do not replace a daughter. I held my great aunt while she cried and told me how terrible it was to survive one's own child. An elderly person such as she does not have a long future in which to heal and move on to a new life.

It is extremely difficult to let go of a parental role. Therefore, for some of us, the preparation and the event of a wake gives us the opportunity to prolong that role for a short while. But for parents who lose an older child, the funeral can be a trying experience. Young people generally have lots of connections, and we may be meeting many of our children's friends and acquaintances for the first time. While some derive comfort from this experience, others consider it an invasion of their privacy. For still others, the presence of large groups of people at the funeral serves as an acknowledgment of their loss.

After the funeral our needs are different. We are faced with all of the physical reminders of our child—an empty room, clothes, toys, or books—that make his or her absence more poignant. Our child's friends might stop in, which makes us experience fresh waves of sadness as the full reality of the death takes hold of us. Some people eventually redecorate the child's room or give away some personal things, keeping only a few mementos. There is no absolute calendar for this. It's a matter of feeling ready.

In the case of an accident, some people decide to move to a new house or a new town, far from the site of the collision or drowning. This can also help us to move to a new place inside ourselves as well as help us avoid painful reminders. The timing for such a decision will be similar to the timing for decisions about the child's personal effects. During the first few months after the death we will experience periods of great confusion and sadness. We may not be ready to let go of those particular memories.

A child's death leaves us feeling as if our lives were shattered and our emotions were in chaos. Maintaining a sense of continuity in our daily routine, especially our outside connections through work or friendship, serves as a step to our eventual recovery. However, in the early weeks and months after the death, we should be careful about burdening ourselves with too many tasks. Just getting through the day after such a tragic loss is a great accomplishment and requires considerable energy. Initially, we are grateful just for the day's passing. Then we make it through weeks. Then, gradually, we begin to think of other things. But those weeks of seeming inactivity are actually periods of hard work for our emotions. It is helpful just to allow our sadness to well up and our tears to flow during these times.

Everyone fears and imagines the loss of a child, so people may be unwilling to see us or to talk to us after the death of our child. We must be especially responsive to our own needs and not worry about sparing others. We need to be able to talk about the death, weep, and find time for ourselves as well as turn to friends who will be sensitive and supportive. Family members might want to have separate supports, because we all grieve in different ways and have different needs.

Single parents have the additional pain of handling all the burdens alone. It is helpful to reach out to supportive friends and special programs. We need to talk about the sadness we feel for our child and to be accepted in our grief.

Couples generally have expectations of mutual support. However, when both parents are affected by a tragedy, the relationship is subjected to great strains. Men and women have different coping styles, which can cause irritation, friction, and misunderstanding. A woman may express her grief through tears and talking, whereas a man may seem stoic by maintaining silence and plunging himself in his work. Although he is in great pain, his wife might conclude that he's not feeling anything. It can be difficult for a man to act nurturing or supportive of his wife, holding her, putting his arms around her. The same is true of a woman. Perhaps each expects responses when the other is having a bad day. It's important to communicate with each other as clearly as possible regarding our own grief and our feelings for our spouse.

Chapter Seven
STILLBIRTHS AND MISCARRIAGES

Michelle

We took it for granted that you'd be with us.
You had already gone far for your age.
You did the subways of New York
Flew with us to Jordan and walked through Petra
Wondered at the tulips in Holland
Visited Washington
And you jumped, startled at the Firebird Suite in Upstate New York.
Along with us, you even survived when our car was hit on the
    highway by a truck.

We often spoke and sang to you from the outside of Mommy's belly,
especially your sister, Angie.

Girl, were you feisty!
Kicking up a storm.
We would watch you turn,
Turn Mommy's tummy into a gymnastics show.

When I saw your limp, lifeless shoulder fall,
gracefully twisting out from Mommy's womb
—though I knew you were gone—
I still waited
hopelessly hopeful
for your cries and kicks

only to hear my gut sliced by the silence
and to feel my body quake under the weight of your stillness.

Michelle, we all bowed our heads in awe of your mother's mythic
    journey.
How could God conceive this?
In full health, strangled by your own cord.
They were driving cars on Mars
and still, we let you fall like this.

If only.
If only we could rewind the tape
and take this story down a different branch
And help you blossom, bloom and conquer.

How is it that you've left us
and yet
You'll be with us always?

Surely God will love your company.

Amin Bishara

Amin

Brenda was sounding a bit distraught because she knew she hadn't felt the baby kick for a while. That was on a Monday morning, and the midwife said, "Come on in. Ninety-nine percent of the time this isn't anything," although she said after the fact that she felt in her stomach that something was wrong just from hearing Brenda. So we drove to the hospital. The nurse who usually checks you out before you get checked in to the labor room took the Doppler sensor and put it in one spot where we normally hear things, and there wasn't any sound, and then she put it in another spot, and there was no sound. She put it in a third spot, and there wasn't any sound, She said, "Well, you know, sometimes we have to do this by ultrasound." So she started doing an ultrasound of Brenda. I liked the way she handled it. She kept moving the ultrasound around so that we could see the baby in the screen. She wasn't saying anything. She'd focus in, and I knew that we were looking at a heart because we'd seen it so many times before, and there was no motion. And then she still wasn't saying anything. And then Brenda said, "Well, I'm not seeing any heart-

beat." And that's the point at which the nurse said, "You know, I'm not either. I'm so sorry." She gave Brenda a hug, and gave us a few minutes to call Brenda's parents. We told them what was going on. Brenda was distraught at that point. Then the midwife came in and began to talk about the things that we would need to do, which was good, because it got repeated later on, got repeated several times.

We went to do an official ultrasound on another floor to determine that the baby was in fact dead. That, I think, was unnecessary. But they had to do it for records and legal purposes. When we got back from there, both the midwife and the doctor on call put us in a room in a quiet area. The doctor explained that it was completely up to us when we wanted to deliver, but that they felt that it was better in general to deliver sooner than later. And they alluded, I think diplomatically, to the fact that it's better for the body to go through the stress of delivery sooner than later.

What I admired was the selection of words. It's a fairly gruesome thing; instead of saying, "The body is beginning to decompose; we'd rather get it out of you sooner than later," there were just subtle allusions to the body and skin tearing and stuff like that. We discussed what the options were and how they would induce labor. I asked at several different times whether we could just surgically extract the baby and get it over with, because that is the male reaction—"I don't want to deal with this. I don't know why you are putting us through this. Just get it out of there and get it over with." Brenda felt very strongly that that wasn't what she wanted to do. They explained that on one level there were risks of surgery associated with a Caesarean: The recovery period is a lot longer after a Caesarean than after a natural delivery. All the literature says that even though in the short term, it's more excruciating to deal with the baby as a real person, in the long run it was much better in terms of getting through it and getting over it to treat it as a normal delivery and to spend time with the baby. That certainly rang true to Brenda. At the time I was still thinking, "My God, this is morbid. Isn't it morbid to hold a dead baby?" But, you know, the male of the species goes through transitions a little bit differently than the female of the species.

I made it clear to Brenda that I wanted to talk to a lawyer before we got started. I know that sounds weird, but my first reaction was, "These people screwed up." The reason I felt that way was because three days, or four days earlier, we'd been at the hospital in order for them to do what's called a "version." Because when the baby is breached, when the head is at the top and the feet are at the bottom, and you're sufficiently near labor—she was within two weeks—in her 38th week—they turn the baby around by manipulating it from the outside. So that's what they had done on Thursday. And this was Monday. A part of me was really making the connection between the cord accident and that event. So partially, I wanted to get the lawyers to start thinking.

Prior to their letting us go home, they had us meet with the chaplain. She was very helpful and warm. Brenda is a Methodist, so it was very important for her to be able to speak to a chaplain at that point. The chaplain was helpful in terms of entertaining the cosmic discussion that I wanted to have, which is, "Why did this happen to us? And if divine inter-vention saved us from a truck accident we had recently, what does that mean about divine intervention at this point?" She expressed the opinion that there was no divine intervention in the accident, and therefore there was no divine intervention in this situation. I wanted to know what they had to say about cosmic questions, but basically their position was "Oh no, you can't blame God for this one. God is not a micromanager. He sets up the big picture and doesn't handle these little things."

Then they made us wait until a social worker arrived, who told us about the variety of resources that the hospital would make available. It ended up being really a set of handouts about the grieving process, a set of booklets that were in fact very helpful as we were going through the process. I give the doctor and the midwife, the chaplain and the social worker credit for asserting over and over the importance of delivering the baby, spending time with the baby, naming it, having a service and being ready to go through a grieving process, and ultimately, the importance of talking with other parents who've been through similar things.

I also give them credit for focusing us on how we were going to start inducing and deliver and the preference to do that sooner than later. It gave us a very definable thing to do in the short term—just to get home, make whatever calls we needed to do, pick up whatever stuff we needed to pick up, and come back to the hospital at a reasonable time. The mid-wife who'd been seeing Brenda throughout the pregnancy most frequently also delivered our first child and assured us that she would be there until 7 A.M. the following morning, but even if it took longer than that, she wanted to see to it that she was the one. That was very helpful.

We were back at the hospital by about 4:30 A.M. They intelligently put us in the delivery area along with everybody else—that's their point—

you're delivering a baby just like everybody else is delivering a baby. But they also chose a room off in a corner where you don't hear sounds from anywhere else. You have privacy, but you're still part of the normal delivery process. They were very smart about the nurses that they chose. They were clearly more competent and more mature than the ones we had seen when we delivered our daughter Angie. These were clearly women who knew what they were dealing with and apparently had had special training in dealing with these situations.

I give them credit for managing a lot of the details very well. If any one of them were to have said the wrong thing or done the wrong thing, it could leave a bruise. And I think, in hindsight, that they were also sharp enough to have picked up my vibes, to know that they had probably better handle things well, because I was really concerned.

Brenda and I started making calls—before people came and while people were there—to some close relatives that we wanted to tell what was happening. It was very helpful that Brenda's parents made it clear that they were going to stick around for the delivery process. At one point, Brenda's father and I went out and did a grocery run at the twenty-four-hour Star market so we would have food and stuff to drink. The midwife said, "Make sure you get a whole bunch of food, because you're going to need it."

The nanny brought our daughter over. Actually, the original plan was that our daughter Angie would go back with her grandparents to Weston either after the baby was delivered or late at night, depending on the sequence of events. My cousin showed up, which was very helpful—she's a nurse. She ended up volunteering to take our daughter to spend the night with her in Cambridge, which was right nearby the hospital, and that she would bring her back in the morning. So that was a great help. The reason I bring that up is that what is most helpful in these situations are the little things that people do for you. The next day, for example, a friend of mine who lives nearby brought us some Lebanese food from Watertown for us to eat. It's the little touches that make a big difference.

To make a long story short, we delivered the baby at 4:30 in the morning. I was very touched that the chaplain was willing to get called up by the midwife at around 3:00 A.M. to tell her "I think this is going to happen in the next hour to hour and a half." The chaplain got out of bed and came to the hospital and actually helped deliver the baby. I was not up for holding one of Brenda's legs. I was next to Brenda, comforting her. But the chaplain held one of Brenda's legs. I think that was nice.

As soon as the baby was delivered, they made a point of letting Brenda and me hold her. It took me a while to want to hold the dead baby. There was this voice inside me constantly saying, "God, isn't this a morbid thing to do?" But it struck us that the baby looked amazingly like Angie when she was born. As the baby was coming out, you could see that the cord was tied around the front of the neck, and there was no blood flowing through. It was very white, as was the area around her neck. So that sort of confirmed their hypothesis that this was a cord accident.

Throughout the evening, even at the late hours of the night, the doctor kept coming in and answering questions that we had, about what the blood tests were that they were doing, everything we could possibly ask about cord accidents, about the connection between the version and the cord accident, and whether proper practice was followed or not. In any case, we spent several hours with the baby.

We slept a little bit after the delivery. They bathed the baby, measured it, weighed it. We made it clear we wanted the baby to be called Michelle. They insisted, prior to that, that we be sure to have a name ready. By morning they were focusing us on these details, that they were bathing the baby, that they wanted to make the name tags, that they wanted to take pictures of the baby. They helped us take pictures right after the baby was delivered. You know, your male voice says, "Why are we dwelling on all this? Why are we taking pictures? Isn't this a little weird?"

The nurse that was helping the midwife from 7 P.M. to 7 A.M. was brilliant. Whenever we asked her a question, I always admired her selection of words. Again I think the selection of words that these people use is so critically important. And there are some pretty gory aspects to this. They were communicating what they needed to communicate without using words that open the wound.

It was painful for us to notice that three hours after the delivery the baby was beginning to turn blue, which was what they had warned us. They said they'd be taking more pictures, but they wanted us to be aware that as time went on her color was going to be turning increasingly blue or purple. What I give them credit for is that they had slipped those observations in at different times so that we were ready for it.

The nurse that came in then ended up being absolutely wonderful in the way she handled everything. At the time, we were contending with what to tell Angie when she came back. We had already told her that the baby was dead and that Mommy was going to be delivering. But do we have her go through the experience of touching the baby and holding her and seeing her, or do we just tell her, "You know, this is a done deal"? Now the hospital was a 150 percent on the side of give her the choice. Even though she agreed with giving Angie a choice, the nurse wanted her to hold the baby.

Angie did eventually come in, and she was unambiguous about the fact that she wanted to see her sister. So I brought her the baby, and she held her for a while. She cried, because she knew she was supposed to cry. She held her hand and touched her skin and said how soft it was. We told her that she looked very much like her when she was born. Then she and I put the baby back on the warming table. We were out of camera film, but we had my father-in-law's video camera, so we videotaped Angie holding the baby up next to her Mommy and touching her. Then, before Angie left, she asked me to take her back to the baby, and so one more time she touched her and kissed her several times and then went away with her nanny. Patty, the nurse, said that if somebody were to write a textbook about the perfect way for a child to handle a situation like this, not in terms of impressing others, but in terms of going through the steps instinctively, it would be the way Angie did it.

It seemed pretty clear that the midwife had told the nurses to observe some of the exceptional things about Angie, and there are exceptional things about every child. So I think that was also a good touch that everybody had. I mean, they weren't saying, "Oh, at least you have Angie." Nobody was saying that, although in the books you find out a lot of people tell you that, and believe me, a lot of people said that. They mean it in the best of ways, they mean celebrate that you have another child, as if one could substitute one for the other. But what they were doing, instead of saying that, was at least remarking and observing the exceptional things about Angie, and that helped create a positive atmosphere.

Another midwife came in for the next shift, and she went over to the baby and cried for a few minutes. Nice touch. And then the nurse was giving us the time, still in the same room with the baby, to hold her and touch her and talk to her even though we knew that because of their schedules, they'd like to get us out of that delivery room and into the post-delivery room. It was interesting that they had talked to us about where we wanted to be after we delivered the baby. Did we want to be with the other mothers, where the advantage was that the nurses knew what they were doing, or did we want to be with people elsewhere in the hospital recovering from other things? I think they were very gracious in giving us all the time we needed to shower and spend time with the child. We were very impressed. Every nurse made a point, and again, I think this was pretty diplomatic on their part, of letting us know that we were getting the best nurse on every shift. Brenda was actually there for about two days after delivering, because they wanted to monitor her and make sure everything was all right.

Everybody who walked in would say, "I'm so sorry. This is so sad." And that was smart and pleasant on their part. Everybody took the time to have discussions with Brenda about how this kind of thing happens, what else they've seen in their experience. They weren't there offering commentary, but they were there offering information every time a question was asked.

The big issues, as soon as Brenda came out of the hospital, were what were we going to decide about an autopsy, and did we or didn't we want one. We'd already begun the discussion while she was in the hospital, and it was coming down to "Is there anything that we would find out from an autopsy about the cause of death that might not otherwise already be known or discernible? And might we find out something from an autopsy that would be important information for us to know in a subsequent pregnancy?" That was one set of considerations, versus Brenda's desire to leave the baby in peace. So we'd gotten actually a number of different opinions on that while we were there. It's a tough choice.

The day after, we had to start dealing with the question of when would the service be, and the timing between the service and an autopsy. Brenda's father had been very helpful. I'd let him know Tuesday morning after delivery that if there was one thing he could do it was to help us figure out this whole thing about funeral homes and where the child would be buried. So he did a lot of homework and that was very helpful.

Now, I'm going to go into some details here because it just shows you what you have to navigate through. On Thursday, after we came back from the hospital, Brenda started calling places because she wanted to do it all in Bedford right near our home. She wanted the baby to be close so she could visit. And the long and the short of it was, we did end up finding that we could put the baby in a baby plot in Bedford. Brenda contacted the one funeral home that we knew existed in Bedford. We had questions about the casket, because they make them so that they'll survive for a long time and they won't break down and they'll withstand a lot of weight if they're not in a vault—all this kind of stuff that I'd never thought about before. They didn't have any of the answers to those questions. So there was a bit of a conflict between me and her. But then I put my foot down that we weren't going to trust a sloppy place with handling our child.

That's the point at which I called Waterman. They were there at 6:30 at night, and they were able to answer every single question, and they were extremely professional and warm about answering all the questions. That's the point at which we resolved that all we wanted was an external autopsy without their cutting the baby up. But in any case, Waterman assured us that they wouldn't pick up the baby until we had heard from the pathologist or from the doctors talking to the pathologist about what their findings were from the external autopsy. And that was helpful. One of the areas where I do fault the midwives is I often felt that we had to extract answers to a lot of our questions. Because I think they felt at one point it's a cord accident, and it's terrible, and then they move on. And I'm still looking for answers to every question. But I got the message through that I wanted answers to specific questions from the pathologist, and we finally got those. Then I called Waterman at 9 in the evening, and they said, "We'll pick up the baby right away." And then they called first thing in the morning and said to Brenda, "Don't worry, your baby's with us," which was a very nice thing to do.

We agreed that there would be a service on Saturday afternoon at the church, and then the graveside service Monday morning. The other thing we had to deal with, I think, that Friday afternoon was the clothes. Somebody had said at some point, "Think about how you want to dress up the baby." And I thought, "My God, why do people dress up a dead body? What are they thinking?" But anyway, Brenda had brought a dress—a little baby dress that Angie had chosen for her sister when they had gone shopping at one point. And that's another spot in which the funeral home had a lot of finesse. Basically what the woman at the funeral home said, although she didn't use these words, was "You can't use this skirt and this sleeveless setup you've got because the skin of the baby is damaged in different areas, and it's not going to look pretty." That's my paraphrasing of what was stated extremely diplomatically, about maybe you want something long-sleeved, or maybe you want a blanket that can help us cover the arms a little bit. We understood what she meant. And so we went to a couple of stores. In one, they were showing us dresses, thinking we were buying things for a baby, and Brenda started crying. Now, it was a humorous situation, because we explained to them that it wasn't that we were upset by the quality of things they were showing us. Then we went back to the other store and found some nice stuff. But it was weird having to deal with selecting.

And then the minister came over Friday afternoon. We talked about what service we wanted. We hadn't really thought about it, but we went through a variety of options, and we told them that I was working on something that I wanted to read, and there were specific pieces of music that I wanted played. We were very pleased at their position, which was "You get to define what the service is."

Saturday morning we had to be at the funeral home so that we could have a private viewing, which is what we wanted, at 11. And then Brenda's family who had flown in would join us at 11:30 to 11:45. The day prior, when we'd seen the casket by itself, that opened up just a flood of sadness. Then, Saturday, when we went to see it, with the baby, with Michelle inside it, it was even that much more heartrending. But one of the touches was that the funeral home—we'd asked for a sign-in book for people—selected a nice sign-in book for a young person. And they had Michelle's name up, just Michelle. We viewed the body. Angie got to touch the baby, and she spoke to it. And she asked us to put the casket on the floor so we could all hug it.

Having the event reminded me that back in the Eastern religious tradition, they create all these ceremonies. For example, there's a service the first day after a person dies. There's a service the third day. There's a service the tenth day, the fortieth day, and over and above that there are pretty well-defined traditions about food and who brings the food and gatherings in the person's home.

So having the service to worry about was actually a good thing. It focuses your energy on doing something. Now people could see the baby at the church, not inside the church itself, but in the gathering area. We played some music that I chose that I think was particularly ethereal. Every time somebody showed up who was close, it would open up a lot of tears, which is good. It meant a a lot to us that people came. I feel very good about the fact that I wrote this poem, and that I read it. I think that and the music had a very positive impact in terms of capturing the feelings of the moment. One person in particular who was there for the service had lost a child six months into her pregnancy said that she found the whole thing very cathartic and helpful for her.

Monday morning we had a graveside service and a lot of people showed up. We had the same music from Saturday playing in the background. The minister read a few things from the Bible. I read that poem again. Then there was this moment of awkwardness—we made it clear that we wanted the burial to be private except for a few very close friends and family. Then there was the question of how do you lower the casket into the grave. I made clear that I wanted to do it, or help do it, and the funeral home guy was the one who got on his knees, helped me carry the casket and put it down underneath. And then people who were around each got to throw a flower in. At that point Brenda said she didn't want to see them cover it up, so she left. But Angie wanted to stay, so she did, and we stood and we watched them gradually fill the grave. And then there was a question about one remaining white rose, and we clarified that Brenda told Angie that she wanted it on top, so Angie went and put it on top, and you could see her footprints in the soil where she had walked in to put the flower. And then she decided that rather than the white flower lying down, what she wanted to do was put it standing up. So she put it standing up, and then we took pictures of that, and that was basically it. And then a few people came home with us afterwards, spent a few hours, and that was the end of it.

It's interesting to observe yourself go through a variety of phases as you're dealing with it on the spot and then afterwards. There's this guilt. I thought, "Oh my God, this happened because I'd said too many times to Brenda and admitted too many times to other people that I had looked forward to having a boy as child number two rather than a girl." And so I wondered, whether on some cosmic level, or some spiritual level with Michelle, that if somehow I'd killed her off by having that emotion and by expressing it. Then there was the sense that, given how focused I'd been in the last six to nine months on my own career, my own life, what I'm going to do next—there are lots of profound issues around those things— I had sometimes felt, "Gee, was this the wrong time to be getting a second child?" I often said to Brenda, "Are we a little crazy? We moved to a new, expensive house. I left my work. We're getting a second child." So because I'd had those feelings of ambivalence, I ended up thinking "Oh my God, maybe on some cosmic level I created an environment that made that cord accident more likely to happen."

Marilyn

The quick summary of what happened is that I had a stillborn child, a little girl. I didn't know it was a girl until I gave birth to the child and I went through a regular labor and birth. I held her after she was born and we named her. Subsequent to the birth we found out that it was due to a genetic problem that my husband and I have and, subsequent to that we tried again. The second pregnancy was problem-ridden. I didn't get to the point of genetic testing as I hoped to and we terminated the second pregnancy because of problems. Then the third pregnancy miscarried.

My own physical health was very much a problem through all of this because between pregnancies I had to be operated on for a fibroid and that fibroid was a problem during the first pregnancy. The second pregnancy was mostly a problem with stress, not knowing from moment to moment what exactly was going on with that one. It was not clear from the beginning whether we would ever get to genetic testing and to term. The third one miscarried. After the miscarriage we found out we had problems with the pregnancy. I have had to have blood tests since then.

One of the problems throughout this whole thing is that I began to see myself as unhealthy, and in some ways I was. It was a tremendous physical as well as an emotional drain. I'm only really feeling myself again now after several months.

My reaction is also very much colored by the second and third experience. The great tragedy was not only the first time, and the others were not minor losses. I had hoped after the first one that I would try again and someday have a child. I lost hope. I've really given up, which is very hard to do, and it sounds very negative, but I see it as positive and so does my husband.

Although the grief over a miscarriage or neonatal death is not always recognized by society, it is nevertheless very complex and profound. Because no one else got to know our child, and because the event may not have seemed real to others, there is a tendency for many to deny our sorrow. We feel as if we are caught in a black hole where, just as the laws of physics as we know them are not operative, the waves of emotion that assault us seem equally uncontrollable. Yet people who are not close to us may not grasp the depth of our loss.

Fortunately, many hospitals, such as the one where Brenda delivered her child, have now established comprehensive programs to deal with stillbirths and miscarriages. Some hospitals have created a nursing protocol that provides specially trained nurses to handle neonatal deaths, and Brenda and Amin's experience is an example of how healing such competence can be. The nurses who took care of Brenda after the delivery were experienced in such situations and were both tactful and supportive.

It is not unusual for hospitals to also provide special boxes that hold momentos of our infant such as the baby's hospital bracelet, locks of his or her hair, a footprint and photographs. Keeping these mementos and sharing them with others affirms our baby's brief passage and our important role as parents.

A few outstanding hospitals have multidisciplinary teams, so that when there is a difficult pregnancy the woman is seen by social workers as well as her obstetrician, and there is an integration of physiological and emotional care. Unfortunately there are still too many institutions where parents are left without support or guidance in the case of miscarriages or neonatal deaths. In such cases we have to seek counseling or check for support groups in our area which might be listed on the Internet, a difficult task when we are feeling so sad and empty.

While it may seem strange to some people, holding our baby is very important, for our love, which was constant throughout the pregnancy, is best expressed through touch. The presence of such a cherished person cannot be measured in weeks or years. The fact that she or he existed, however briefly, and that we held her or him is a moment that will always be with us. While Amin initially felt the strangeness of holding a dead child, when he saw Michelle's resemblance to her sister Angie, he was deeply moved. Angie's opportunity to hold her sister will illuminate a most perplexing reality for her as she grows up and is better able to process such an event, for nothing is more fearful to a child than secrets around the death of a newborn.

Chaplains of various faiths can advise us on ceremonies or address our important spiritual questions. One of the chaplains in a local hospital typically holds a naming ceremony for the child as well as helps the parents arrange for a graveside ceremony. She makes sure that the parents have a key role in preparing the ceremony while she selects the prayers and blessings in accordance with their wishes. Sometimes a family has a graveside ceremony a year after their infant's death to honor that child's presence in their lives.

While ceremonies are more commonly performed after a stillbirth caused by genetic or other problems such as cord accidents, some parents may wish to have a ceremony after a miscarriage when there are very few remains. A chaplain recalls performing a service for distraught parents over a bottle containing fetal tissue. Some people deny the importance of a burgeoning life, but we are entitled to our feelings as parents and to our grief.

It was very helpful for Brenda to speak with the chaplain after the birth of Michelle; her presence created the safety and assurance they needed after such a heart-wrenching experience. As Amin makes clear, what helps are people who accompany us during such painful moments, who speak with us in a manner that acknowledges and supports our feelings. He also stresses the importance of words after a loss, for words are not neutral. They have the power to wound or heal. Not only the chaplain, but the doctors and nurses advising Brenda and Amin were able to communicate the necessity for delivering their child without letting the more grisly aspects of the infant's death overshadow her personhood. The tears shed by the midwife who came on duty after Michelle's death were as important as words and perhaps more touching. In their selection of a funeral home, the couple was able to find one whose staff referred to their child as "the baby" rather than "the body." Given that the world continues with its business and dailiness while we are suspended in time by our shock, the way people communicate with us can be important steps in the healing process.

A chaplain can address the question that assails all of us who have suffered such a loss: "Why did this happen to us?" It is a question we need to repeat over and over again as we search for meaning when there are no ready answers, when in the rawness of our grief we may question the role of the Creator while blaming either the medical establishment or our own behavior. While the chaplain assured Amin that God did not want their child to die, a chaplain in another hospital recently told an anguished parent that "even stars die."

Holding a ceremony for our baby not only focuses us when we may be feeling disoriented, but also gives us an opportunity to express love for our child and share his or her passage with family and friends. It is a way of bringing our child into society. Amin's moving poem and his choice of medieval choral music for the services provided both beauty and catharsis for all who attended. He discovered that music and the arts speak on a much deeper level than ordinary words. The service also gave family and friends a way to accompany Amin and Brenda through their ordeal and helped everyone concerned to feel less powerless. The act of arranging such a ritual will help us feel that we continued our parental role in the best way possible.

Massachusetts General Hospital in Boston holds a yearly two-hour nondenominational service for such losses in one of its loveliest auditoriums. Parents are encouraged to participate by contributing poems they have written and by saying their child's name during the service. These are then included in an "Honor Book" along with poems and other writings by the parents. Afterward there is a balloon ceremony outside with a child's name on each balloon, and a reception with refreshments, a very sensitive touch since people need further accompaniment after such an expression of grief. Despite the size of the auditorium, there is usually standing room only, a testament to the need to express our sadness and honor the memory of our child.

The death of a newborn is the death of a wish and the death of our dreams. During the pregnancy, both parents have invested their energy, not just in painting a room or buying furniture and clothes for the new child, but also in planning for their life as a family. They may have spent much time discussing scheduling arrangements at work or have taken important steps to reorganize their lives in anticipation of parenthood. For instance, the expectant father in one couple made arrangements to take a consulting job so that he could spend more time at home with their new baby. After a death, the focus of our hope is gone, and we are left with an emptiness, a feeling of having been cheated. As a chaplain so aptly phrased it, "Our bridge to the future has been blown up, and we are faced with the task of reconstruction." We grieve for the child we didn't know. Just because we never did see the color of his hair or get to know him doesn't mean that we will stop thinking or wondering or caring about him.

In the case of a miscarriage, we examine our own behavior or the state of our health during the pregnancy, searching for causes, wondering if we were careful enough. A friend of mine who lost a child through miscarriage worried for months afterward about her responsibility for the loss. Even though she had taken good care of herself during her pregnancy, she kept looking for possible causes. Because we identify so closely with a child during pregnancy, we feel responsible for the development of that child. After all, during pregnancy, a baby is part of a woman's body. If we lose that child, we will not only face physical and emotional adjustments, we may also feel that we have failed.

Sometimes other people's comments about our pregnancy reenforce our belief that we ourselves were somehow to blame for the miscarriage. Because such an event seems so meaningless (there has been no comprehensive study made of the causes of single miscarriages, although more is known about the reasons for multiple miscarriages), we are particularly vulnerable to veiled suggestions that we were somehow at fault, or got what we deserved. We should be especially protective of ourselves during this difficult period and seek out friends who will be supportive.

We face different but equally complex sorrows around an early miscarriage, a second trimester miscarriage, or a late loss, and we feel an especially difficult grief if we had to terminate a pregnancy because of severe genetic or other defects in our child. In the latter case, even though our decision was based on love and a wish to spare our child a life of terrible pain, the political and religious debate over the termination of pregnancies causes many of us to remain silent about our decision and thereby lose the support we so desperately need. That debate also masks the realities and the spiritual anguish of our choice and complicates our grieving.

Women who miscarry often do not receive the same attention and concern as women who deliver a stillborn child. They are left to their own devices and treated as if they were just having "a medical procedure." Women have D&Cs (dilation and curettage) for many different reasons and are often grouped with other day-surgery patients who are not pregnant. After our procedure, we are left alone in the recovery room as if we had not lost a child. Even if we did not get to hold a baby, even if we lost tissue or a three-inch fetus, it is important for our friends and acquaintances to realize that from the moment our pregnancy was confirmed, we became parents, and the child growing within us was the source of our concern, joy, and future. Even if we have other children, this child is and always will be unique.

Unfortunately, like Marilyn, many women have multiple miscarriages and enter a second or third pregnancy with much trepidation and the memory of the grief of the first or second loss. While some women do eventually have a child, many must make the painful adjustment to the fact that they will never have a child. A friend of mine tried to have a baby for ten years and grieved for an even longer period over the loss of her dream. While she took refuge in writing a book of poems about her experience, and while she and her husband have fulfilling careers, it is still difficult for her to be in a room where women are discussing their children. It has also been much harder for her than for other people to lose elderly relations, because she has been robbed of the future.

In her narrative, Marilyn makes very clear that each of the three losses was significant to her and her husband. When each pregnancy ended, they experienced the loss of hope and the denial of a deeply felt wish. They were also anxious about Marilyn's health and their own future as a family. Marilyn is seeing a counselor, and she and her husband are thinking about adoption. She discovered that after such a difficult loss, she has to be very selective about friends and spend time only with those who respond to her and her husband's pain with tact and sensitivity.

Many hospitals hand out pamphlets with other parents' stories. Unfortunately, because they depend on volunteers, few institutions are able to provide support groups for parents who have suffered these types of losses. If we are lucky enough to have access to such a group, it will be very helpful, and we will be less alone with our burden. For some of us, talking about the event with other parents is a way of healing ourselves, of untangling events that feel meaningless and represent a terrible injustice to our dead child and our family. On the other hand, others of us prefer to read and reflect in solitude. We need to choose the path that is most comfortable for us.

There is sometimes a tendency to consider this kind of loss as one only mothers suffer. However, we must remember that even though the father's body is not at issue, his dreams and hopes are, as well as his concern for his wife. It is doubly difficult for him to lose a child and then to have his own pain ignored. Also, men and women enter the grieving process with very different approaches. Few men are as willing or able to speak as freely about their feelings as Amin, for our society constricts male expressiveness as well as women's ways of thinking. In addition, regardless of the fact that it is now typical for both parents to have careers and not unusual for a woman to earn more than her husband, men are still socialized to think that they must be in charge. Like Amin, they see it as their role to take all the necessary measures to ensure that their wife and child are adequately cared for and to stand as a buffer between their family and the world. Amin's desire for legal advice is an example of this extra burden of responsibility and guilt men often carry in such situations.

The grandparents of a stillborn or miscarried child face a dual burden of sadness: the pain their child endured and their own terrible disappointment at the outcome of the pregnancy. Friends of mine watched their daughter struggle through a difficult pregnancy that resulted in a miscarriage. They were concerned about their daughter's well-being and left with an enduring sorrow over the loss, for grandparents cherish dreams of a new baby and the transformation a grandchild will bring to their lives. Often they are so busy supporting their son and daughter that their own grief is neglected. I remember how crushed my friends were when we visited them and how palpable the air was with the weight of the absence they both carried. If there is little social recognition of parents who have suffered such a loss, there is even less of grandparents, yet grandparents do not have the same time for healing or for hoping for the successful outcome of another pregnancy.

The siblings of a stillborn baby face their own fears and sadness, and we may be uncertain how to tell them about the death or how to support them, for young children do not have the capacity to understand the full implications of such an event. Brenda and Amin involved their daughter Angie in their plans from the beginning of the pregnancy and are a model of how to include a child in both the joy and the grief of such an occasion. Angie shared her mother's exercises and went shopping with her for baby clothes. Her participation in holding her stillborn sister and in the funeral services will be very helpful as time progresses.

Such an event assaults children's sense of safety and prompts them to question all the givens of their universe. They may feel guilty about such a loss and wonder about their own mortality. Angie resolves her hurt and confusion through play. She delivers babies and then announces to her parents that either she delivered a healthy baby or unfortunately the baby died. She is also trying to understand the enormity of her sister's death and keeps coming up with new explanations. For instance, she told her mother that she had spoken to God and he promised to send her a new baby sister who would make her parents happy. *But this time,* she added, the sister *would not come through Mommy's tummy.* For a child of barely over four, she was extremely perceptive in her realization that the cause of her sister's death was complications in the pregnancy.

After a miscarriage or a neonatal death, we are faced with the difficult task of telling our coworkers and all those involved in different aspects of our lives. If we have other children, we must contact our children's teachers and the parents of their friends. Some of us find it easier to write letters than to make phone calls at such a difficult time. Amin and Brenda decided to make an announcement of Michelle's birth and death with Amin's poem included, a way of honoring their child and helping people understand the gravity of what had happened. If this task is overwhelming, we can ask a trusted friend to help us or seek guidance from the social services at the hospital or a therapist.

A miscarriage or stillbirth is a difficult topic to talk about with others. Some people want to know the details. However, if the details are too painful for us to discuss, we should respond that because it is hurtful for us, we would rather not talk about it or limit our answers to the simple facts. Some people tell us with the best of intentions, "You can always try again," or "You have a child already." These are not exactly comforting replies, and they minimize our loss. Those of us who already have a child at the time of our loss know that one child never replaces another. We have had years of deepening parental relationships, of discovering day after day the person who came into this world, perhaps wearing our features and displaying flashes of our personality. If we lose our first child, our dreams and fantasies of these relationships go up in smoke. After time passed, Marilyn learned to respond to tactless comments by saying that she didn't feel that it was for the best and that it was a painful loss.

Guilt is one of the most trying feelings we deal with when we lose a child. It is curious that while we are feeling utterly powerless because we have *failed* to prevent our child from dying, we somehow endow ourselves with a power that is almost cosmic. Like Amin, we mull over our thoughts and words as if somehow they had the capacity to unleash the events that led to the death. We review our every decision and blame ourselves for taking steps that many people would have taken in our circumstances. It is important to allow ourselves to feel this guilt, no matter how irrational it seems to others. Such powerful feelings cannot be dismissed, for guilt is the necessary stirring of conscience, a repeated questioning of an incomprehensible occurrence. We need to experience it in order to move through it. A clearer sense of perspective comes only with time and after we have allowed ourselves to be battered by anger and self-blame.

When our child dies, the grief is apt to be with us for a long time, and the anniversary of the birth of our child or of our miscarriage opens up our wounds for some years. Even though we eventually move on to new concerns and occupations, and even though the pain moves away from the center of our lives, it will always be part of us. Whenever we enter a new social situation and people ask us about our families, we will suffer the pain of having to say that we had four but lost one, or that we lost an only child in stillbirth or had one or repeated miscarriages. We will always be a parent to the child we lost.

Chapter Eight
WHEN A SIBLING DIES

Jim

As I look back at it, there were two very difficult times for me: the time right after she died and the anniversary of her death. I found myself writing poetry as the anniversary of her death approached. Her death in some way was an expression of a lot of the pain and emotional distress in our family. It was a drug abuse-related death. She was a nurse. She was three years younger than me, the middle of three children. She always felt that she was different. When we were kids she used to insist to my parents that she was adopted. There was something in our family that produced that feeling in her. All three of us escaped the house as soon as we could. One of my avenues for escape was college. Ellen never felt that she could go to college, so she went to nursing school. She always felt that she didn't have a lot of ability. The first guy she ever dated she was very attached to and when he graduated and went to college, he cooled it off, and that devastated her. As soon as she got to nursing school she met another guy and married him after she finished nursing school.

For some reason, she started taking Darvon and then started to take it on the sly and gradually got more and more involved in drug abuse. Initially it was drugs that she would only pilfer from the hospital. Eventually she got caught and lost her job. But she had figured out the system and called pharmacies, pretending to phone in prescriptions. About three years before she died, it first became apparent to everyone how serious the problem was. She went through several periods of treatment. She developed epilepsy secondary to drug abuse.

They still don't know what happened. She was working in a nursing home and apparently had a massive seizure and fell down the stairs. One of the strangest things that happened was this incredible need I had to find out how she died and the anger and frustration at the coroner who took so much time in finding out what had caused her death. But they ended up saying the immediate cause was undetermined, that it was probably related to this seizure which was secondary to chronic drug abuse. It happened at a time when she had appeared to be doing much better. My mother and sister had just seen her the week before, which was significant because there were often extended periods when we wouldn't be in touch with her.

There was a very miserable and tragic period that led up to her death. It was very difficult for me because my relationship with her had grown strained. But there was this intense period when her drug problem surfaced and we became very close. She came out to visit us, supposedly having gone through a residential treatment program and having improved. We wrapped up all the medicines and hid them away. We had a visit and it was reasonably good, although she still seemed pretty depressed, and we talked a lot about our parents. My father is currently a recovering alcoholic. My parents have a terrible relationship. For the most part, my father drank heavily, and my mother is an extremely devout—an almost pathologically devout—Catholic. Though if I think hard, I can remember some happy periods in my childhood. I was trying to provide as much support for her as possible in that drug thing. When she left, I found that she had taken all the medicines that I had hidden. I called her on the phone, and at first she denied it and finally she acknowledged it. Then I got involved in this role I always played in the family, this role of "I was going to save her." I tried to set up another admission for her. I flew to her home to try to get her into a program, and when I got there, she refused. Her husband was not helpful. He said that it was just a problem of willpower, that if she tried to stop she could. After, she went into another treatment program, and during this time I stayed in touch with her.

The last time I talked to her was about a year and three months before she died. She had just gotten divorced from her husband. The last thing I said to her was that this was a time when she should really be careful. She should try to meet a number of new people, and just to take time because she was still young and there was no need to rush into anything. She seemed receptive to that. I think that when she took off with a guy, she couldn't face me. Then I couldn't contact her when she was moving around the country. And then I got angry at her for not contacting me. I stayed angry for at least a year. About three or four months before she died I was feeling less anger and more of a sense of missing her. By that time she and this guy had come back and were living in New Jersey. I knew now that I could contact her, and I had gotten the address and phone number from my mother. It was one of those things I kept putting off, and I didn't do it before she died.

That was very horrible for me, to have had that period when I was not in touch in with her. I know it is normal to feel guilty and responsible under circumstances like these. I felt and still have not really worked through a very pervasive sense of guilt, that I was treated more favorably than she was in the family, that I did a lot more crazy things with drugs than she did and yet I survived. But it pulled her down and destroyed her.

Maureen

I'm twenty-five now. My sister was nineteen when she died. I was in the ninth grade. I was fifteen. It was really quick. One summer she became sick and went to the doctor. Within two weeks her right side was paralyzed. Then her hair started to fall out, all within a month. I didn't see much of her because I was living down at our Cape house. I was being a bum, being a kid on the Cape, and she was home working. She had just finished her first year in college. Then she spent a couple of months in the hospital having tests and getting all this medicine that made her cheeks really big and her hair fall out. She looked like a chipmunk. Her speech slurred a lot. You could only understand her if you were living with her. She was at Children's Hospital with a bunch of babies, and it was real hard because she was nineteen years old. When she came home from the hospital, she was in bed all the time

The worst thing about it was that I didn't know what to ask or who to ask about what was happening. I didn't want to ask my parents because I was afraid of learning the truth and I was afraid of hurting them by making them talk about it. It was really hard.

One day I was driving to the hospital with my father and I asked him, "Well, what is wrong with her?" My father said, "Well, the doctors have told us we have to be honest with you or you'll never trust us again. We can't lie to you and tell you she is going to get better or tell you that things are great." He said she had a brain tumor or something, that it had probably had been dormant all her life and that something happened that brought it out. It wasn't inherited so there was no way that I would become sick.

My sister and I always used to hold hands until I was about twelve years old. When she became ill, we started to hold hands again. At least we could do that. I think that was our closeness. When my parents would go out, we would just lie on the bed and watch television and hold hands. I wish I could have said things.

In the end, she was in a coma for about a month, and then my parents said that she was in God's hands. That was the toughest time to go and see her. She was in a nursing home for retired nuns, and there were all these old, whacked-out nuns. It wasn't my sister. She wouldn't respond. I'd just go there and hold her hand and hope that she knew that I was there. That was the hardest time to go and see her because I didn't want to remember her being that way.

The day she died I was coming out of an art course and I was blowing it off kind-of-like I'd go to the gym and talk to my friends and then I'd go to the bathroom and then come back to class. They had been paging me all through the class. Finally I answered the page, and they told me to go down to the guidance office cause "your mother is here." I saw my aunt's car outside and I said, "Oh, shit." And when I got to the office my mother was there. She just said, "Honey, Joan died. We loved her, everybody loved her. God loved her so much he wanted to take her." That's how she justified it. In my mind I was saying, "That's just bull." I didn't know what to do. I went to get my books. I just wanted to walk out and get away, just leave and cry. I stood alone at my locker for three minutes, and then I went to the classroom and grabbed my books. And the teacher said, "Where are you going?" I just felt like turning around and yelling, "My sister just died, all right?" I was in tears and I just walked out and got in the car with my aunts and mother. She said they were going to pick out flowers and a dress and said if I'd like to come I could. I said, "Definitely." I wanted to be there. I wanted to take part in that. That took about an hour and a half. Then we got home and I got on my bike and left for about three hours.

I just went to a field and cried and smoked cigarettes. I was thinking, "Why her? Why my sister?" She was the sweetest girl. You know, I'm a tyrant. She was sweet. She wasn't really smart, but she tried a lot. She was beautiful. I always thought of her as very insecure, and losing her hair and her face looking awful was so terrible for her. I always used to think, "Why her? Why not me? It should have been me. I'm stronger than she is. I could deal with the things that she's been going through." And that's all I basically thought. "Why her? Why her and not me? She was a sweet person and she shouldn't have died. Why did God do this to somebody? What about my parents? They have to live through this. Why did they do this to us? What have we done to God? She missed so much of her life. Why was I a jerk to her?" I remembered the time we went to a drive-in and couldn't get in because it was full and I was so furious at her. I was pounding on the back seat of the car. She was driving. I was in the eighth grade and then, I just hated her. And she said, "Why? I don't hate you." And I was feeling so guilty that day she died. I kept thinking, "Does she know I love her? Gee, I hope she knows I love her." That's what I was thinking in the field that day. I had been so bad to her. You know little sisters. Sometimes she'd try to kiss me and I'd say, "Get away." I kept thinking, "I hope she knew that I loved her, and I hope she'll forgive me for all the crap that I pulled on her."

I cried all that night. I was thinking about my parents and how much it hurt them. I tried not to cry in front of them. They were so hurt. My mother was a wreck.

I remember the funeral and the wake. What I remember is that my friends came. They came to the funeral too. Some of them came to the wake, and they came through the line and I wasn't even there. I was in the bathroom crying, and I felt terrible that I missed them. There were tons of people there. I didn't cry except when my brother yelled at me for something. And I cried when my friends came, especially when one of them gave me a big hug. I loved my sister's dress. She looked great except for her chubby little chipmunk cheeks, and then I began to think, "What am I doing here? I don't want to be here. Why am I staying here?" And what do you say when you are standing there? People don't know what to say and you say, "Oh, it's nice to meet you." You meet a lot of people that you've never met or that you've met but never talked to, and you try to make a conversation. "Thank you for coming." It sounds so insincere. I started thinking, "Why am I thanking you for coming? You're not coming for me. You're coming for my sister. I'm the one who is getting the pity here, and I shouldn't. I shouldn't get this pity. I'm not the one that's dead. I'm not the one who is never going to see any of you again."

There was this one girl that my sister hated who showed up. I felt like saying, "God, you're such a hypocrite to be here." Instead I said, "Oh, Ann, you look great. Thanks for coming. I'll see you this summer."

At the funeral, my mother was crying. My father was crying. And I think my brother was crying. I didn't cry till I was walking down the aisle in church following the casket and I saw one of my mother's best friends and I started to cry. I began to realize, "This is it. You're saying good-bye right now." Somehow I didn't think it would be over and gone forever. I wanted to be alone a lot and I wasn't.

We went back to the house for coffee and doughnuts. You have to sit there and be phony and talk about things you don't care about. You have to pretend and say to people, "Yes, we're glad it's over." You almost have to pretend it didn't happen.

Losing a sibling is particularly difficult because the other people in our family are considered the primary mourners. When we lose a brother or sister as a child, all the attention is focused on our parents and we feel invisible in our sadness. When we lose a sibling as an adult, the sympathy is offered to the spouse and children of our sibling. Our own loss is very wrenching, and yet there may be no acknowledgment of it.

As in all relationships, whether we identified closely with our brother or sister or felt rivalry and resentment toward each other will affect our reactions to a loss. However, we might feel guilty even when there were deep feelings of mutuality with a sibling. We remember the times we quarreled or think of things we wish we had done. Maybe we feel that our brother or sister died because of something we did or said. It's helpful to remember that a sibling's death is not a judgment on us.

Perhaps we feel survivor's guilt and wonder why our brother or sister died instead of us, as Maureen did when she asked, "Why her and not me?" This is a question that many of us ask after the death of a sibling. We identify so closely with our sibling or admire him or her so much that we wonder why we were spared.

The quality of our relationship during the time before death is also going to affect how long we feel guilt and anger. That Jim did not have the opportunity to be with his sister before her death affected him profoundly.

However, this was a relationship to which he had made years of significant contribution, and this positive side will become clearer as time passes. But even though he had made contributions to his sister's well-being, he was unable to save her. We often feel powerless in the face of death.

The relationship Jim had with his sister carried over into their adult years as Jim became almost like a parent to her in assuming responsibility for her health. Often when parents are unable to function as such, an older sibling assumes that role. In a sense, Jim is grieving for the loss of a child as well as for the loss of a sister, with the added difficulty of not having either the status or the influence of a real parent. In acting as the conscience of the family, he bears a heavy burden.

There are differences between losing a sibling as an adult and losing a sibling as a child. When Jim's sister died, he was already established in his career and had a family. These were available to him as supports, and he also relied upon the wisdom of his accumulated experience. When Maureen's sister died, she was still a teenager facing all the turmoils of adolescence. Her behavior toward her sister, which troubled her so much after her sister died, was the normal acting out of adolescent stress. When we lose a sibling during our teenage years, we may not have the perspective to remember all the nice things we did and loving thoughts that we had for our sister or brother. This is a difficult burden to bear. It's helpful to remind ourselves of the good moments we had in our relationship with our sibling.

When our sibling dies after an illness, we may have been very confused by the illness, as Maureen was. She saw her sister's face swollen from the chemotherapy but did not understand the acute nature of the illness and the implications of the symptoms. A friend of mine who lost her sister when they were both teenagers remembers not realizing the seriousness of her sister's condition until she heard her father weeping during a telephone conversation. As her sister was taken to the hospital my friend recalls her saying, "Good-bye, house," as the stretcher carried her away. Even when her sister died shortly after, and she was sitting by the body at the wake, she still couldn't comprehend the fact of her sister's death. As young adults we are not apt to understand the nature of our sibling's illness until it becomes critical. We may be very confused by the death.

Younger people may not find solace in the explanations of religion or in so-called systems of justice. We might see religion as part of our parents' world and as having little meaning for us. Perhaps our parents tried to explain the death of our sibling as "God's will." This is small comfort to us when we resent our brother or sister's absence. We might be turned off by religion and angry at a God who took away our sibling.

As Maureen did, some resent the funeral for its "phoniness," for all the people present at a time when perhaps we would rather be alone with our parents. Ritual which is a source of comfort for our parents can seem like an empty charade to us. Perhaps we weren't included in or even consulted about the funeral arrangements and are feeling left out. Some of us would rather be with our family at this time or would rather not participate in the funeral. However, even if we would prefer not to go to the funeral, we would like to have the choice of taking part or staying home. Maureen's disgust with the funeral is not unusual. We might feel uncomfortable with other people's display of feelings and don't want others to see our distress. There are times when we just want to express our sadness in the privacy of our room.

Our parents may react to the loss of our brother or sister by being overprotective or demanding. A colleague of mine who had lost her sister as a teenager had to contend with her mother's anguish every time she went out. At the time she couldn't understand why her mother always wanted her in sight. It was difficult for her to understand that her mother was afraid that something would happen to her. All she could see was that her freedom was suddenly restricted. It's not unusual for parents to change their behavior toward us after the loss of a child.

Because our parents miss our deceased sibling, they may idealize him or her. It usually takes many months or even years after a death before we see our relationship with the deceased in perspective. Parents remember above all the good qualities of their child and the joy he or she brought them. They may seem overly concerned with the memory of our brother or sister. A friend of mine remembers asking her parents in frustration some months after the death of her sister, "Do you still love me?" Her parents were astonished by the question, believing that their deep love for her was obvious. In their grief, it was difficult for them to see that their surviving daughter felt left out.

Not only will our parents be absorbed in their grief over our deceased brother or sister, but the whole atmosphere in our home will have changed. A friend of mine who lost a brother when she was young remembers her home as a place of gloom that she wished to escape from. Eventually she went off to college and a new life and later on was able to have a close relationship with her parents. However, the year after her brother's death remains in her memory as a very unsettling time. When we are children what happens in our home after a death affects our sense of security. After all, our home is our universe when we are young, and we are likely to be deeply upset by changes in our daily life, our routines around school or friends, or the way we spend our free time.

When we lose a brother or sister, our grief is often ignored in our parents' preoccupation with their own sorrow, causing us terrible loneliness in the face of our parents' sadness. Our parents might be overly preoccupied with their feelings and with guests who are pouring into the house. This is a time when we may want to have the attention of our parents and resent the intrusion of outsiders.

In the face of such difficult circumstances, we feel that we must avoid any behavior which might cause our parents further pain. It's terribly upsetting to see our parents grieving, and we will do everything possible to avoid causing them further sorrow. We may try to keep our room as tidy as possible, to be very quiet or not make any demands on our mother and father. However, it's important to recognize our own grief and realize that expressing our own sadness will not add to our parents' sadness. It's normal to want to assume responsibility of our parents' pain. However, it is a great relief to realize that their sadness has nothing to do with our own behavior. Feeling sad or angry over a sibling's death will not hurt our parents and instead will help us on the path to healing.

If we shared a room with a brother or sister we must now face an empty room. For some of us, it will be comforting to be near our siblings' things, whereas others of us will find this fearsome. If we are one of several children, our sibling's bed might be taken by a younger brother or sister, and we might resent the intrusion. Besides the reminder of the room, there are all the places we went together—the drive-in, the park, the family excursions—which are occasions for sadness.

Many of us who lose siblings when we are teenagers or young adults find that all the attention is focused on our parents and that we have no one to whom we can turn to discuss our sorrow. Sometimes our parents' friends or our own relatives urge us to take care of our parents. They tell us to "be strong" for them. It seems as if our own grief is invisible and somehow inappropriate. It's helpful to remember that while everyone grieves in his or her own way and that while our own grief is different from that of our parents, it nevertheless deserves our attention. Perhaps friends at school who have experienced loss through a divorce or a death in their own families will share our feelings with us. Maybe we are ashamed of or uncomfortable with the depth of our feelings. But a true friend will want to share our sadness as well as our happy times.

Our friends and perhaps even our family may not want to mention our deceased sibling because of their own pain or because they are afraid of hurting us, causing us to interpret this silence as an admonition not to grieve. But losing a sibling is like losing a part of ourselves. It touches the core of our identity. As survivors, we need to express sorrow and our anger in a way that is comfortable for us.

Chapter Nine
WHEN A PARENT OF
MATURE ADULTS DIES

Writing about a father who had just died, an author referred to middle age as the "final orphanage." This may seem like a paradox. People in their thirties, forties, and fifties usually have families, careers, lives of their own. We hardly think of them as children. Yet we are still the children of our parents, and we carry this relationship with us as long as our parents are alive, no matter how old we may be. A friend of mine who teaches psychology at a nearby university described this situation very simply. He told me, "I had teenage children when my father died, but even though we never communicated very well, I felt lost without him. But I still had my mother. When things got tough, I could say to myself deep inside, 'Ma.' Then when she died, I really felt abandoned. There was no more calling out to Ma when things got rough." Even though we are adults with responsibilities for others, we still have powerful feelings and relationships with the people who nurtured us and raised us from infancy.

In middle age, we discover in a new way what we had perhaps always taken for granted—our parent's unconditional love. As my friend so aptly described, they are the ones we think of or turn to for acceptance and support in the difficult periods of our lives. Even if they do not fulfill these expectations, we nevertheless continue to feel them. If we have had negative relationships with our parents throughout our lives, we experience this legacy with renewed impact as we age.

Our parents also give us a sense of belonging and identity. Even if we rebelled against them when we were young adults, in later years we often discover traces of that parent in ourselves. Writing about his father in the

New York Times Magazine column "About Men," Clark Blaise mused that "as I enter my perilous years, I find that he is inside me, we are becoming one." Having confronted our own failures and weakness, we are now ready to accept the parent we may have found wanting or are ready to accept the love we feel for that parent.

By the time we reach our middle years, we have had the parent-child relationship for a long time, time for it to grow, perhaps to transform into friendship or at least mutual understanding. We will have had plenty of opportunity to think about these ties. Men often think about the issues of their professional identity, trying to do better or as well as their fathers or perhaps wanting their approval.

Both men and women gauge their accomplishments according to their fathers, either by trying to measure up or by trying to compensate. However, women also develop closer ties with their mothers as they age. A psychologist who studied marriages found that frequently a woman's mother provided the closeness and support or companionship missing in a partnership. Mothers often provide moral support and advice during periods of change associated with child-rearing. A woman who loses a mother in middle age mourns not only the end of that relationship, but also the loss of an intimate friend, someone who knew her better than anyone else. Sometimes men experience a closeness and communication with their mothers that they couldn't achieve with their fathers. They suffer great loneliness and a sense of abandonment after a mother's death.

As we grow older, we think about who we are over and above the roles we play. Rumination about our identities inevitably involves our parents. In a nontraditional and highly mobile society, our sense of rootedness comes not so much from place or lineage as from our nuclear or chosen family. When we lose our parents, we lose that sense of belonging. Even though we may have families that we created ourselves, we still feel a terrible emptiness after the death of a parent.

If we have children when our parents die, we also lose grandparents for those children. Our parents shared important events with our families and spent holidays with us, and during these celebrations we feel a renewed sense of grief. After our parents die, we become the older generation. As a friend once described, "After my parents died, there was no longer any shelter from my own death." Just as our parents provided a buffer against life's problems and hurts, they were also a buffer against our own deaths.

Many people live with their parents after they become adults. If we are single, our parents may have been our chief emotional tie. We experienced with them not only the sharing of a household, but also the intimacy and companionship others find in a partnership or marriage. Perhaps our parents were in poor health and we provided them with physical and financial support. When our parents die, we are left without the resources that our married friends have. I remember talking with my unmarried cousin after the death of her mother. When I told her that I also lost my mother and understood the pain she felt, she looked at me and said, "But you had a husband and children."

Sometimes a single person feels burdened with the responsibility of living with an elderly parent and resents the loss of his or her own separate space. It's not unusual for the single family member to be expected to shoulder this responsibility by his or her married siblings. Maybe we have separate housing and arranged for our parent to live in the neighborhood or in the same town, and after our parent dies, we feel guilty for not having shared a roof with him or her. Even though we are entitled to our own lives and our own space, we are torn between a sense of responsibility to our parent and a desire for privacy. This is not an easy conflict to resolve. The death of a parent under these circumstances leaves us feeling confused and complicates our grieving. It is helpful to remind ourselves that it's all right to have made our separate lives and that we did care for our parents, even if it was not within the same home.

Mature adults are not always expected to grieve over the loss of a parent or parents. I remember the silence that greeted me both at work and from acquaintances after my mother's death. It was as if the pain I was feeling and the importance of the ties I had with her were completely invisible. Also, because older people are not as highly valued in a society that places so much emphasis on productivity, consumption, and health, their loss is not considered in all its fullness. The widespread perception is that it is easier to let go of loved ones when they are older. "It's all for the best," or "He had a full life," we hear. But that is small comfort when we are grieving for one of the most important relationships we have had.

The age we were when our parent or parents died, the quality of the relationship we had with them, and the way our parents died will affect our grieving. We react differently to a death after a long illness than to a sudden death, such as through accident or heart attack. A troubled relationship with a parent complicates our experience after his or her death.

Even if we believe that we came to terms with the difficulties and frustrations in relating to a father or mother, we are struck by the finality of death. We know intellectually that we couldn't bridge the distances and misunderstandings between us, yet in life there was always the possibility and the hope for change. After a death we suffer years of bitterness and regret for what we did not have or were unable to achieve. Even though we may continue to feel responsible for our parent's failings, we needn't blame ourselves or feel guilty about resenting his or her negative qualities. We can love someone whom we have difficulty liking. It's not unusual to be angry at the inadequacies of a parental relationship.

If we are in our late twenties or thirties when we lose a parent, we lose a very important emotional support just when we are establishing our own identities, either getting married or starting families of our own. A former student of mine who had lost both parents went through some major life events with great loneliness and yearning. Although friends and siblings came to her college graduation and wedding, they could not replace her parents. Years later, when she had her first child, she suffered depression. This is a period when a mother's guidance and support is very important in helping us face new responsibilities. The birth of Andrea's child filled her with a resurgent grief and a renewed sense of the dimension of her loss. A young mother whose own mother died of cancer just before she had her first child told me, "There's not a day that goes by that I don't think of my mother and how she would have loved seeing her grandson."

As adult children, we want to share our accomplishments and our important passages with our parents and suffer deep loneliness during these times if we have lost them. We feel a sense of abandonment if we lost a father when we were young men establishing ourselves in a career or a family. A father provides us with advice and guidance when we are establishing our professional identities. Even in our twenties and thirties, we need parental approval to assess our life journey.

If we are in our forties and fifties or older when our parents die, we had a different relationship with them than when we were younger. We face the dual responsibility of adolescent children and parents whose health is declining. While it's possible to resolve these responsibilities without conflict, often the challenge taxes our patience and stamina. Sometimes we face the agonizing decision of having to place a parent in a nursing home and have to run between visits to the home, errands for the children, and our jobs. In addition we may be burdened with the financial costs for our parents' support.

If we are caring for elderly parents, we find ourselves in the uncomfortable position of role reversal, parenting our own parents. We may be angry at them for not being able to fill their parental role, and conversely, they probably resent their helplessness. Much as we love our parents, these conditions can cause mutual resentment and misunderstanding. Quite naturally, we feel emotionally and physically drained by the responsibility.

Caring for an ill parent often means juggling this with our jobs and attention for our children. In some instances, we make frequent trips to another city to visit our ill parent. A friend of mine whose mother suffered a stroke dealt with her family, her job, and her own painful arthritis as well as repeated flights to New York City from Boston. These are trying circumstances, and after a death we sometimes feel great anger over the burden we carried as well as for the suffering of our parents.

Some illnesses, such as Alzheimer's disease or a stroke, transform our parent to such an extent that we feel we are caring for a stranger. Losing the parent we knew through such circumstances is a separate grief. We feel as if we had lost our parent before he or she died. We have very complex reactions to such a difficult situation, wishing our loved one freed from a life which hardly seems like a life and then feeling guilty about this wish. Or we wish for the relief of being able to grieve for the death of a parent rather than living in a twilight area where our parent is in a coma or totally inaccessible. We spend our time, energy, and emotion caring for our parent, but he or she is not the person we knew.

When a parent dies after a long and difficult illness, we experience guilt, relief, and regret as well as great pain and sorrow. We go over and over this period, wondering if we made the right decisions about care, whether we did the best we could. Even the most conscientious son or daughter finds reasons for self-blame. This is a time to be easy on ourselves and remember all that we did do in the face of many competing claims for our emotions.

Our reactions to the death of a parent are different depending on whether our parent died suddenly or after a long illness. If our parent was ill, we had time to prepare ourselves for his or her death. We could grieve in anticipation of the loss, experience denial, disbelief, anger, and sadness, though in a muted way. If our parent died accidentally, we suffer a more intense and prolonged shock immediately after the death. We also must cope with the meaninglessness of an accidental death.

My aunt was a very active woman. She lived on a farm and was always on her feet, milking the cows, making jam, tending the vegetable garden. It seemed as if she was never still. While she was driving into town, exactly one mile from home, she was killed in a head-on collision. Her family reacted with extreme shock and disbelief. When someone we love dies suddenly, our sense of shock is usually heightened and lasts much longer than the shock we experience after a death from a long illness. How can we take in the reality of being separated forever from someone we had just spoken to hours or minutes ago? It is too much to assimilate in such a short period of time. This is especially true in closely dependent and deeply loving relationships.

Sometimes our shock is expressed by numbness. My cousins methodically prepared for the funeral, setting up tables on the front lawn, trimming the flowers, arranging for the reception. Shortly after the funeral, one of my cousins came down with pleurisy. After such a shock, we are overcome with sadness and pain and may develop acute physical reactions as a result. When a death is sudden we are not only brutally cut off from a loved one, but we are also faced with a whole new set of circumstances at one blow. We have to deal not only with lawyers and wills but with new responsibilities. The period of shock is actually a protection for us until we are psychologically ready to accept the fact of death.

When I was in my thirties, my mother died of a heart attack while she was reading in bed. Because she was alone in her apartment when she died, a neighbor called the police. When they arrived, they removed her jewelry and passport. I flew in from Boston and found a police officer in the apartment and my mother's body covered with a sheet. The image of her body and the eerie unreality of going to a police station where the air was thick with mace remained with me for weeks. The circumstances surrounding her death added to my shock and bewilderment. The night before we had spoken on the telephone, planning for a family celebration. In her bedroom there was a pile of unwrapped gifts. I felt as if I were left hanging in midair.

I dealt with the lawyers, called relatives, and arranged for the funeral as if I were in a dream. It took me weeks to feel the full intensity of my pain and months for the anger to surface.

My mother and I had a close and loving relationship. The horror and the images of her death eventually faded, and I was able to retain the joy of our time together. However, if our relationship with our parents was conflict-ridden, a sudden death often heightens the guilt and resentment we feel, and we struggle with our grief for a longer period of time. My father also died suddenly while traveling in Europe. We had a distant and difficult relationship and had not spoken to each other for years. My reaction of shock was curious. I interpreted my numbness as a sign of not caring. But even though I knew intellectually that there was no possibility of reconciliation, I was haunted for years by our unfinished relationship. A sudden death can be like a door slammed shut in the midst of a quarrel. There are no more opportunities for resolution.

The grief we feel after a sudden death is often more complicated and problematic than our grief after a long illness. Immediately after such a death, we may feel as if we had gone insane: We hallucinate the smell of our dead parent's pipe or feel their presence around us. This is a perfectly normal reaction. We were thrust headlong into a new reality, like being hurled into the deep end of the pool for our first swimming lesson.

Chapter Ten
WHEN A LOVER DIES

Lovers, whether heterosexual or homosexual, have the same powerful emotional bonds as those who are living together or married. However, while living together without marriage is becoming more accepted, homosexual relationships and extramarital affairs are not sanctioned by society. When we live outside of prevailing social norms, we suffer discrimination, hostility, and rejection. Often the extramarital or homosexual relationship is known only to a few acquaintances. In this case, when our lover dies we are without the usual supports of family, friends, and coworkers.

A friend of mine who had a ten-year relationship with a married lover handled this relationship with great discretion, and very few people outside of her family were aware of the connection. However, the man was very close to her children and acted like a father to her younger daughter, bringing her to college interviews, keeping in close touch with her during her years at school, and attending her wedding. Although her lover participated in events with her family, only a few of his friends and acquaintances knew about the relationship. Then he was diagnosed with terminal cancer and immediately hospitalized. Suddenly my friend was completely cut off from her lover. Because his family was constantly at his side, she was unable to visit him. By disguising her relationship to him she was able to call the hospital and find out how he was. After an agonizing few months in which she managed to get bits of information about him, he died.

My friend received the news of his death while she was in another city on a business trip. Because she was excluded from his company during his illness and because of the way she received the news, she reacted as if she had just received news about an accidental death. Under the circumstances she was not able to attend the funeral services or go to the cemetery. Even though she felt widowed, and even though she lost not only a friend and lover, but someone who was like a spouse to her, she was unable to experience the solace of a funeral ritual. Her exclusion from the supports these events provide added to her loneliness and grief.

An elderly friend of mine experienced the same situation when her lover died. Since she was denied all the socially sanctioned outlets for her feelings, she designed her own memorial service for him. She invited a few close friends to a service in which she gave the eulogy. After this event, her friends felt as if they too had been given permission to comfort her and talk about her lover with her. No matter what our situation is, the loss of a loved one is a devastating blow, and we are entitled not only to our own grief, but to share this grief with others and receive support.

Although gays and lesbians have received more understanding in the past few years as a result of political and educational efforts, we may still experience or expect discrimination. Because social hostility is so painful, some of us conceal our relationships from family, friends, or coworkers. In such a case, when a lover dies, we may have no one to turn to.

The grieving process can be very lonely, but this is especially true in these kinds of relationships. Our friends may feel that we shouldn't be experiencing such deep sorrow, or people may be surprised at our response. These reactions confuse us or make us hide our feelings. But the loss of a lover is as painful as the loss of a spouse. This is not a time for others to judge our relationships, our identity, or our behavior.

Chapter Eleven
WHEN A FRIEND DIES

A friend of mine who recently lost a close friend after a long illness told me ruefully, "Water is thicker than blood." Her comment revealed the importance of friendship in a society where nuclear or fragmented families rather than extended families are the rule. In a society with an increasing number of singles, friends frequently function as family. And even when a family has all of its members living together, we still might share our more private selves with a friend.

The importance of friendship varies with our age and with the length and intensity of the relationship. While friendships are significant to us at all ages, this is particularly true when we are in the throes of critical periods of our lives. When we are adolescents and young adults, friends support us as we develop our own identities and begin the long process of separation from our parents. When we are bringing up young children or are newly married, friends share the stresses and difficulties of parenting. As we age and our children become independent and our careers and marriages no longer seem so absorbing, friends answer our needs for emotional bonds and companionship. Some elderly people have had friends throughout their lives who know their history and who have shared important life events with them. In addition, for the elderly, friends are the carriers of the values and culture of an entire generation. Losing a friend in old age is like losing a large part of the world.

In a highly mobile society where the circumstances of our lives change frequently, a friend is one who knows our history and who shares our most private thoughts and feelings. A friend not only has known us over a period of time, but may also have shared with us the high or low points of our lives. Because of this, we continue to feel deeply about such a person even if we no longer see each other frequently, or even if we live in distant cities. If that person dies, it's as if we were losing a part of ourselves, leaving us with a feeling of emptiness.

When a close friend dies, especially if that friend is the same age and sex as we are, we suddenly face our own mortality. We are suddenly aware of our own fragility and vulnerability, especially if we are adolescents or young adults. We tell ourselves it could have been us who was struck by a car or who died of cancer. Even if someone who was not a close friend dies, we feel intense grief. As young people we do not expect anyone in our age group to die. A woman in her early twenties explained to me, "You mourn for anyone you know who shared your space, whether you liked them or not."

A student of mine who lost one of her friends kept writing poems for her as she struggled with the finality of that death. A young person may agonize for years over the horror and injustice of a death at an early age. As adolescents or young adults, we are less likely to find people in our age group who have experienced the death of friends. We may think we are unusual or abnormal because of the pain and confusion we feel and therefore keep the pain of that death inside us.

When a friend dies, we do not experience the wrenching changes in status and role as when a member of our own family dies. However, while we will not necessarily have to face major changes in our lifestyle, we still go through all the phases of grief: shock, waves of pain, and sadness. Watching our friend's family grapple with their own sorrow might make us think that our sadness is of little account, yet we are entitled to our own feelings of loss and need to give ourselves permission to mourn. Love is mysterious and complex. It exists in its own right and transcends the roles which hold us together in the web of our lives. Anyone we have truly loved is irreplaceable, and the loss of a cherished person will always cause us to mourn.

When I was in my late twenties, my closest friend became ill with cancer. We both had two very young children, and the six of us used to spend many hours together every week. Once the tumor was discovered, she deteriorated rapidly. In less than a year she died, leaving a mother, siblings, her husband, and her children. During her illness, I took care of her children. Having been so close to her family during that period, I felt as if I experienced their pain.

However, in the difficult period of disruption after her death, when the family struggled with the problem of childcare as I returned to my teaching, I was surprised at the depth of my grief and the anger I felt for my friend's suffering. Although my own life didn't change outwardly, I was shaken at the roots. I was outraged that such a young and vibrant person should die when she had just begun her life as a wife and mother. She had everything going for her, a very happy marriage, two beautiful children, and an intense enjoyment of life. "Young people shouldn't die," I thought to myself.

I carried this sadness and pain for many months but was unable to discuss it with anyone, as if I had no right to mourn for someone who wasn't family and who had left a grief-stricken family behind her. I have since learned that it helps to discuss and express our pain over the loss of a friend. It is important in our own lives and merits sharing.

Losing a friend when we are middle-aged has its own complexities. We lose friends with greater frequency as we become older, and therefore death may not be such a shock to us. However, as we see more and more of our friends die of cancer or heart disease, we perceive our own mortality not so much as a revelation but as a daily reminder. We grieve the evanescence, the short span of our lives. "A life passes so quickly," my uncle said after the death of his friend.

If we are elderly, losing a friend adds to our increasing sense of solitude, a grief in a long string of griefs as we let go of our jobs, change our places of residence and our lifestyles, and experience changes in our health. Losing a friend means losing yet another thread which connects us to the world. When our parents are gone, a friend may be the last person who shared our memories and histories.

Losing a friend causes us to look at our own lives and perhaps rearrange them in some way. When my father's close friend and colleague died of a heart attack, leaving a large family, my father changed his highly charged lifestyle and began to take better care of himself. Because I found no "recognized" place for my grief and my newly awakened sense of mortality after the death of my friend, I began to write. We can be carried to new places inside ourselves by the shock of death.

When we lose a member of our family, whether spouse, sibling, child, or parent, we are hurled out of our roles and status. For a period after the death, we feel as if we were without moorings, so closely do we identify with these roles. The changes we experience after the death of a friend may not be as disruptive but they are significant and painful. Our perceptions of life change, as do our views on the meaning of life, our sense of our own mortality. Ultimately we may change the way we spend our time.

"I care too much about my friends," someone commented bitterly when telling me about the death of a friend. To love someone is indeed to take a great risk of loss. However, not many people would want to trade the poverty of a life without friends for protection against the pain of loss.

Chapter Twelve
LOVE AND GRIEF

Love is one of the most powerful emotions we experience, but if we dwelled on it constantly, we would have difficulty functioning. We express our love for others subconsciously in the hundreds of small chores and routines of the day: driving our children to school, filling out insurance forms, preparing supper, repairing a bicycle. But when we lose someone close, we suddenly feel at one blow the depth and magnitude of our love for that person. A poet once wrote that whoever was struck by the shock of love would return to his work with an altered face. Along with the shock of loss, we feel the shock of our love for the person we have lost. We need time to be with that discovery as much as we need time to let our anger and sadness surface.

If we had a troubled and difficult relationship with someone close to us—a parent, lover, or sibling—we may be surprised by our grief. We do not expect to feel so deeply about someone who disappointed us so often or with whom we were in conflict. However, the death of such a person strikes us by its finality. There are no longer any opportunities to improve the relationship. This can leave us with a burden of bitterness and regret. Or we discover how much we loved someone who was difficult to like or who taxed our patience time and time again. If we feel responsible for the difficulties in a relationship, this is the time to forgive ourselves.

The depth and extent of our love often catches us by surprise. Love is one of the freest emotions. It transcends the many roles and categories that hold us together as families, friends, church members. Literature is full of stories of love that moves across social barriers. We grieve profoundly for a grandmother, for a friend's child, for a neighbor, yet because we had only loose social connections with the person we are grieving for, we may feel that our sadness is unwarranted. We try to minimize it or hold it inside. We have an endless capacity for loving different people. The more one loves, the more one is able to love.

Each person we love has a unique place in our feelings. When my mother died, I felt the loss keenly, even though I had a wonderful family of my own. She was my best friend and was more than a parent to me, since our relationship was one of equality. We had such a quiet understanding and such a sharing of each other's burdens that I felt as if I had been widowed when she died. Since there was no place to discuss the love between parents and adult children, I began reading articles about widows. Only we can define how important a relationship is to us.

We take our cues from society and the larger culture. However, when someone we love dies, our emotions and feelings might be out of sync with society's expectations. We are bewildered and confused by the welter of emotions assailing us. However painful our emotions seem, eventually they will bring us to a new place in our lives and within ourselves. The core of ourselves which feels the shock and hurt of loving fully is the very essence of what it means to be a human being.

Part Three
LOSING A LOVED ONE THROUGH SUICIDE OR HOMICIDE

Winter Rain
"Drama Student Stabbed to Death on West Side."

Under the dazzle of lights and rain
I can't see the signs, the familiar
curbs jutting out before the black trees,
the blur of oncoming traffic.

I careen through a landscape of skids
and precipice. **She was leaning over
the roof edge screaming for help.**
Instead of snow, this December rain,

denser than flesh, the warm air
eddying above the pavement,
rising like smoke above a pyre.
I hear a voice, youth's sweet lilt,

in the dressing room before the play.
Svanheld, Ibsen's swan lifts her face
in expectation. Her ivory skin, pale red hair
light the passageway. She's ready

to enter, say her lines. The season's
all wrong, the fog rising in coils,
warm rain that will not clot spattering
on the roof, beneath the man without a face.

I skid on a bed of water, the water's like oil,
the road an oil slick. Who knows
where it will carry us, where the spill
first gushed and the blind hand pumping.

Marguerite Guzman Bouvard

Chapter Thirteen
WHEN SOMEONE WE LOVE
COMMITS SUICIDE

Merryl

In 1982, my husband committed suicide. He was thirty-three at the time and I had just turned thirty-four. Carl had been in a doctoral program at the University of Chicago for eight years. At the time of his death we had been married for six years, although we had lived together for a few years before that. We had been trying to have a child for the past six months. In a way I really felt that I lost two people. There was the potential child that was very much a part of my life at that time. That's been one of the harder griefs to deal with. It's still an ongoing grief.

Carl had been in a doctoral program for child development. It's very difficult to find a job in that field in academic teaching. For three years he sent out letters, but many weren't even answered. He met with lots of rejection. Meanwhile, his dissertation was taking longer and longer and his vita was always being updated. In spring of 1982, a part-time job that he had at Children's Hospital was ending, and he just didn't see what was ahead. He discovered what he thought was a serious flaw in his dissertation. He went into an agony of despair, believing he was worthless. He perceived the world saying no to him as his own failure.

The last week of his life he did speak of suicide. He had never spoken of it before except once, a year before when he woke up one morning and said, "If I ever have to go through another job search like this, I'll kill myself." At that time I didn't pay much attention. There was no context for it. He never mentioned it again. A year and a half later, I thought of his having said that. But even his supervisor at the Children's Hospital who was herself a psychologist said that she saw Carl as someone who was very much in control of his own life. I was the only one who knew he had these conflicts inside. His parents didn't have any idea. He had been tops in his class at the university. He was very good looking. He was president of the honor society. On the outside he looked like Robert Redford. On the inside he was like Woody Allen.

The last week of his life he was immersed in a kind of despair, and I could not reach him. I stayed home to be with him. I called a psychiatrist. He did see a psychiatrist, but the doctor said that Carl would not have the courage to commit suicide.

Carl left the house on Friday of that week. He was to meet me at my office at six o'clock. He never showed up at my office. I got home in a frenzy because I knew that there was something very wrong. In eight years of being together he had never left the house like that without telling me where he would be. I noticed his suitcase was gone. The nightmare weekend began.

I called my parents and his parents. We had a vigil, his parents and I. We just waited by the phone. We had no idea where he was. He had taken the car. I reported him as a missing person.

I knew in my heart of hearts that there was a danger of suicide, and we talked about it that weekend, although I tried to imagine that he might be in Atlanta looking for a job. He had always talked of the South. A policeman came to the door on Sunday night. He gave me a phone number to call. I think he knew that something had happened, but he wouldn't tell me and just walked away. I ran to the phone and called that number. It was a New York City number. The man at the other end of the phone said, "Medical." I knew that he was probably a coroner, and I asked, "Is this a hospital?" desperately hoping that this was a medical ward. He said, "This is the morgue, lady."

I threw the phone down and ran and jumped off the porch. I started screaming. I didn't care if I broke all my bones. The police came because my neighbors called them. They really didn't know what was happening. The police came and brought me in the house and said I needed some kind of sedation. I remember talking about killing myself, and they said, "If you talk like that we'll have to put you in a hospital," so I just said nothing and they went away. That really was the beginning of the worst. The reason I jumped off the porch at that moment was that I had total and intense knowledge that I would never see Carl again. I had no illusions. It hit me in one solid moment that I would never see this man again whom I totally loved and with whom I wanted to have a child.

He hanged himself. He was in a hotel with a closed door. A chambermaid found him. It wasn't this cry for help that people talk about. It was this final act when Carl decided to die. There was no way to help him.

It was the christening weekend for my sister-in-law's baby. They named him for Carl. The very moment he was found dead was the christening of this little baby which was assuming his name.

The suicide person is really a victim of his own crime. Sometimes I felt as if Carl had committed murder, and in a sense he did. He took the life of the person I loved the most in the world. In a way I did get angry at him for murdering the person I loved. You start to feel angry and then you short-circuit it with the feeling that somehow you could have saved the person. You were responsible.

Although I don't think so now, at the time I found every single way of feeling responsible for what happened. I had three categories of guilt. One was our marriage, that I wasn't a good wife. Or that because we had returned here to Boston where I had found a good job, that may have limited opportunities for him, and therefore I was the cause. The third part of the guilt was the last week of his life. I really was the only one involved in his life at that point in terms of knowing his suicidal feelings. I would circle around with those guilts like a mad person for a long time.

I kept short-circuiting my anger. It's slowly that the anger will come in. You make a lot of excuses for the person because you keep feeling how they suffered. It took me a long time to realize that you can have understanding of the person that they did something terrible and you can be furious at them for what they did to themselves and to your life, but that doesn't change the fact that you loved them. Sometimes you feel that you'll stop loving them if you are angry, but that's not true. Anger is a tricky emotion with suicide.

The "if only" syndrome with suicide is one that can almost drive you crazy. You have these scenarios in your head: If I had gotten home earlier, if I had listened harder. You can find a million of them waiting in every single fact. I've spoken to many people who have had suicide deaths in their family, and it's a universal reaction. It's natural and necessary in the beginning. You need to rerun that movie in your head. I even had myself in the hotel room in New York. You need to exorcise that guilt to work it through. No one can speed it up for you. But if you go on like that for years, something has gone awry. It could take over your whole life.

I'm going on with my life, and I'm living with another man. But there is still this issue: When do I bring Carl up? He's still part of my life. I still think about him three times a day even though it's been almost three years. It's been slowly getting easier. Telling people that I had this whole past other life isn't such a problem anymore. I feel I can bring it up when I want to.

In the first year I used to go around hunched over. I had lost weight. I was like a totally different person physically. I hardly spoke to people, and usually I am a very outgoing person. I took a month off from work, and then I went back on a part-time basis for a while. I didn't look or act like myself for eight months. I was crying all the time.

I went to Safe Place for survivors of suicides for two years, every other week, and that really helped. I had a lot of support in my mother and one very good friend and a therapist. You have to make a network for yourself. If you're isolated, it's worse.

After I got through the first year, I thought, "I survived a year, but he's still not here so, so what." The anniversary of his death was okay. I made a memorial for myself. I went to a beach and I just watched the waves and I really felt peaceful. But the next month was horrible because there was that backlash feeling of so what, who cares. He's not here. That's the absolute fact of death.

For me it was talking that helped, a great deal of talking. I really feel that when you do communicate the pain, it does ease it. It's a long, slow process. I would talk to anybody about it. My mother was wonderful. She was there night and day whenever I needed her. Right after Carl's death I lived with my parents for three months, being taken care of. I had no children. In an odd way that was a blessing, because I could be totally selfish with my grief. This woman I worked with offered me her home. I needed a transition between my parent's house and getting back into a normal life in our apartment. She offered me a room in her house. She has a family. It was a wonderful place for me to go. She was my dearest, closest friend suddenly. Then there was a therapist I saw three times a week. Those three things, in addition to the strengths I found inside myself, are what helped.

I was lucky in the sense that I could scream. My parents have this place off on the water, and I could just go there and scream. If you live in the city, you can't do that. There's no other reaction.

I've imagined the scene of Carl hanging himself. I've read about asphyxia. In the beginning I read everything I could get my hands on. I remember my mother saying, "At least it's a merciful death." Well, I read about suicidal hanging. The person is suffering at least seven minutes before they die. I knew all the details. I was spared that agony of finding my husband. Many people are not spared that and have terrible stories to tell and nightmares recurring for many months. I'm happy that Carl was not in the home. Any kind of violent death like that you suffer with the person. With empathy you want to take it away but you can't.

What I didn't find and what I wanted to find was a young widow two years down the line looking normal in her life. When I went to the Safe Place, all I really found were people in agony and terrible suffering. Even if it had been two years, they weren't the ones that had put it together. I didn't have any role model and that is one of the reasons that I would like to go back. It is very important to see someone who has been through it and who has managed to move on. The nature of a self-help group is that when people start to feel better they don't come anymore. Slowly, in this miraculous way, I became one of the ones who was making it. People would come in who were worse, and I would measure myself and say, "I'm better off."

When someone dies through suicide, it doesn't come out of nowhere. I really feel that this came out of Carl. It came out of the person he was for whatever reason. It did come from him, and therefore it might have happened again. He had in him that terrible sense that he could get to those black depressions that are the feeling of worthlessness. That had happened to him when he was eighteen, as it turns out, and it could have happened to him when he was thirty-nine or fifty. Perhaps he might not have gotten tenure later on when everyone around him was getting it. I have envisioned that it could have happened later on in his life. From my reading and from my therapist I feel that I have learned a lot about what makes people, the comparisons between me and my husband, him and other people. There isn't this sense that a random act took him away. In an odd way that's been a kind of a good feeling for me. For the spouse of a suicide, a way of understanding is to see the person as a whole person and that they came to the relationship with certain problems.

Because of the therapy, because of really facing the worst of it, I kind of moved on from it the first year. I did face it constantly for almost a year, and that's what freed me up to feel as much love as I do for the man I'm now involved with. I don't feel that that's in any way a lessening of my affection for Carl. One of the first things I told this man on our first date—about fourteen months after Carl died—was "My husband committed suicide, and you really need to know that." I thought if he can't handle this, this is not going to be a relationship. He was able to talk to me about pain. We don't talk about Carl a lot, but I know that he understands.

Writing about his experiences during World War II, the Italian author Primo Levi claimed that some events are unspeakable and some wounds are so deep that there are no words which could possibly console. Sometimes language is inadequate to either express or acknowledge our pain. As the narrative makes clear, people who have lost a loved one through suicide or homicide often scream when they hear the news. Merryl jumped off the porch and screamed until the neighbors called the police. Weeks later, at her parents' home by the ocean, she sat on the beach and yelled out her anguish. When someone we love commits suicide, the shock, pain, and all the emotions associated with loss are heightened. They are not only more intense but occur simultaneously. The struggle to find meaning, which may be postponed in other types of death, assail us immediately after a suicide. We anticipate the death of a terminally ill person. We are periodically aware of the possibilities of death by accident, but how can we ever imagine a loved one or a friend taking his or her own life? How can we possibly include it within our frame of reference? The meaninglessness of such a death prolongs the period of shock we experience afterward. The utter mystery of motivation for suicide baffles and overwhelms.

Suicide not only defies our sense of the meaning of life, but also calls into question our most profound social beliefs. Society considers suicide offensive. We regard it as a blot on our family name and a source of personal failure. Many families try to cover it up and are deeply ashamed of it. Two close friends of mine attempted suicide without success, one, a single professional woman, the other, a mother of three, yet a year passed before they could tell me, even though we were trusted friends. The brother of one of my daughter's closest friends committed suicide years ago, the family never speaks of it. It's as if they sealed a door forever, as if by this means they could push away the torment and shame. Suicide elicits both guilt on the part of survivors and shame before what is perceived as a social stigma.

Yet suicide touches so many of us. Although it is rarely discussed in social settings, it would be difficult to find a person today who did not know someone affected by such a tragedy. As any other kind of death, suicide knows no differences in age or economic or social circumstances. Perhaps because suicides among the young are so widespread and such a source of social concern, newspapers frequently carry stories of such events. Yet suicide afflicts many different types of people, not only the young or the chronically depressed.

Among those who commit suicide are people with a history of mental or emotional illness. Perhaps they attempted to kill themselves without success before, or perhaps they had repeated hospitalizations. If we had a troubled family member or friend, we might have struggled through his illness with him for years, but always we hoped for his eventual recovery. Often, just before the suicide, our loved one seemed better. But even when the person we love suffered from mental illness for a long period of time, we never expect suicide.

Perhaps the suicidal person suffered from depression for only a few months or weeks and had no previous history of depression. Maybe we friends or family suffered through the depression too and sought psychiatric help for him. Sometimes, the suicide occurs just when that person seems to be finally emerging from depression. The decision to end his life might have been the source of relief which accounted for the turnaround. However, perhaps the person who committed suicide expressed some kind of hope, talked of a new job or changes in his life. One man who had been suffering depression made plans to do something with his son during the week, yet he committed suicide the weekend prior. In all these cases, survivors are left with a mystery. We look desperately for clues, but clues are most evident with hindsight and are frequently ambivalent.

Many people who take their lives had no previous episodes of depression. It seems as if this terrible tragedy simply came out of the blue. The perfectionist who imposes very high standards on herself, who expects herself to perform with equal brilliance in a number of areas, may be masking deep feelings of worthlessness. Some people who commit suicide are solitary, not given to talking with others or not wishing to impose on other people. For most people who commit suicide, it is a solution to a deep and searing inner pain. They may leave notes behind saying, "It hurts too much," or "You'll be better off without me," or "Life is too hard." A person suffering such anguish is unable to see any options to cope with her pain. Suicide seems the only way out. As survivors, we can see other ways to cope, but no matter how much love or help we provided to our loved one, we could not prevent the suicide, and that is difficult to accept.

We try to enter into our loved one's last moments in order to understand his point of view, but how can we possibly imagine a pain so profound that suicide seems the only way to end it? A woman whose husband committed suicide had a sudden revelation of his inner logic when she was lying in his study one morning among his books and papers:

A primitive awareness took me over. The pain he had spoken of weighed itself against the failure and worthlessness of his life as he saw it at that time. To trade away such pain—and the only thing required, to give up a worthless life. When I lived through it as I did that morning in the absolute terms that had gripped him, it appeared to me for a moment as it had to him: there was only one choice.

How and where we discover the suicide affects our grieving. Discovering a suicide in our own home shakes us to the core. We relive that discovery through nightmares for months afterward or can't go into the room where our loved one killed himself, or even follow the same path we took when we found him, whether opening a certain door or going up the stairs. Our house seems tainted or changed.

Miriam's husband had been depressed for three months. It was the first time during their married life that he had been through a period like this. He was always concerned about being healthy and physically fit. He seemed very contented with his life and his living arrangement with his brother and sister-in-law and their children. There were four parents and four children living in harmony and enjoying their closeness not only in everyday life but also during vacations and weekends. When Miriam's husband became depressed, all three adults rallied around him. They showed their support in a number of ways, by talking with him, offering him the option of taking a trip or stopping work for a while. Finally Miriam arranged for a visit to a psychiatrist. He did go, and he made an appointment for another visit. But he hanged himself before the second appointment.

That fateful morning, Miriam had stayed in bed a little late because she wasn't feeling well. Her husband got up around seven, and when he came downstairs to the kitchen he met his mother-in-law, who was staying with them at the time. They greeted each other, and then his mother-in-law went out for her usual morning walk. When she returned, she found that Miriam's husband had hanged himself in the kitchen. Her screams sent Miriam racing down the stairs.

When the suicide occurred, Miriam's two children were away for a weekend with the rest of the extended family. She telephoned them immediately and had to face the terrible burden of telling the children. She did this in stages. First, she told the boys that their father had died, and as they asked questions about how and why, she gradually told them. As a family, they had always had very open communication and were used to leveling with each other. Although the door where her husband hanged himself was eventually taken down, the family continued to use the room, and the children were soon coloring and playing there again.

The family arranged the funeral rites so that everyone could participate. The father's body was cremated, and his ashes were scattered over the sea. The children included messages and letters of farewell with the ashes.

Some families have a much harder time coping with the shock and horror of discovering a suicide. One family whose fourteen-year-old son committed suicide arranged for a cremation and private funeral within twenty-four hours of the death. They were trying to push the horror of it away as soon as possible. Eventually they realized how precipitous their planning was, and with great difficulty they rearranged the ceremony to allow close friends to participate. Sometimes the shock of such a death makes us want to deny it, and it is easy to temporarily lose sight of the many years of joy we shared with the deceased. We want to get the body away fast, and above all we don't want anyone to know what happened.

For some the discovery of a suicide comes at the end of a painful search for a missing person. Spouses and parents sometimes have premonitions of the possibility of suicide when a child misses his or her usual schedule, or as in Merryl's case when her husband failed to show up at her office as planned. Then follows what Merryl referred to as her nightmare time, when the family reported him missing and began the long vigil by the phone. Even though the way the news was conveyed to Merryl was heartless and impersonal, she was grateful that she didn't find her husband herself, in their home. But people who receive news of a suicide by phone often experience a phobia of phone calls for months and years afterward.

The method of suicide, whether by hanging or slashing the wrists, for example, is a continuing source of anguish. We relive both the mental and the physical pain our friend experienced in the months before the death and in the seemingly endless minutes of dying. In our images and in our replay of events, the mental and physical anguish our loved one suffered is reinforced. Knowing how painful such a death can be, we can only imagine the depth of emotional pain that chose such an ending as a relief.

Because suicide is so difficult to understand, we go over and over the last moments or hours we spent with our loved one. We examine our last conversations and the final events in order to find some sort of explanation. We spend many hours going over the details of the time before the death as if we could find a reason for what happened, some cause to blame. We are haunted by these details, because our belief structure has been undermined. While we may dwell upon the last months or weeks of suffering a loved one endured during an illness, in time we are able to return to the better times and the joys we shared. We can let go of those months of suffering.

We need a much longer period of time to get through a suicide. We are obsessed with trying to pinpoint the specific circumstances that led our loved one to such a tragic ending, more so than for any other type of death. We focus on our loved one's working conditions, the pressures, or perhaps his or her struggle with alcohol. In some cases we request an autopsy or spend time talking to hospital personnel in our effort to comprehend the unanswerable question. It is only months or years later that we can separate the immediate circumstances of our loved one's life from the decision to end it.

Behind the details that we sift like ashes after a fire is the feeling that we are responsible for the suicide. We think that somehow we could have prevented it. We say to ourselves, "If only I had heard what she was saying, if only I had been there at the time, if only we had not made the decision to go away." Our imagination unfolds an endless list of "if onlys." This is one of the biggest issues suicide survivors face. We need to go over our roles in our loved one's lives and to be allowed the months and even years it takes to examine our own conduct. We have a powerful sense of responsibility to those we love, and this feeling of responsibility is closely related to conscience. It is simply not possible to sidestep this process. Even when we begin to see that perhaps we could not have prevented our loved one's death, this is still a purely intellectual perception. The heart and the stomach are slow to follow the mind's reasoning.

Following our initial shocked reaction to a suicide, guilt and anger predominate. Our guilt can be paralyzing. We know that we need to continue our lives, turn our attention to our jobs and surviving family and friends, and yet just when we feel it is finally possible to move on, the guilt returns and pulls us back. We think a lot about whether our loved one planned the suicide for some time and look for evidence, such as failing health or paying bills and attending to financial matters much ahead of schedule. Then we think of living with the person and wonder what we could have done to prevent it had we only noticed and paid more attention. We may be able to function, to go through the motions of our lives, but we are caught in an internal struggle as we face our guilt and the unfathomable nature of such an event.

Guilt continues during the bereavement period until we are finally able to let go of it. At one point, Merryl realized that she would never be whole again if she didn't let go of the self-blame. That realization has to come from within. But we can gain a sense of perspective from friends who listen and talk to us during this period. Our friends will remind us of all the things we did to help our loved ones which we may have forgotten in our agony. Our friends will remind us that we see clues and symptoms only with hindsight. A good friend will keep repeating these insights to us, which will help us internalize them and ultimately see our loved one in relation to himself and not only in relation to ourselves.

After a suicide we are not only shaken by guilt, but we also experience profound anger. We are not necessarily angry at the person who died, given that person's extreme pain, but we may be angry at the pain we are left with after the suicide. "She took away her pain, but left us with it," or "How could she do this to us?" we ask ourselves. It is helpful to think of the deceased as two people. the one we love and the one who murdered her. We can be angry at the murderer while loving and accepting her victim. In some cases we perceive the suicide as a rejection of ourselves. We are angry that our wife or lover didn't consider us important enough to live for. In a moment of humor, a member of a support group for survivors of suicide exploded, "If I could have him back for just five minutes, I'd kill him."

A suicide in our family or among close relations can arouse fears that other members of the family or even we ourselves are prone to suicide. Perhaps the suicidal family member was the one who always seemed in control. When the unlikely person commits suicide, we look at the more fragile or vulnerable members of our family with new concern. Or we become afraid that we ourselves might be vulnerable to such a tragic end. After the death of someone we love deeply, it is normal to feel that we don't want to go on. But there is a big difference between thinking that we *don't want* to live and thinking that we *shouldn't* live.

The brother of a young man who committed suicide became depressed after his brother's death. Unlike his brother, who had mental difficulties, he had always been balanced and had felt positive about his own life. Then he began acting like his dead brother. He dressed like him, took on some of his characteristics. It was his way of taking responsibility for his brother's death. Ultimately, the young man regained his health and stability after attending support groups and after seeing a psychiatrist. However, as family members, we can be vulnerable to the thought that we don't deserve to live.

Living in a home where a suicide occurred is especially difficult. We may feel our home is somehow marked and yet may have few options for alternative housing. Merryl lived with her parents and then with a friend until she could confront her own apartment again. It will take some time for us to see our home as a place where we and our loved one had a very full life together.

Holidays, which are always difficult for those who have lost loved ones, are especially trying for survivors of a suicide. When Thanksgiving arrived, Miriam didn't feel like getting out of bed. She wished the whole day would disappear or that she could ignore it, but this is impossible for families with children. Miriam gave a special reading for her husband at the beginning of the Thanksgiving dinner, and that helped her through the day.

There are also painful daily reminders that make our passage through this period difficult. Our children continue to ask us questions or express their pain and confusion in their play activities, by the pictures they draw, or by acting out the suicide with a stuffed animal or toy. Not only do we have to answer our own questions, but we have to address the pain of those around us as well.

If it is awkward and sometimes impossible to talk about the death of a loved one, it is even more difficult to talk about suicide. Some friends and acquaintances are willing to listen to us talk of our deceased, but it is very rare to find someone who is able to listen sympathetically while we air our pain over a suicide. Support groups where suicide survivors can discuss the particular issues around suicide are extremely helpful. Many people stay with these support groups for two or three years and then return to help others. It is good to talk about this kind of death, to share our experiences with others who have had similar ones, to see people in various stages of the grieving process, and especially to see those who have left the most difficult phases behind them.

It is hard to admit that we can't control the circumstances and fate of our loved ones. Our society puts a great deal of energy into suicide prevention, and therefore we feel like failures when someone we love takes his or her own life. However, even when we knew what was troubling a spouse, child, or sibling and even when we did everything humanly possible to help that person, ultimately we could not reach him or her. Only time can help us accept our powerlessness to save those we love.

It is always hard to talk about a death and our grief over that death with our friends and coworkers, but it is particularly difficult to tell people about a suicide. We want to protect ourselves and our family because of the powerful social taboos against suicide. We may feel a sense of shame and dread adverse social reactions. Consequently some of us try to cover it up by telling people that our loved one died of an accident or a heart attack. We may feel protective of some members of our own family, the elderly, very young children, or the emotionally fragile.

The way we deal with the problem of facing the outside world depends on our own style of communication and our own way of coping. When Merryl returned to work, she sat down with her new secretary and explained to her that her appearance and withdrawn behavior was due to the recent suicide of her husband. Some people can talk about suicide, but others play it down. However, many of us experience a deep sense of isolation on returning to our lives as workers, students, or parents. It's as if such a terrible tragedy sets us apart from others. As suicide survivors, we are also victims. We carry the burden of it our whole lives.

Chapter Fourteen
WHEN SOMEONE WE LOVE IS MURDERED

Margaret

My story begins on June 9, 1988. At that time I had three children, a son, seventeen, and two daughters, aged fifteen and ten. My son, John, was learning to drive and drove me and his friend to a graduation party. He was happy, in love, and looking forward to a great future for himself. I was very happy. He had caused me a lot of problems when he was in his early teens, but now he was turning seventeen and he had seen the light. It was wonderful.

At 12:30 on June 10th, I was awakened by a doctor calling me from City Hospital, telling me that my son had been stabbed. Since I was alone, he arranged for the police to pick me up. There were three policemen in the car. They didn't speak a word to me but chatted with each other as if I weren't even there. The first hospital that I was taken to was the Cambridge City Hospital. Looking back, they were really great. They had a crisis center counselor there, and she put her arm around me while the doctor told me what condition John was in. They had decided to move him to the Massachusetts General. When I arrived there I was immediately asked whether I had Blue Cross/Blue Shield and put in a room by myself. I remember saying the Hail Mary out loud. That was something I hadn't done in a long time. My heart was pounding.

A doctor came into the room and matter-of-factly told me, "Your son has expired." I ran outside the hospital and I screamed and screamed and screamed. Thank God I was able to do that. Then my defense system took

140

over and I was anesthetized. From the moment he died, I was consumed by the loss. I just couldn't be concerned about how he had died, it was just that he had died. I didn't know what was happening to the person that killed him. I didn't want to believe that John had suffered and that he knew he was going to die. I wanted to believe that he had been stabbed in the back and never knew anything. I couldn't bear to feel that he had suffered, so I didn't ask any questions.

I was told by my brother that a probable cause hearing was being held and that later a grand jury hearing would take place. During this time, the person who had stabbed my son was in custody and had been since the night of the murder. I read in the paper that sufficient evidence was found to have him stand trial. I was under the delusion that I would be notified when the trial was to begin. Not so. I found out the date of the trial when I contacted the prosecuting attorney just to find out what was happening. At the trial I was totally ignored. I was the person who was the most deeply affected by the crime, and yet I was treated as if I didn't exist. Perhaps the attorney could have told me how things were progressing in the case before the trial or even talked to me during the trial. It was humiliating to be ignored.

The person who killed my son was convicted of second-degree murder and was sentenced to life in prison. He will be eligible for parole in fifteen years. I'm lucky, because somebody is paying some price for the crime. Many people don't have that luck, if you want to call it luck in this situation. At least I had somewhere to go after the trial. I could get on with my life.

I felt nothing except pain in my head for the first month. At some point somebody said to me, "You must be angry at God." That gave me permission to feel angry. I hadn't felt angry until that moment, and then I was totally enraged.

I feel lucky that I had some therapy before John died. I got some of the other stuff out of the way. During 1982, I had a love affair that ended, and my father died. I was suffering terribly. The psychiatrist kept mentioning grief. Now, this was thirteen years ago. I thought grief was some psychiatric term. I really didn't know that grief was something that everybody experienced when they lost someone, because people didn't talk about grief. I kept wondering would I ever feel better again. I kept asking people whether anyone ever recovered from it. No one was able to give me an answer, and that was one of the reasons I thought I would write a little of what I felt when John died so that someday I could say to someone, "I felt this bad and I got better."

The week after John's funeral was just a blur of pain. I ran around looking for someone, for anything that I could find out about grief. I called people. I looked in the death notices to see if I could find someone whose child had died, and I wrote letters to people who had lost children. Nobody responded, and I believe now it was because my son had been murdered. Their children had died from illness or accidents. Even people who are grieving can't relate to homicide.

My son died on June 10th. On June 29th I wrote in my journal, "I can't imagine parting with John's clothes. I feel like this will never heal up. It's so awful I can't believe it. Everything I do reminds me of something I did with John. I love him so much. How can I have a decent life without him? What a terrible pain to have to bear for the rest of my life. There's no consolation. I keep picturing John, so full of life."

On August 15th I wrote, "I feel a lot of anger toward a lot of people. They are so smug in their security. Everyone except me and my daughters seems to be getting over it. I feel like everyone has forgotten it. I feel like I'll never stop crying."

On September 27th I wrote, "I feel so bad I just can't comprehend it. It's so horrible. All I can say is, 'Oh my God, Oh my God.' I feel as if I'm going to split into pieces. Why did God ever let this happen to me? If there's a God, I hate him."

The trial took place that November and lasted for two weeks. At that time, I felt as though John had just died. I was back to square one. People couldn't understand why I had to attend the trial. I had to. He was my son. I had to complete that journey. When the defendant was found guilty, I was elated, for one day. But then, so what? John was still dead.

The months of December, January, and February were the worst I experienced in the whole mourning period. There was no relief from pain. The only way I could tell people how badly I felt was to say that I didn't want to live. I didn't think of suicide, but that was the only way to express my feelings. Paradoxically, it was just at this time that people were letting go of me, feeling that I was now able to stand on my own two feet.

On January 2nd I wrote, "I'm in agony. My son is dead and I will never see him again. For the first time since he died, I feel as if I can't stand it. I can't get him out of my mind. I feel like screaming all the time. I feel very angry toward people. I guess I'm not getting any special treat-

ment any longer and I think I should. What I'm contending with is so intense, I can't believe I can go to work. It almost feels worse now than before. People ignore the facts of my life. They expect me to be happy."

People who have lost children agree with me that one's public grieving is over in eight months. After that people are no longer interested. They don't want to know you are still feeling bad.

On April 3rd I wrote, "I looked at pictures of John growing up today. I thought I was up to it. I wasn't. It broke my heart. I know I've healed somewhat because I don't think about John all the time. I think I'm letting go of him a little, through no choice of mine. I don't want to. The space in the house is filling up a little."

After the first anniversary I wrote, "I've survived." I think there was a high in getting through the first year. Now I'm stuck with it. I have to live with it day in and day out.

I hardly wrote in my journal after the first year. I was reinvesting in life. I took some courses. I continued to attend Compassionate Friends for two more years. After three years, I had recovered sufficiently so that I started doing some work on victim rights.

I had a good support system, but they were all grieving too. My mother was very upset. Looking back, I got little, but my children got nothing. I wish they had some supports in the school system. If I feel guilty about anything, it's about my daughters, because I was totally unable to help them. No one mentioned it in school. They went back to school, nothing was said about it. If only people would acknowledge what happened or at least say, "I'm sorry." People feel that you might cry. You probably will, but that's okay.

I met Charlotte Hollinger shortly after her daughter was murdered. She started a group called Parents of Murdered Children. She said, "The church was no help. I was getting platitudes: 'It was God's will.' Or 'God wanted Lisa so badly he took her early. She's much happier now with God.'" There's nothing more maddening or patronizing then to be told this. Another thing I hear from other homicide victims when they talk about the clergy is that they are told they have to forgive. I don't know how you get around to forgiving. I haven't even thought about it myself. I think it's asking a lot to ask people to forgive someone who murdered their loved one.

I went to Compassionate Friends, a support group for bereaved parents. I did not talk about the fact that my son was murdered there. I used what I had in common with these people. I didn't feel as if they were comfortable with the fact that John was murdered. Maybe it was in my own head. I never did have a lot of opportunity to discuss the fact that John was murdered. I think what happens to homicide survivors is that they constantly relive the murder scene. I could be drying my hair and I will suddenly picture John getting stabbed and staggering across the street screaming, "I've been stabbed." Even now I think more about John than my children who are alive because all I have are memories. There are things from John's childhood that will pop up. I drive a long distance to work, and that's when I'm by myself and that's when I'm very sad.

If I hadn't gone to a group, even though I didn't meet anyone who at that time had lost a child through homicide, I would have thought that I was the only person in the world who was suffering. At least when I went there, there were other people who were suffering, and it helped somehow. You hate everybody else who is having a good time. You're totally obsessed with this death experience. It's just on your mind morning, noon, and night.

I was lucky because I was in pretty good shape when this happened to me. Not everyone is in good shape when something like this happens to them. I had suffered before, so I knew something about suffering, and that helped me.

It's been seven years since my son died. I feel I have recovered to a certain extent. It's below the surface. I live above it all the time. I'm very sad and very angry. I can talk about the rights of crime victims without crying, but when I talk about my own son John I can't do it without crying. I don't mind, but it's very hard for other people to deal with. One of the things that's very hard about losing a child is that people won't let you mention his name. It's like he never existed.

To me the best thing that could ever happen is that somebody would say, "Do you have a picture?" When it's your child you feel like you want to talk about them. But when I talk about John, I will cry. Then there's this thing about murder. If I tell people that John was murdered then I have to take care of them. It's hard to decide whether or not to mention it. In fact, one person did say, "Why did you mention it?" I say, well, I did have three children. I hate to leave him out of my life. I had him for seventeen years, and I was very proud of him. I still want people to know that he was very good looking and that he had a good personality.

I don't know what this experience has taught me. I've had other

*grieving experiences to which I could look back and know that I've
learned something. I can't say anything good about this experience except
that I didn't lie down and die myself. I have learned that the human spirit
is amazing. We don't know what we have inside us, no one knows. You
live, you survive.*

Though murder is the focus of so many television shows, movies, and
newspaper articles, we never imagine that it could possibly happen to
someone we love. Although statistics tell us certain types of people are
more frequently the victims of murder, we are all vulnerable to drunk dri-
vers when we are on the highway and we may all be prey to wanton
murder.

Murder is commonplace in the pseudoreality of the mass media.
However, the drama of murder that we witness on our television screens
focuses on investigations, arrests, and courtroom scenes. These programs
rarely give us any view of the terrible emotional impact on the survivors
of a murder and often even the victim is given little attention.

It is only when the Oklahoma City bombing occurred on April 19,
1995, that the stark reality of such a loss was brought home to us through
television and newspapers. We were assaulted with scenes of parents
grieving the loss of young children who were in the daycare center in the
devastated building and even of rescue workers' grief as they sifted
through the debris in search of survivors. That our first reaction was to
blame foreign terrorists attests to our desire to hold on to assumptions that
our world is safe and that we are somehow exempt from such senseless
killing. Our subsequent national obsession with suspects and the trial is a
normal hunger for meaning and justice in the face of such wanton murder.

When a loved one is murdered, the emotions of grieving, such as
anger, are more intense and long-lasting than in other kinds of loss. The
elements of horror and cruelty in such a crime throw us into acute turmoil. We are shocked and confused, perhaps for much longer than for
other kinds of loss because such an event is so difficult to comprehend.
We are frequently obsessed by an overwhelming need to know the details
of our loved one's death and the depth of his or her suffering. We replay
the event both because we want to know the extent and nature of the
victim's suffering and because gathering the details is a search for understanding what seems incomprehensible.

We are caught in a kaleidoscope of emotions: rage at the murderer, desire for revenge, sorrow at the pain of our loved one, intense anxiety about the security of our world. We think we should have been able to prevent that death and are tormented by guilt. We have a hard time sleeping, and when sleep finally comes we have terrible nightmares. We feel out of control in a world which seems arbitrary and unpredictable. Those of us who lose a loved one through murder have all the symptoms of post-traumatic stress, such as flashbacks if we witnessed the murder and a fear for our own safety. We may be also hypersensitive and easily startled by sudden or loud noises.

The father of one of my students, a policeman, was killed while he was on duty. He was killed by an inmate who was temporarily released from prison to take part in a new study program at a nearby university. After the murder, the university offered my student a scholarship, which she refused. Within the same year, her uncle, who was also a policeman, was murdered. During the next two years of her college career, Doris was disruptive in class, frequently interrupted her professors during their lectures, and stormed out of a room for the slightest difficulty. Her anger was a heavy burden for her to carry. Eventually, she joined the police force when she graduated. The violence which shattered her family life had a profound effect on her life choices.

It is not unusual for the survivors of a murder to want to kill the murderer. We simultaneously feel sorrow for our loved one and a deep rage toward the person who killed him or her, perhaps even a desire to avenge the death. Amy's husband was stabbed in a quarrel after a hockey game and then dumped outside and left to die. The killer was never charged, but Amy thinks that she knows who did it and fantasizes killing him herself. When she blurted out this wish in her support group, instead of chiding her, the members remained silent. They understood this feeling and probably experienced it themselves.

When someone we love is murdered, we are victimized, too. The stigma of murder can be overpowering because we feel marked in a public way. If the crime occurred in our town or city, we may want to move away. We need to be assured that there is nothing wrong with us. It is normal to feel helpless and violated after such a horrible event.

For many of us, the anguish of surviving a murder is compounded by the way we were notified. Margaret's experience of being driven to the hospital by three policemen who were absorbed in their own small talk and then being matter-of-factly informed by the doctor that her son had "expired" is not atypical. Some are notified by telephone or are given inaccurate and incomplete information. We are entitled to know what happened, when, and how. Some of us discover the news through the media, and that causes additional pain. Being notified by trained policemen with the aid of a crisis counselor makes a great difference in helping us deal with our initial shock.

A violent death presents us with its own special demands, such as identifying our loved one's body, dealing with medical personnel, notifying our friends, and dealing with the media. We may be subject to the intrusiveness and insensitivity of newspaper reporters who seem more concerned with the story than with the suffering of our loved one. And if our loved one died in a sensational or newsworthy crime, we may feel harassed by the constant presence of the media, even as we leave the funeral services.

The type of murder and the way in which our loved one was killed will affect our reactions. If the victim was sexually violated before he or she was murdered, the assault will cause as much anguish as the murder itself. We can't even think about such a horrible event or feel guilty that somehow we were unable to protect the victim. We might have difficulty with normal sexual relations. We are caught in our images of the terror and degradation our loved one suffered.

In many murders, the body has been repeatedly stabbed or otherwise mutilated. Viewing the body for identification and prior to burial is an excruciating experience. We wonder whether our loved one was unconscious while the act took place. Like Margaret, we don't want to know, because that knowledge can be unbearable. My aunt was killed in a head-on automobile collision that resulted in an explosion. Her children and husband could not bear to see the body and made arrangements for the funeral and burial without ever viewing it.

If our loved one was killed by a drunk driver, we suffer additional outrage and isolation because of the way vehicular homicide is viewed by society. We tend to excuse drunk driving and to refer to drunk-driving deaths as "accidents," not as criminal homicides. Assailants are generally given light sentences and may even have caused deaths before the one that took our loved one. If the assailant is young, we are sometimes urged to forgive and forget, to consider the assailant's life. This can leave us with deep bitterness, a sense that justice has not been done.

Elaine's twenty-year-old daughter, Susan, was killed in a motor-vehicle homicide. She was driving home from a party with her friend Marie, who had had too much to drink. The car crashed into a pole and Susan died, while Marie survived. The absence of skid marks near the pole attests to the level of alcohol Marie had in her body.

Marie was charged with motor-vehicle homicide, but this was by no means the end of Elaine's efforts to deal with the crime. This type of homicide is not a priority in court, and Elaine arrived at the court ready to make her statement four times, only to have the trial postponed. When the trial finally took place, Marie was given a very light sentence, six months in an alcohol clinic, five years probation, and the loss of her license. Marie appealed to have the sentence cut in half, and eventually, after a rehearing, she did get two weeks off the sentence.

This seemed like an extremely light sentence to Elaine. But in similar cases, some sentences are never served, and often the person charged is placed on probation. The result of the case heightened the anger that Elaine already felt over the death of her daughter. And along with the anger, Elaine was left with the profound grief over her daughter's absence. When she returned home after the trial, she felt that nobody had won. Her daughter was gone forever, and even though Marie got off with such a light sentence and was presented with a new car by her father, she didn't win either.

Because murder is such a distasteful subject, we often suffer additional pain from the reactions of our friends and even of the religious community. Our friends may be distant or may even try to avoid us. Some members of the clergy unintentionally minimize our anguish by either saying that "your loved one was called by God" or by advising us to forgive the murderer. But when someone murders our loved one, we want to avenge it ourselves. This is a perfectly normal response. Not only is it difficult to experience such profound rage, but it is difficult to see ourselves as vengeful people. We need support in our struggle with these emotions, rather than what often seems like a cavalier dismissal.

Sometimes members of the clergy receive the murderer in forgiveness and ask him to forgive himself. In the late seventies, when Richard Herrin murdered his girlfriend with a hammer, he turned himself in to a Roman Catholic priest. The priest embraced the killer and told him he must immediately begin the process of self-forgiveness. In a more recent case, a young man choked his girlfriend to death in Central Park. At a bail hearing the accused killer presented a letter from a Roman Catholic archbishop testifying to his character. Although many of us find solace in our religious beliefs, many others are alienated by the misguided compassion of members of the clergy.

People don't like discussing the painful subject of murder and may try to distance themselves from the event by blaming the victim or the survivors. When an aspiring young theater student was brutally stabbed in New York City in a much-celebrated case, many people blamed her for struggling with her assailant. Women are taught that being passive is more likely to save them in such a situation. Others blamed her for not being more cautious, ignoring the fact that she was attacked in her own apartment building by the son of the superintendent. People feel that if they can somehow place the blame on the victim or on the victim's family, they will be invulnerable to murder themselves.

When someone we love is murdered, our view of the world as a safe and predictable place is shattered and our view of the justice system is called into question. One of our fundamental beliefs in the social and political systems is that they provide us with protection and justice. However, dealing with our criminal justice system often exacerbates the pain and stress of facing the murderer and leaves us feeling disillusioned with the court system.

We learn firsthand that the justice process is lengthy, that many murders are never solved, and that the killer can be acquitted or receive a very light sentence. Even if the killer is convicted and receives a life sentence, we don't always feel the emotional relief we expected.

When the suspected killer is arrested, we are relieved that the process of justice has begun and believe that things will be all right. However, arrests do not always result in prosecutions, and prosecutions do not always lead to convictions, or convictions to stiff sentences, or sentences to actual time served. Further, what appears to be a clear instance of murder to us can be understood by judges and juries as manslaughter, negligent homicide, or accidental death.

If the case goes to trial, the trial can be postponed or delayed for months or years, leaving us suspended in our grief and outrage. We strongly desire closure, an orderly process that corresponds to our sense of the injustice of the murder, only to realize that the process has its own calendar. As we sit through the trial we must also face the relatives of the defendant, a terribly upsetting experience which may be compounded by the hostility sometimes displayed by that family. However, we are not permitted to show emotion, or the judge will dismiss us because our feelings can influence the jury.

It is important for us to know about the federal Victims of Crime Act (VOCA), which ensures that all states have a Victim Assistance Program, (see appendix A). Although the programs vary from state to state, some being housed in courts, others in various state government offices, we are all entitled to services such as advocates to keep us informed about the investigation, upcoming hearings and trials, and to assist us during the trial.

We face different dilemmas if our loved one died in another state. If the district attorney asks us to be present, we have to decide whether to travel across the country. We may hesitate to make such a trip if we have no friends or relatives to support us during our ordeal. But if we do not undertake such a journey, there will be no personal representative of our loved one, and we will worry whether our family member will be fairly represented, especially since the perpetrator's family will be there.

We must face other painful choices during the trial—like whether to leave or stay when evidence is presented, such as grisly photographs of the crime, bloodstained clothing, or other personal property of our loved one. These belongings have now become public property, since the victim is represented by the state and his or her possessions are confiscated. It seems to us that the intimacy with our family member and our privacy have been violated.

If the victim was a young woman who was raped during the killing, the trial will likely focus on her reputation, not on the question of whether she was assaulted. A professor of evidence and ethics at New York University School of Law has stated that not only is it not unethical to question or malign the victim's character, but it's the defense lawyer's duty to do so if it will render a not guilty verdict or a conviction on a lesser charge. During the trial, public opinion and the media might be concerned more with the suspected killer than with the victim. Added to our profound grief over the loss of our loved one is a sense that we are living in a world in which right and wrong, accountability and social good are discounted by the justice system.

If the suspected killer is found not guilty, we feel intense outrage and disillusionment. We might even fear retaliation by that killer. In some cases a convicted murderer appeals and has the case thrown out on a technicality, and we as well as the jurors in the first trial could be endangered. If the suspect is found guilty but receives a trivial or inappropriate sentence, we will be as distressed as if a not guilty verdict had been handed down. It is easy to understand how the parents of a child killed by a drunk driver feel when the person charged receives a minimal sentence, even though the current crime might have been only one in a series of similar criminal acts.

Even if the killer receives what we consider a just sentence, we may be surprised at our response. Perhaps we expected that the end of the trial and an appropriate sentence would lessen our pain. But as Margaret discovered, her elation at the defendant's sentencing was short-lived. Her son was still dead. When the trial is behind us, our emotions surface with full force, for we are no longer focused on that external event. We are left with the terrible emptiness created by the murder and the knowledge that we have to live with it.

The sentencing stage in a trial is of great concern. Because of legislation providing for "victim impact statements," survivors in most states have a right to have input on sentencing. Sometimes this takes the form of a written statement of how the murder affected the survivors. In most states survivors are allowed to speak to the judge at the sentencing hearing, helping them feel that they've made a difference.

There is always the prospect of endless appeals and the overturning of the conviction or even an acquittal in a second or third trial. Such dealings with the court system draw out our suffering even longer. Margaret felt lucky because someone was paying for the crime and she could go on with her life.

Many murders remain unresolved because there is not enough evidence to arrest and convict the murderer. A woman whose sister was murdered in her home agonized for a year while the police looked for a possible intruder. They then began to suspect her sister's husband and spent years gathering evidence, even arresting him at one point, only to discover that they did not have enough evidence to convict him. Meanwhile, the husband is free and has custody of the couple's only child, and the victim's sister suffers not only from the loss but also from her outrage that the killer is free. In another case, a mother whose daughter was also murdered in her home suspects a man her daughter had been dating for a few weeks. She believes her daughter tried to end the relationship and was stabbed as a result, but she does not have enough evidence to support that theory. Both of these survivors are very involved in the cases, keeping in touch with investigators and the police and putting up money for rewards.

Their assuming responsibility for helping the ongoing investigation miti-
gates their sense of helplessness and eases the grieving process.

Sometimes the murderer is known to both the police and the victim's
family, but the witness refuses to testify for fear of his own life. There are
also cases where the murder is utterly random, and we are left with the
anxiety of knowing that such a person is out on the streets and liable to
commit a similar crime.

One of the difficulties survivors face is a sense of isolation. As Margaret commented, when she tells people her son was murdered, she has to
support them, rather than being supported herself. It is very difficult to talk
about the pain we suffer. People may be frightened and repelled, yet we
need to talk, not only about the sorrow and anguish of our loss, but about
the person we lost and how much we loved him or her. We never forget
either the murder or the victim. Margaret had a good relationship with her
son and many happy memories. Thinking about her son's life is healing for
her, and her private times are devoted to his memory. What other people
consider an unhealthy focus on the past is the route to our survival.

There are few support groups that focus specifically on the needs of
murder survivors. Sharing our anger and sorrow with others who have
had similar experiences helps to break down our sense of isolation, the
feeling that we are the only ones in the world who are suffering this grief.
Margaret attended Compassionate Friends, which provides support to
parents who have lost a child by any cause. She also attended a local support group called Omega sponsored by a bereavement counseling center.
Omega is for survivors of homicide or motor-vehicle homicide. Those
who come are welcome to stay as long as necessary to regain fullness and
meaning in their lives. In addition to sharing feelings and experiences,
participants get support in preparing for and attending the trial, gain
coping skills, and have someone to talk when they are in a crisis. Parents
of Murdered Children and Mothers Against Drunk Driving also provide
support for the bereaved.

Our families are subjected to stressful changes at this time. Margaret
faced the problem of continuing to be a mother to her daughters and keeping the family together as a single parent. This is a heavy burden, because
after the murder of a child, we are obsessed with the child we lost, which
makes it difficult to attend to the needs of the siblings. Our swirling emotions leave us with little energy to devote to our other children.

A two-parent family experiences different reactions to a murder.

These may correspond to the roles society has ascribed to men and women. It is not unusual for marriages to end in divorce after such a traumatic event. Those who survive a homicide death become different people who think and feel in new ways, which may cause tensions in marriage and in relations with other family members.

Survivors of a homicide are also victims. Many never recover from such a blow. However, some not only reconstruct their lives, but also become involved in volunteer efforts on behalf of victim rights and other causes. Three years after her son's death, Margaret helped establish support groups and started working for victim rights. She has lobbied extensively for legislation on behalf of families affected by homicide.

A loved one's murder changes our lives irrevocably. A young European boy whose mother was murdered during World War II shaped his whole life in response to that event. He emigrated to the United States and became a reporter for a large newspaper. When he reached middle age, he took time off from his job to return to his village, unearth the details of his mother's murder, and write about her life. His whole career as a reporter was shaped by his desire to find out what happened to his mother. After a year's painstaking research, he tracked down the name and address of his mother's killer. Armed with a gun, he paid a visit to the killer's home. He had been waiting for this moment his whole life, but when he finally confronted the man, he put the gun away. Face to face with the murderer, he finally understood the futility of his thirst for revenge. His pilgrimage home ultimately resulted in a book and then a movie about his mother and the events that led to her death.

Reconstructing our lives means remembering the murder victim, not just the murder. Margaret's son is very much a part of her life. She was very proud of him, and talking about him, sharing her memories of him with others is a way of acknowledging that precious life which was cut short. Recovering does not mean either forgetting or the end of our pain. It means that we have found something positive to do with our sorrow. It means simply that we have more good days than bad days and that we have learned to separate the horror of the murder from the victim's life. We discover the depth of our inner resources and what it really means to live.

Part Four
LOSING A LOVED ONE THROUGH AIDS

Wanting a New Language

In the hospital room with its grim
routine, the nurses' cheery
clucks, the doctor hides behind
his terms. I want to say that
I'm on the threshing floor
flailed from within, that pain
is tedious and does not create
symphonies, I want to say that grief
leaves us gasping for breath
and does not dissipate like clouds.
I want to shape a creole stronger
than the ruler's tongue, invade
the calm of unknowing.
I want to storm the circle
of polite exchanges, become visible
again, cloaked in sharp-edged words,
the raw colors of battle.

Marguerite Guzman Bouvard

Chapter Fifteen
WHEN SOMEONE WE LOVE
DIES OF AIDS

Greg

My lover of three years broke up with me in early 1990. Then Christian and I became involved and were together the rest of the year. At the end of that year my former partner came back and wanted to get back together. About a year and four months after Christian and I broke up, in March of '92, he was diagnosed with full-blown AIDS. He had less than thirty T cells. At that point, people didn't live that long if T cells dropped under fifty.

I found out he was diagnosed through a friend, about a month after he got out of the hospital for pneumonia. She knew about Christian and I and what it meant to me. When I heard the news, all I wanted to do was run out and try to find him. I got home, and I did call, but he didn't return my call. He actually says he never got the message. We ran into each other a couple of times over the next year or so. Then, in 1994, under very chance circumstances, Christian and I ran into each other again, and pretty much, from that day to the day he died, we were inseparable.

It felt like there was no hiccup of time between the beginning of our relationship and the last year or so. I always told him I had felt like we had been together a very long time. It must have been some connection between our energies or perhaps our spirits.

When we ran into each other again, he did not know that I knew. He had no problems talking about AIDS with anyone, or anyone knowing, but for some reason through the years, his best friend told me he could not tell me. He was so afraid he had made me sick. I had been tested constantly all those years, and had been negative, and I could have relieved the sort of load he had been carrying, if only we had talked.

Within a week of us running into each other again and getting back together, we talked about everything. From that point on—I don't want to say it was the center of our life, but when you are living with AIDS, and it wasn't just him living with AIDS, it was us living with AIDS—it's never out of your field of vision. It shouldn't be, because there are issues and things you need to pay attention to. But it was no more so for me than had it been something involving my career or a hobby or an interest. It was just another one of those things for him too. He made it very easy for me in a lot of ways. His outlook and his attitude was so positive, not that he had false hope or anything, it's just that his opinion was "I've lived more in my (at the time twenty-nine years—he did make it to thirty) than most people have lived in their lifetime." And he did. He was pleased with what he had done in life, and he felt a lot luckier than some people who just sort of plodded along for their eighty years. It was never a big huge weight that was dragging us down.

There were one or two evenings when he had fevers, and we both did get upset, and we would cry and he would say he was not afraid of dying. He just didn't want to die yet. We had a few of those moments together through the year, but for the most part, it was just living. There was a lot of joy in this house. So many people who are the uninitiated into AIDS or any terminal illness have a perception of this "death house," a home where someone is terminally ill, and it's foreboding. It wasn't that way. This house was full of laughter, and it was full of people who loved Christian and in the end helped take care of him.

Time did all sorts of funny things during that last year. I guess when you're in a relationship with someone, and there's a very definitive end, it stares you in the face. It's tangible. It's real. Everything becomes more concentrated. When people ask me how long Christian and I were together, I always stumble because I want to say, "Forever," because that's what it seems like. Especially that last year when we were together constantly and dealing with his illness. We did more living than many people do in a lifetime.

I had some friends who couldn't understand how I could get back together with someone who I knew was going to die. I felt like I had no choice because I could not turn down the opportunity to have what did turn out to be the best year of my life and to spend it with someone who loved me unconditionally and would have done the very same thing for me. Even though on the surface it looks as if I did so much in the relationship, dealing with the illness and taking care of him, he did so much for me in return. You can't throw everything on a scale and measure it.

One thing is as I march forward alone without Christian, there have been advances in medicine. I think back to the health care decisions we made—Christian had the opportunity to get involved in the clinical trials for Protease inhibitors because of his low T cells. We talked about it, and he decided no. There was a chance he would have gotten a placebo, but he also had an attitude about antivirals at that point, and he just didn't believe it was going to do any good. And so I find myself thinking as I continue to read more and more that perhaps if we had, maybe he would still be here. Obviously the prognosis is still the same, but it does not consume me.

I really believe he felt so much was outside of his control, that those were decisions he did have. And even though he trusted me implicitly, one of the hardest things he did was sign a power of attorney for me to make decisions once he would not be able to. He was afraid his family would take him back to Pennsylvania. It worked out that once they knew his wishes, they honored them and came here.

Christian's mother and brother were very supportive. His mother was here when he died. Once he needed twenty-four-hour care, then they were here often. And that period lasted for two months: it started in late October, and he died at the end of December.

The entire last year, he was never in the hospital. . . . During the last few months, [Christian] had no active infections, no fevers, no night sweats, nothing. He had dementia, and once it crossed the blood-brain barrier, it very systematically and very kindly started shutting down his abilities. But it left him able to enjoy what he could. A lot of people who have been involved here said it was the most uncanny sort of last few months that they had seen. I made the decision about what drugs we would continue to give him that would keep away what I felt would cause a difficulty like pneumonia, those sorts of things. Everything else we tossed.

When the time came that I knew he was going downhill, I just kicked into automatic, from scheduling his twenty-four-hour care, to dealing with his $100-a-day drugs, either getting them through the drug compa-

nies, finding out how, what, who Medicare would pay for, what Medicare wouldn't pay for—I was his case worker, and of course working my full-time job, which actually became a refuge for me during the day. It's where I went to relax and focus on something besides AIDS and Christian—not that it ever left my mind. What no one warned me about—I've dealt with a lot of death in my family—my father died of a massive heart attack at forty-seven when I was nineteen—I've lost grandparents and uncles and aunts. But I had never dealt with a long illness and done this sort of thing. No one told me what it would be like afterward.

After he died, there was such a loss of not only Christian, but of purpose. I still was focused at work to a certain degree, but I just felt like I didn't belong anywhere. Not even really in my own home, except for the two rooms he and I lived in during that time. Once Christian started going downhill, some of the caretakers felt we should get a hospital bed. I thought a lot about it, and decided no, absolutely not. He would feel too alienated from everybody, plus at night we were going to sleep in the same bed. So every morning, when the nurse came, when the aide came to bathe him, she would put him in a wheelchair and roll him to the study at the other end of the house. He'd sit on the sofa and watch TV. We'd sit him up so he didn't lie down all day. He could talk to people a little, and they were sitting around him and watching TV.

Then, at the end of the day when it was time to go to bed, he and I would walk together to the bedroom. I put his feet on my feet, on top of my feet, so that he still felt like he was walking. I couldn't stand the wheelchair, so I came up with this way: I would get behind him and hold him. Christian was very small, even before all of this. He weighed 130 pounds when I met him. And he was only about 5'6". But he weighed about 100, or 90 near the end, before the last couple of weeks when he really lost weight.

Every night I'd ask him if he wanted to put his head on my chest, and he would say yes, so that's how we slept, all wrapped up like a pretzel even through the night before he died. Something happened that last night. (He had some kind of seizure or stroke in mid-November and then leveled off pretty much through December, but was getting a little worse.) When I got up the next morning to go to work, there was an obvious change in his breathing. I woke his mother and said, "Look, I'm going to work, but please call me if anything changes." She called me after I'd been there for thirty minutes and said his breathing had changed and it didn't sound good. So I came home. That was about 9:30, and he ended up dying at 5 P.M. that day.

In the past, death had seemed very mysterious, looming, scary. But, you know, when you—and this sounds trite—but when you literally walk someone to the light, it mutes the fear. At that point, Christian knew it was time to go. Although he was not speaking that day, if I held his hand he would squeeze my fingers, and if I put my lips down to his face, he would purse his lips. So he knew, he was there. He was conscious at some level. His mother was here. I was here. Christmas was past. The new year wasn't here yet. It didn't have anything to offer him. And he went. Afterward there was a shattering realization of how much a part of life meant.

Having experienced the horrible shock of an unexpected death with my father, I was surprised when I felt some of that shock set in immediately after Christian died. I wondered, "How can you feel shock when you've known someone was dying?" I suppose it is a numbing mechanism to get us through the time immediately following someone's death. It makes it possible to deal with all of the logistical issues following a death. Right after Christian died, one of my overriding concerns was how to get his body out of the house. I live in an old-town neighborhood where the houses are close together and very close to the front sidewalk. I had great difficulty with Christian's body being wheeled out of the front door on a gurney. The back door was up a flight of steps that the gurney could not negotiate. Suddenly I felt a great need to carry Christian's body out of the house myself, so I carried him out the back, down the steps and laid him on the gurney in the driveway behind the crematory van. I am so grateful to the people there for not trying to stop me from doing what I needed to do. They understood.

We had talked a lot about what he wanted and what he didn't want, and I promised him three or four things I would do. And it was sort of this quote unquote "Constitution" or "Bill of Rights" or "Magna Carta" I balanced, once he was not able to communicate his needs anymore, for instance, to his mother. And that was one: He was not to be taken away from here. If he had wanted to go home, that's where he would have gone—back to Philadelphia. But he wanted to stay here. And he didn't want to be put on any antivirals. And he didn't want to be given IV nutrition. The only thing he wanted was hydration if he needed it. His mother and I got into an argument when he stopped being able to eat. I said, "Look, he had a living will." She respected that. As difficult as the year was, this year has been so much harder. It's gotten a little better, but my whole purpose is gone, and so many people say so many platitudes.

Terms like quote unquote "moving along" or "putting it behind you" or "getting over it" are too small a framework for me. My whole purpose and intent is how do I move forward in life—move forward and take Christian with me—how do I integrate him in where I am now and where I am going. I am not going to get over this, and I am not going to put it behind me. It is a part of who I am and will always be. Some people feel I'm trying to hold on longer than I should. There's this general lack of understanding.

It has been so interesting for me in a lot of ways. My grandmother died at the beginning of December, the year after Christian died. She became very ill and went downhill with me and my mom sitting by her side for two weeks and holding her hand and talking to her. It was like a repeat of last year. So it made it all the more poignant. When I sat there talking to her and crying, the two got so mixed up I didn't know why I was crying or even who I was talking to, but it didn't matter.

I was controller of the company, a pretty important job. I made sure I was there the time that I needed to be. I might be gone between 12 and 3 in the afternoon with doctors' appointments and be back in the office from 5 to 8. So my job didn't skip a beat. I made sure things were done, and people were verbally supportive. I did ask for some financial support since we don't offer benefits to spouses of significant others. I asked the company to cover the cost of four hours a day of a sitter so that I didn't have to take time off, which would have cost the company far more. It ended up not getting approved, so the company was not supportive when it came to money.

Most companies have a lot further to go than we do. We recognize sexual orientation under our company guidelines for nondiscrimination. We have several homosexuals in the office, and it's no problem. But there are tangible differences in how people treat a homosexual relationship, even those people who are verbally supportive. For instance, I received more acknowledgment of my grandmother's death than I did with Christian's. This is partially because no one sent out a memo after Christian died. It was more word of mouth by people who knew. What was interesting was that people who had been so supportive of Christian and I sent flowers when my grandmother died but did nothing when Christian died. The reaction is very different when it's a heterosexual couple.

Even my mother's reaction has been difficult for me. She knew Christian. She knew about us. She was supportive. She'd been through the death of my father, and she and I were very close. She was out of town when Christian died. I called her and talked to her when he died. I didn't hear from her again for days—until she got home. The reason she didn't call me was because she didn't want the friends she was visiting in South Carolina to know. A year later, she's back up there during the same period of time. It's the anniversary of Christian's death. Nothing. No call. I'm still fuming over that one. I've called her every June 4 of every year since my father has died—for the past fifteen years. I was there, sitting with her when her mother was dying—my grandmother. And I know she cares, and I know she loves me, but I know that if it were my brother, if it were his wife, it would be a whole lot different. It's these aspects of AIDS, even when you've got an accepting family, those differences of how people treat grief in your workplace—it becomes so obvious to the person who's left behind. It hurts. And you know, people need acknowledgment.

After Christian died I got very angry with my mother, and while she apologized, she got mad at my anger. She understands, but there's the added layer, and it's something my therapist pointed out to me was, that oftentimes when parents find out, even when they are accepting with their children, they go in the closet. The children come out of the closet, but they go in. And this is what the group PFLAG (the Parents and Friends of Lesbians and Gays) is all about, bringing parents out of closets. While Mom does have friends who know, and she can talk with them about it, she's got friends that don't know, and she's very guarded with them. What hurt more than anything was just the fact she didn't call me each night. I would have done it. Hell, I stayed with her the summer after my father died.

Christian's mother and I have gotten very close, and we talk very frequently. She has given an enormous amount of support to me, and I think I've helped her a lot too through this year. I'm her connection to Christian's adult life because they lived in Pennsylvania, and he left home at eighteen. She's my connection to his childhood.

Christian didn't want a funeral. He didn't want a memorial service. He just wanted to be cremated. I had taken care of all the arrangements for the cremation prior to his dying because I didn't want to have to deal with it when he died. So when I was just focused all day at work, it just became another task. I asked him if we could have a party. He said "Yeah, that would be fine." So we had what we called a celebration at the bar of a local restaurant on Sunday afternoon, which was New Year's Eve, from 3 to 7, just people to drop by, have some drinks, chat, maybe eat if they wanted to. And it was very nice. But you know, I have a lot of difficulty with it, and it doesn't have anything to do with religion. Organized religion just doesn't do much for me, but I am a firm believer in the importance of ritual in our lives. And this was one of those milestones in life where there needs to be some kind of ritual.

I think some of my grief process has been very rough at points in time because I didn't have this memory of a ritual. Whatever it would have been, whether we all had gathered and stood around a lake and read poetry and thrown roses in the lake, lit candles, written notes and burned them in a fire, I don't know. I would have liked a communal sharing, not just a dropping by a bar and having a drink, or even haphazardly eating food together, but something symbolic of the loss we shared. If I could have it to do over again, I would have broken this promise to him. And I wouldn't have had a problem with it, because you know what, it's not for him. Intellectually I knew this, having been through this with my father— I mean my father specifically said, "I do not want to be buried in Newnan, Georgia, in Oak Hill Cemetery." You know where he's buried? In Newnan, Georgia, in Oak Hill Cemetery. My mother's comment was, "Well, he shouldn't have died first."

People who are adamant about what they want their funeral or their services to be like or not to be like are hampering, in many cases unknowingly, the grief process for the people who are left behind. I would like to have a place to go, and I've been thinking about just putting a stone down with Christian's name on it. I've got some of the locks of his hair because his hair was long at one point and we cut it. Even if I put his hair in a box and buried it in the ground in the cemetery just so there would be something there.

There's a park in Atlanta that's dedicated to people who have died of AIDS, and it's in my neighborhood, up the street. It's much like Centennial Park in downtown Atlanta, where you can buy a brick and have your name in it. So I bought bricks, and they're not in yet—they'll be put in at some point. While I don't say everyone needs a funeral, there is some ritual which needs to take place, that needs to be more than just the wake. When I was sitting at my grandmother's funeral, I just sat there thinking, "This is so incredibly wonderful." And as much as I tried to include some of those needs about Christian, it was still my grandmother's funeral. It was really then I realized that what had been missing for me this past year was a requiem mass.

His mom took his ashes. I think she was so afraid I was going to keep them. I told her, "I promised him I would cremate him. He didn't care what was done with his ashes. I don't need them. Take 'em." So she's got those and keeps them very close—too close. She keeps them under the pillow next to her in the bed. She's having a very hard time. She can't look at pictures of him without getting hysterical, saying she feels like she is being stabbed, and that someone is sitting on her chest. She still hasn't opened the suitcase where his best friend packed some of his things for her.

I'm very different. I surround myself. I've got pictures and notes from him. His work is on the walls. He was a clothing stylist for fashion photography. For all shots they have the photographer, the makeup artist, and then the clothing stylist. And if you really look at the fashion shots, the clothing stylist has a big impact on the finished product. I had his portfolio framed. His career was really blasting off when he was diagnosed. He would have left Atlanta. He would have gone to New York. He was too talented for Atlanta. He did a lot of really good work and was respected.

I had a good friend who came over from Augusta the day after he died. She and I are very close. She's very supportive. She asked me a day later if I wanted help changing the bed Christian had died on. I told her no, I didn't intend to change the bed. And I didn't. I slept on the sheets for a week.

I struggle with when to stop wearing my ring, because he gave me a ring, and I had given him one a couple of weeks later, and I took it off of him after he died. I wear it on a chain around my neck. But you struggle with those kinds of things.

When you're like a piece of flotsam just being washed around wherever it takes you, that's when it's ultimately been the easiest for me. You know, letting the pain be painful whenever it shows up, letting the tears come whenever they want to, to stay at home and pull the sheets over my head when I want to, and then going out. I spent part of the year after Christian's death traveling. I traveled more this year than I have done in many years. I took nearly two months off from work. The company let me carry over all my vacation from the prior year, which they don't normally do. So that was one good thing. But as much as I enjoyed the traveling and what I did, I realized a good bit of it was me—not running. I mean I don't feel like I was ever running away, but I was avoiding it.

I feel like earlier in the year, shortly after Christian died when every-body was saying, "You're doing so well," it should always be a red flag. Instead of praising you when people see you're happy and you're out and you're doing things, they should be saying "What's wrong with you?"

Christian's birthday in August had the biggest effect on me during the year. It was like a Mack truck. And from his birthday through the rest of '96, I was very down, grieving very hard. It lightened up a little bit during the holidays, which was surprising for me because I thought it was going to get worse as we approached the 28th of December, which was the day he died. That day was difficult, but it was not so horrible that I would pick it out as a specifically terrible day. I had trouble deciding what I wanted to do.

The middle of the afternoon, I decided to have a dinner party that night—my friend Bon came over from Augusta. We got on the phone, and we ended up having a lovely dinner party. But I had a little "foxhole interval": about 4:30 that afternoon I went back to my bedroom, shut the door, got out my diary from last year, lit a couple of candles, hopped up on the bed, read, and let the time pass. I cried. I spent the time with Christian as much as I could. I know I carry something of him with me. But I feel like he took something of me with him.

There's been a lot of pain, but joy too, and you can't experience those levels of joy unless there is pain at times.

You've got Couple A, where they found out that one member of the couple is terminally ill after they've been together. In Couple B, one person is terminally ill, and the other person knows it, and they go into a relationship. Couple B's pain is discounted from Couple A's at times. It's like the question is "Oh, my God, did he know he had AIDS?" Most people should be intelligent enough to realize that love is love and pain is pain and grief is grief. The circumstances may vary. You can't place values on whatever people are feeling. I couldn't have loved Christian any more or hurt any more if he had been diagnosed after we had started our relationship, or if we had been straight.

AIDS plays a very unique role. It's not the disease, but people's perception of it, their lack of knowledge and their fear. You add their fear of death on top of the fear of AIDS, and that is pretty powerful.

Although grief is a lonely pilgrimage, the public and social dimensions of sorrow are an important factor in the healing process. Those of us who mourn the loss of a loved one to AIDS undergo a complicated grieving, a layering of burdens, because, as Greg so aptly phrased it, fear plays a major role in social perceptions of this illness. Just as the issues of living wills, assisted suicide, and health care rationing are forcing our death-denying culture to confront mortality, the AIDS epidemic has created a wave of alienation and dread. The strident public reactions of figures such as Jerry Falwell, who defines AIDS as God's judgment on society, and Jesse Helms or Pat Buchanan, who equate AIDS with moral bankruptcy, deeply affects those who mourn the loss of a loved one. Our sorrow is heightened by the tasteless jokes of certain politicians and by our society's tendency toward blaming and judging.

People who did not contract AIDS through homosexual behavior or drug use have been categorized as "innocent victims," thus suggesting that there is a blamable group. Consequently, people respond to us not as survivors of a terrible loss, but as someone who is mourning the loss of a gay man, an IV drug user, or a member of an ethnic minority. We may be a mother mourning the loss of an extraordinary adult child, a sibling, friend or lover, but the lack of social understanding of this illness and of different sexual orientations delegitimize these very important relationships. Frequently homosexual ties are seen as short-term and based only on sex, whereas many of us are mourning deeply satisfying spousal relationships. We are caught between the reality of our personal life and intolerant social portrayals.

Surviving partners in homosexual relationships have distinct legal and economic disadvantages after the death of a loved one. Except in certain cities in California where domestic partnership legislation has been enacted, we face the harsh absence of institutional recognition of our relationship. Even in San Francisco, where legal protection has been extended to gay and lesbian families, there is currently a great deal of controversy regarding both the economic and the religious implications of such provisions as the Catholic Church hierarchy and out-of-state businesses balk at honoring legislation granting legal status to homosexual couples. As Greg emphasizes, his employers were unwilling to give him the financial support he needed to care for his partner while carrying out his job. However, they granted him a flexible schedule during Christian's illness and a long leave after his death. Many workers are denied bereavement leave or are hurt by the failure of their employers or coworkers to recognize their loss.

The social discourse around AIDS has become so charged with prejudice and so exploited for ideological and political purposes that it is practically impossible to speak of our grief and be heard. We are not only subjected to indifference and a lack of understanding, but also to outright hostility. Consequently, some of us react by withholding our thoughts and feelings from everyone, retreating into a deadly silence, which compounds our emotional devastation. We are isolated just when we need caring responses the most.

Even though AIDS spread among heterosexuals in its country of origin and is increasingly affecting the heterosexual population, it has still created social images and metaphors that have given it moral overtones and delineated a separate group. AIDS is perceived as occurring within certain risk groups, a community of pariahs engaging in promiscuous or deviant behavior. Because of its current prevalence among stigmatized groups — homosexual men, bisexual men and women, IV drug users, minorities, sexual partners of these groups, and infants and children of infected parents — many people view AIDS sufferers and their survivors as *the other.* People categorized as outsiders are made to feel less valuable, so our loss may be minimized and disparaged. Given the physical disfigurement often associated with AIDS, the lack of a known cure, and the unrealistic fear of contagion, we too are stigmatized by our relationships with the deceased. Besides losing a lover, child, sibling, or friend, we experience self-doubt, anxiety, or self-blame. As survivors we grieve both a painful and a difficult death and the unjust assault on our status within the community.

Many of us face the additional anxiety that we might also be infected. This may mean facing the wrenching decision of whether to be tested for HIV. Some of us won't want to know the results, or if we decide to go ahead find the waiting period for results unbearable. The diagnosis might be the first time some parents or spouses learn that their child is gay or spouse is bisexual or that a blood transfusion had terrible consequences.

Recent in-depth discussions of AIDS in the news have defined it as a medical problem. Although the spate of articles on medical breakthroughs is certainly a result of the efforts of AIDS activists to obtain increased funding for research, there is still no public space for acknowledging the emotional toll of this illness on the infected person and his or her loved ones or for mourning a loss. As a society that values people according to their contribution to the economy, we tend to regard people who are ill with AIDS as we have come to view our elderly population: as a drain on our health care system and resources.

Unfortunately the heroism of so many young people cut off in the prime of life is unacknowledged. The arts have taken up the role of commemorating them and celebrating the grace and anguish with which they face their trials. Movies intended for mass audiences, such as *Philadelphia,* are a welcome addition to social images of illness, even if they portray an unreal vision of social triumph and family cohesion. Among the more interesting efforts to voice such a painful reality is a video by a young filmmaker who is HIV-positive, comparing the fate of his generation to the Holocaust. As a Jewish person, he has a history to draw on. The novels of Paul Monette, playwright Tony Kushner's *Angels in America,* and John Corigliano's *Symphony No. 1* also serve as bridges to the wider culture.

Those of us who have lost friends, families, and partners can testify to the telescoping of years our loved one experienced during the illness as he or she acquired the perspective of age and a sense of life's preciousness. Greg speaks of how Christian's positive outlook helped him during Christian's illness, and a mother has written to me that her son, Peter, who died of AIDS, was her hero:

He never complained about how unfair life had been to him. He did get angry at times at the difficulties of getting his insurance to pay up and he would mention one of the many complications of AIDS which plagued him on a daily basis, such as neuropathy in his feet, which made walking difficult. He coped with commuting during ice storms as well as the ongoing home emergencies of an old house. I certainly don't have that kind of determination and sheer grit, and I don't think many people do. He also knew how to enjoy the good times: dinners out, friends, his family. In sum, he always made an effort to get the most out of what became a more and more limited number of things he could do as his strength slipped away.

This mother was outraged at the emphasis on the bravery of war heroes during TV documentaries on World War II, while in contrast society condemns rather than supports the generation of young adults suffering from AIDS, and it certainly does not honor the surviving families with medals or ceremonies. A young woman whose close friend died after struggling with Kaposi's sarcoma and dementia drew an analogy with the young men who returned from World War I badly scarred. Except, she added, the veterans would have been respected, while people turned away in fear at her friend's disfigurement.

Often AIDS sufferers continue to care for loved ones and serve the community, counseling the young and others who are ailing. For instance, a man who was a counselor at the Birch Summer Camp for HIV-positive children and their families is remembered by his colleagues as a person who was particularly sensitive and helpful to the adolescents in his charge, which are such important traits, for there is often no social recognition of the courage and endurance of children who have AIDS and yet revel in the simple pleasures of childhood when given the opportunity.

A man named Forrest was diagnosed as HIV-positive, and he decided to spend the years before he became ill working as a volunteer in Los Angeles for the Northern Lights Alternative, an organization serving gay men with AIDS. Forrest spent four years organizing workshops and weekend retreats to help people who were living with AIDS cope with their illness and deal with the community. Overcome with exhaustion, he returned to his home in Virginia and worked for the AIDS Action Council in Washington, D.C., until he became too ill to work. The way he spent his last years is a testament not only to his courage but especially to his humanity.

The gap between reality and the social portrayals of those with AIDS fills us with anger, frustration, and anxiety. Our anger after the loss of a loved one is very acute. We rage at the pain our loved one endured and at the impenetrable silence surrounding us. It is unbearable that such a loss is unspeakable, that there is no one to receive and share our anguish or to understand its depth, for as people mourning a death from AIDS, we are truly disenfranchised mourners. We grieve in secret, but sorrow must be expressed to unfold. Peter's mother said she felt invisible, as if she were somehow underwater, because her and her husband's closest friends never mentioned their son's death.

There is a great difference between solitude and a socially enforced loneliness. When Greg decided to have what he called a "foxhole interval," lighting candles, reading his diary, and honoring the memory of his lover, he took the space he needed and decided how he would express his love and sadness. But when we are greeted by an impenetrable wall of denial, it's as if we were somehow imprisoned in a tiny room without windows or doors, and the only dialogue is with our pain.

As a parent or surviving partner we endure not only silence but caustic social responses that ultimately prevent us from mentioning that a loved one has died from AIDS. Forrest's parents, who now work with an AIDS ministry in their church, found that many people seeking help

suffer from guilt and shame anchored in their particular church's inter-
pretation of the Bible and in concepts of sin. This is a particularly heavy
burden to bear, for it touches on our sense of spiritual meaning and order.
It is common to feel that the clergy has a more powerful grasp of the truth
than we do.

Consequently, some of us lie about the nature of our loved one's illness, claiming that he or she suffered from leukemia, for instance. In
many cases the diagnosis is kept secret not only from friends and colleagues, but from family members as well, and some of us have gone to
a funeral believing our loved one died of cancer. Sometimes our friend or
loved one requests that we not tell others about his or her condition or did
not tell us until the illness was well advanced. Whether the insistence on
secretiveness comes from the ailing person or from other members of the
family, it is emotionally draining to live with the enormity of such a situation: when there are lies and secrets, we are denied the social support we
need and can't express our guilt, anger, and helplessness. Greg underwent
great pain when his mother selectively supported his grief because of her
fear of social censure. He felt that having given her unconditional love,
he was entitled to the same response. The lack of social support in such
circumstances is another loss we grieve.

Often family members do not speak to each other regarding the illness and death of their loved one. They feel shame and fear well beyond
the limits felt in other types of death. A young woman whose brother died
of AIDS played the role of family mediator as well as caretaker of her
brother. Because of her parents' lack of acceptance of their son's lifestyle
and condition, the young woman kept her brother's secrets and finally
arranged for two funeral services: the quiet party with close friends
requested by her brother and the service insisted on by his parents. Neither the sister nor the parents were able to receive recognition of their
sorrow, while enduring the added difficulty of bitter feelings among
family members. The social stigma and the terrible burden of secretiveness tears some families apart, complicating the grieving process and
engendering explosive emotions.

Compounding these emotions is the anger at the untimeliness of the
death—a young person cut off in his early thirties or the loss of a child
through such a difficult and painful illness. Our outrage is often expressed
at the government's slowness in conducting research and making newer
drugs available, interwoven with anguish at dashed hopes, interrupted

plans, and the indifference of those around us. We are angry at the callousness of health care providers, at the withdrawal of friends, the intolerance of neighbors and coworkers.

Some of us blame ourselves for having failed as parents, siblings, or friends. As parents we feel guilty about our distance, acceptance or lack of acceptance, strictness, or other qualities in our relationship. In Barbara Ascher's touching memoir, *Landscape without Gravity* (see appendix B), she mourns the fact that she did not accept her brother's life and that once he died it was too late to undo the years of distance and make up for failed love. Even when parents and siblings were supportive of their loved one, they suffer the inevitable anguish of having been unable to protect him or her and believing they failed.

Some of us are uncomfortable with our sexual orientation and blame ourselves for who we are, unaware of the immense social presence in our consciousness of self. Our society prides itself on its "individuality," but the focus on the individual enshrined in our Constitution and anchored in the philosophy of our founding fathers often makes us discount the role of culture and society in the development of self-images. We internalize values and negative judgments unconsciously, believing they are our own, and as a result may be tempted to turn the negative social judgments about homosexuality on ourselves and see AIDS as a punishment for our sexual orientation. The mother who wrote about the heroism of her son also confided to me that her son was the most conventional of her three children and would have had a house in the suburbs, children, and a barbecue in the back yard, that he would have loved to be the average American male. She recognizes that when he was in his early twenties, he grieved over an identity he did not choose, although she was very accepting and commented, "That's who he was." Not all parents are as secure as Peter's. We blame ourselves for situations we were not in a position to change.

In many instances, relations between parents and siblings and partners are warm and accepting. However, differences in lifestyle sometimes create a distance between the two sets of families. In those cases the parents feel anger at their child's choice or blame themselves for having somehow caused it. In one instance, a father severed relations with his son because of his sexual orientation, and after their son's death the mother attended the funeral and took part in support groups while the father wrapped himself in a painful silence and withdrawal. While a partner sometimes joins parents in planning a service, he or she may also be excluded from this very important opportunity for saying good-bye and paying tribute to the loved one. There are myriad ways that survivors suffer the failure of society to recognize the relationship and to honor the ties between parent and child. Peter's mother was stunned that none of her friends mentioned his death, as if somehow he was less valuable because of how he died, as if she should feel shame for her situation rather than pride in his courage.

Even when a family is united, it might be hard for its members to speak of the loss for fear of hostile responses. Some families think they must protect each other, and parents may have difficulty talking to the other children or relatives about a death which remains an enormous and unspoken presence. There are also many instances of families believing that they are problem-free but who actually harbor issues simmering below the surface. Fortunately there are support groups where we can express our feelings with others who have gone through similar problems. Organizations such as People With Aids offer support during the illness of a loved one and can steer us to bereavement support groups as a follow-up (see appendix A). We might have to do some research to find such groups, however, like calling national support organizations which will direct us to local and regional support groups. If our loved one was fortunate enough to die in a hospice, we will have access to such groups.

Like Greg, some of us have a circle of close friends to assuage our anger and loneliness and accompany us into the redefinition of our lives. Forrest and his parents were surrounded by loving friends throughout his illness and after his death. However, many of us live in communities where neither homosexuality nor AIDS is considered acceptable, and we find ourselves alone and unable to go to a priest, minister, or rabbi for fear of rejection. It was only recently that former President Jimmy Carter, renowned for his human-rights advocacy, announced from the pulpit that he was "uncomfortable with homosexuals."

Many of us feel guilty discussing issues other than our loved one's illness while he or she is alive. When that person dies, certain issues connected with the illness may rise to the surface, such as multiple sex partners or substance abuse, for instance. When these issues surface they can affect our family's stability and structure as well as unmask long-term dependency problems of our own. Support groups will help us deal with the anguish of lying about the diagnosis and even about the cause of death. We may be relieved that our loved one has died because he or she is no longer suffering and because we no longer have to live a double life, but such relief makes us feel guilty. Expressing our feelings in a compassionate and accepting environment will help us move through the devastating randomness of life and the terrible pain of loss. Sharing with others who are going through similar experiences will help our own healing.

Families and friends who were involved in caregiving often feel that they had time to cope with their profound feelings of helplessness. This does not mean that our grief is not as intense after the death, but rather that we are more comfortable with ourselves and at peace with our behavior. Peter's mother was deeply involved in his care and was able to devote considerable time to him. She was also present in his hospital room at the time of his death and had a chance to be with him in his last moments and to say good-bye. Greg mentions walking his lover "to the light" and the effect it had on him. He also has the memory of enjoying quality time with his partner, of capturing precious moments that will remain part of his life as he moves forward. Forrest's parents cared for him in their home as he was dying and used these wrenching months to repair wounds and to be together in a deep and meaningful way. Many of us found our loved ones serving as guides and teachers during their illness, thus providing us with comfort and inspiration after their deaths. The young woman who lost her friend commented to me that during the last months of his illness they became much closer, and he opened up to her in ways that might not have happened if his time were not so limited. Her grief is more tolerable because she can look back on the time they spent together and the intensity of their sharing. She told me, "I felt a certain satisfaction in knowing that I had done what I could, that he felt he could trust me and that our relationship was magnified." The sister who kept her brother's secret and who remained by his side until the time of his death remarked that "when you suffer with someone, you look for the light, and what you find is commonness."

Regardless of our religious beliefs, most of us need spiritual affirmation, especially when faced with such a seemingly senseless and agonizing death. We also need to publicly mark the death of a loved one, as attested by Greg's comments comparing the funeral for his grandmother and the lack of opportunity to honor Christian after his death. Given social attitudes toward AIDS-related deaths and the fact that there are no models or culturally prescribed roles for AIDS mourners, survivors experience yet another loss: the ability to publicly express grief. Consequently, many of us have to be imaginative in honoring the deceased.

Sometimes arranging a funeral gives a dying person a sense of control as he or she loses physical powers. The young woman whose friend died was able to discuss funeral arrangements with him, which proved to be a great gift. Her friend had always enjoyed planning celebrations, and despite his final battle with his illness, he was able to organize his funeral down to the last detail. He had announcements printed asked his friend to read at the memorial service. He was a landscape designer and always loved trees and plants, so he decided on a ceremony to take place under a very old oak tree in his parents' back yard. In fact, he left fifteen pages of directions regarding how the chairs should be placed, what kind of food should be served and when. His family and friends were especially grateful for this because it gave them something to do immediately after his death and helped them through the first shock of their sorrow. The young man's friend also arranged for a memorial tree to be planted at the college he had attended. She was very careful to select a hardy and almost full-grown tree to ensure it would survive the Vermont winters.

Inspired by the Vietnam memorial in Washington, D.C., which sought to reclaim the fallen from anonymity, a number of memorials for AIDS victims have been designed. The Names Quilt Project circulates throughout the country and serves as a public recognition of each person who has died. Greg is planning to buy a brick inscribed with Christian's name to place in the monument to AIDS victims. A woman who lost the son of a close friend, a successful dancer with the French opera, contacted a choreographer to plan a performance in his honor. Planting a tree, establishing a fund in our loved one's name, selecting a charity where family and friends can make small donations, or engaging in social activism are some of the many ways we can affirm our loved one's place in our lives and in the world.

In the long months after the funeral, we experience a unique sorrow. Many years ago, I worked to sponsor and resettle Laotian refugees, and some of us became very close during those intense years of adjustment. One of the many things I learned from these gracious people was the phenomenon of survivor's guilt. After the euphoria of having crossed the Mekong River, avoiding pirates, and living through the stresses of refugee camp had worn off, they became deeply depressed and had difficulty sleeping at night. They wondered why they should have survived when so many of their countrymen perished in such terrible circumstances. An epidemic which takes the lives of so many young people has the same dimensions as a war, and we wonder why we survived when our friends did not. Some of us have lost thirty or more friends since the epidemic started, and our relief at remaining HIV-negative is tempered by the question of why we were somehow singled out to escape such a death. In fact, the social prejudice against survivors and our consequent isolation and lack of self-esteem may reinforce our desire to be part of "the group." We may try to infect ourselves rather than continue living or we may believe that it is useless to practice safe sex. We might also experience "battle fatigue." In such cases, we need special help to regain a sense that life can still hold possibilities and that our former spouse or friends would have wished us to take special care of ourselves.

Many regret the timing of the death and keep repeating, "If only . . ." The recent development of the combination therapy of AZT with protease inhibitors has lengthened the lives of those fortunate enough to have access to them, and AIDS is sometimes referred to as a chronic illness. If our loved one died before these treatments were available, we mourn the fact that he or she might have been able to realize their aspirations. Peter's mother exclaimed that she felt bitter over the unfairness of the timing: "When he was ill a few years ago, AIDS was a disease without hope, and now he might still be alive." So many survivors have spoken of the untimeliness of their loved one's death, remarking that they died just when they had finally managed to build a satisfying personal and professional life.

The response to AIDS is much more complex than the one portrayed in public speeches and the media. In contrast to the devaluation of our pain is an awareness among certain groups that AIDS is a unique challenge to reaffirm our common humanity. The efforts of public figures such as Elizabeth Taylor and Magic Johnson, and fund-raising projects such as Walk for AIDS have brought together different groups and reasserted our interconnectedness. One young participant in a bicycle marathon for AIDS research, which stretched from Boston to New York, commented that AIDS represented for her a different kind of metaphor, one about everyone coming together. The Episcopal church where Forrest's family worships created an AIDS ministry, an extraordinary accomplishment given that the church is located in what the father has described as a bigoted community.

Among those suffering from AIDS, communities have sprung up creating support groups, crisis intervention, and providing an outlet for social action. As hospices have for decades, these volunteer organizations serve as models for compassionate caring and are a lesson to us all about mutual commitment in a society where going it alone is held up as a model of behavior. The sister who stayed at her brother's side throughout his illness and death quit her job and applied for a grant to study psychology, ultimately writing her dissertation on responses to pain. She also mounted an exhibit of books and videos about loss. Forrest's father, a former member of the Marine Corps, has told me that his son's illness and death opened his eyes and gave him a whole new way of looking at things. After struggling for many years and finally accepting his son's homosexuality, he discovered that gay men are "loving and gentle" and marveled at the "caring, nonjudgmental atmosphere" within his son's community of friends. He now works with men who struggle with their sons' sexual orientation and illness. The first he thing he tells people who come for his help is, "We are all made in God's image." Then he adds, "I've become the face for this disease," in effect reaffirming our oneness.

Forrest's mother is helping those around the country who are grieving by talking to them over the phone. She feels that she was fortunate to have been surrounded by supportive people during her son's illness and death and hopes to comfort those who have no one to talk to. Peter's mother tried volunteer work after his death but found that she needed more time to be with her grief. When we are ready, those of us who survive the loss of a loved one have resources to turn to which ultimately lead to social healing as well as to our own growth. Many of us struggle with numerous problems, so the decision to continue our lives as best we can is a significant accomplishment.

Part Five
AS TIME PASSES: THE PHASE OF DISORGANIZATION

Grief

A gray stalk in water
sends out a flower:

nothing is lost forever.
The ones who sleep underground

come back in dreams
wearing the faces of strangers.

We have to learn again and again
what to keep, what to throw away.

by Beatrice Hawley

Chapter Sixteen

THE DISORGANIZATION OF OUR LIVES AFTER THE DEATH OF A LOVED ONE

"It's been ten months, and I'm still in such pain," a young widow exclaimed. We may be surprised by the length of time we spend grieving for a loved one. Somehow we expected our pain and sadness to dissipate sooner and grow impatient with ourselves as time passes and we don't appear to be making any progress. Although the length of time needed to work through grief varies with each individual, some need not months but years for the burden of pain and loss to move away from the center of our lives. While the shock we experience immediately after a death can be measured in weeks or months, the disorganization and disruption of our lives last longer.

Grieving is a long and gradual process that moves unevenly and sometimes in reverse. We have several good days in a row, and then some event or something we see, perhaps a person who reminds us of our loved one, triggers those painful feelings again. These mood swings are normal, and it's best not to subject ourselves to timetables for moving through this phase. Even though our progress may not be evident, we will find that we can see real differences in what seem like small things. A friend of mine who lost her husband remarked that some days she is able to think about other things besides her own pain and can even talk with others about their own interests, moving away a little bit from an intense focus on her sadness.

During this period, the friends who gathered around us for the funeral and in the early weeks after the death may have returned to their own lives and concerns. Perhaps we discover that our old friendships are unsatisfactory, that our friends are unable to be there for us when we need them. Not everyone is willing or able to deal with our pain. Sometimes the only ones who can really understand what we are going through are those who are grieving themselves.

Some of us find new friends in people we knew only casually but who may have experienced loss themselves and can understand us. Perhaps this is the time to turn to a professional helper or a trusted member of the clergy or to join a support group.

At this time we may be receiving subtle messages that we should be pulling ourselves together and returning to our normal activities. Our co-workers might think that we should be resuming our work at our usual pace. We ourselves may think that we should be able to do more than we are doing. But many of us find that on the contrary, we need to spend time on other things. If we have lost a spouse we might need time just to be alone and to withdraw for a few hours from the demands of work and children.

Most women have been socialized to assume nurturing roles, so the self-regarding aspects of grieving are especially difficult. Children, friends, spouses, and coworkers build up expectations that cannot be fulfilled during this period. Perhaps we cannot be as good a parent or spouse or friend as we would like to be, but it's important to recognize the very legitimate need to withdraw. "I feel selfish sometimes," a widowed friend confided, but taking a weekend away from the children or other responsibilities is far from selfish under these circumstances. It's a matter of our own health and well-being. We can hardly take responsibility for others if we ourselves are not in good shape.

We need to reach out to others for support, which may be a very difficult step for us. However, we are doing our friends a favor by requesting specific types of supports, such as talking over coffee or picking up a child after school or simply discussing the new issues we face. By asking for help we provide the structure our acquaintances need. Many people may want to help us, but don't know what to do. Those around us are as baffled by our emotions as we are.

As the numbness of our shock wears off, we face the full intensity of our pain. We have much less energy and find that we need more rest than usual, or we discover that we are unable to maintain our usual pace at work and at home. Some people work a few hours a day and then return home because of fatigue, or work only a few days a week. It is not unusual for people who have some means to take a few months off from work after the death of a loved one. We may be surprised by our diminished energy level given our reduced activity. Even though it is invisible, the work of the emotions is very consuming. While we feel drained for a period of time, these profound emotions are helping us through the healing process.

Some people plunge into activity as a relief from pain. "I try to keep busy to keep my mind off it," a bereaved parent confided. It helps some people to pursue their regular activities; it gives them a structure or provides them with meaning. Yet sometimes we need to give ourselves more space in order to grieve.

This is a time of depression. The death of a loved one is a stunning blow, and we may experience a consequent lack of self-esteem. Just getting out of bed in the morning can seem like an enormous chore, and if we had the choice we might prefer staying in bed. If it is hard just getting up and facing the day, it is equally difficult being at work or at home. We may be unable to concentrate on our tasks or to remember small things and have a very low tolerance for the countless frustrations the day brings. These are all symptoms of depression.

Instead of forcing ourselves through our chores, it is helpful to slow down our pace, to be easy on ourselves. This is a good time to do small favors for ourselves, to take a long walk or to take the day off and drive to the country. Maybe there are things we have wanted to do for a long time but postponed because of all our responsibilities. Now is the time for learning how to ski, taking a course, or reading that book we have always wanted to get to. Some people have even referred to their new situation as a blank page which they will enjoy filling, and they have been able to say this without feeling as if they are betraying their loved one.

Along with depression, we may be feeling anger. We are angry at the person who died and left us with so much responsibility. We think our loved one is in a good place while we are left with all of the problems of family and work. We may be angry at God for the injustice of the death. "Why me?" we ask ourselves. "I've been a good person. What have I done to deserve this?" Or we have a more diffuse anger which erupts at everyday things, a simple demand by our coworker or some small thing at home. "I've been rotten in the office lately," mused a woman who lost her mother. We express this anger in hostile reactions to minor events or in the bitterness of our tone.

It's all right to be angry and to find appropriate ways to express it. A friend of mine who lost a child stayed home alone one morning and let her anger surface. She screamed and pounded against the bed. A woman whose lover committed suicide went to his grave and yelled at him for leaving her. It was a great relief. It is not a denial of our love to be angry about the difficulties that death imposed on us.

Even though months may have passed since our loved one died, we still miss that person and become increasingly aware of the significance of our loss as we struggle with our responsibilities and loneliness. We miss the companionship and emotional support of our loved one, miss the physical side of love, being able to hold our child or sleeping close to our spouse. We may feel a fresh surge of sadness at special times of the day, such as when our spouse returned from work or the time we used to talk to our parent on the phone to discuss the events of the day.

Our sadness is often occasioned by a new event that our loved one would have been part of, such as the birthday of one of the children or a special holiday we used to enjoy celebrating together. The smallest thing, the fragment of a song, the sight of someone who resembles our loved one triggers waves of sadness. We feel like crying for no apparent reason and in the most inappropriate places.

In time we will be able to move that sadness to a more comfortable place inside ourselves. But the events we all share in—graduations, birthdays, anniversaries—are a reminder of what might have been had our loved one survived and a fresh source of pain. On the anniversary of the death we may feel the pain as intensely as we did at the time of the death. It's a common experience to relive those events over again. These feelings may take us by surprise by their intensity, yet they are perfectly normal.

Some people have designed ways to handle these events so that they can be comfortable with them. A young widow I know usually takes the day off on the anniversary of her husband's death. She drives out to the beach to be by herself and reflect. Others call members of their bereavement support group on that day. Some bereavement centers have memorial services in which members of various support groups participate. Our family members may not want to join us for these services, but we can find alternate ways to spend time with them on that day, perhaps just getting together over dinner. Some of us prefer a more private observance, such as bringing fresh flowers to a grave. It's important to recognize the effect anniversaries have on us and to help ourselves through these difficult moments in a way that is meaningful to us.

We may have accepted feeling out of control immediately after the death, but it is more disturbing to endure these strong emotions after the months have passed. However, this period of inner turbulence is perfectly normal. "I feel crazy," a woman who had lost a parent told me. It's frightening to be shaken by such strong feelings, yet they are part of the grieving process. Allowing ourselves to feel these emotions in all their intensity will actually help us move through them.

Some of us had to postpone our own sadness because of family responsibilities. Perhaps we were the member of the family in charge of the funeral arrangements and the subsequent disposition of the home or business. Or perhaps we were the father left with children to care for, and the demands of work and parenting gave us little time to think about ourselves. Months may have passed without our awareness of our feelings, and then our buried grief is suddenly triggered by a seemingly casual event. A woman who lost her mother was so busy in her role as head of an extended family that she didn't even have time to think about her loss. Some months later, she attended the funeral of a coworker whom she barely knew. All of her colleagues were astounded when she broke down and wept uncontrollably during the service. She was finally facing her sorrow over the loss of her mother.

Because our emotions are heightened after a loss, we look for that level of emotional intensity in others and are very disappointed when it is not reciprocated. Other concerns are superficial, and we feel that most people are interested only in trivial matters. We want to scream out, "Can't you see that I just lost a child?" Our sorrow seems invisible at a time when our need for acceptance is particularly strong.

Frequently we find ourselves engaging in unusual behavior during the long months of grieving. We can't concentrate and shift from one activity to another, or aimlessly wander through our home, unable to focus on anything for more than a little while. This kind of restless behavior is a normal expression of our intense emotional activity.

Some people engage in different kinds of "searching" behavior such as following someone on the street who looks like the loved one, wearing our dead parents' clothes, or taking on personality traits of our loved one. One woman who lost her only sister when she was in her late teens began assuming many of her sister's attributes. She went from being the more reserved member of the family to being the outgoing and exuberant one, like her sister. Such behavior reflects the desire to perpetuate our loved one's role in the world, to guarantee him or her some measure of immortality.

Even though we all experience grief in unique ways, our grief occurs within a family setting. The death of a family member places great stress on the family structure. Some of us are very practical and logical, dealing with the disposition of effects and financial arrangements, while others of us withdraw from practical tasks and focus on our emotions. Just when we expect a drawing together of our family, we may experience the opposite.

Because men are more likely to conceal their feelings, their spouses and friends may conclude that they are uncaring and that their lack of expression means a lack of concern. A young woman who had a miscarriage grieved openly, weeping and expressing anger and despair. Her husband became more and more absorbed in his work, and she concluded that he didn't care or couldn't understand what she was feeling. It is difficult for some to express their feelings openly or verbally. In such cases we can find ways to do things together that express our caring, such as asking our husband or wife to stay home with us one evening or afternoon, holding each other without talking or expecting a verbal response, or even watching television together.

Children often withdraw in silence before their parents' grieving and think that their sadness is less important than their parents'. The son of a recently widowed woman told his mother on his birthday, "It's okay. I've known Daddy for much less time than you have, for only eight years, and I can't remember some of them because I was a baby." The way we handle our own grief gives cues to our children. If we grieve openly, they will feel free to do so, and if we try to hold everything inside, they will feel constrained. The important thing is to keep the channels of communication open and try to reassure our children that even though we are not always available to them, we love them.

Although the world around us hasn't changed, we are aware of how much we have changed. The death of a loved one is a searing wound. It alters our perspective on everything. Our values, friendships, and roles appear in a new light, and we are living closer to what is real in life than most people who have not suffered loss. While we may have suffered a crisis in meaning as we tried to understand the death of our loved one and why we were singled out, we may also have gained a new understanding of what it means to be alive.

Some people are able to move through this phase of disorganization and create a new life within little more than a year. A middle-aged man whose wife died of cancer was happily remarried and settled into a new life a year after his wife's death. However, a man or a woman with small children to care for needs much more time to rebuild his or her life. A couple who lost a child may decide to move into a new home or begin a pregnancy or even adopt a child. A teenager who lost a sibling may decide to attend college in a distant city or move to a new town to start his or her own life.

These decisions take years to implement. Usually we make important life decisions incrementally. For instance, a young widow moved into a smaller but similar home a year after her husband's death. It took her two more years to move into an urban setting, which reflected her change in career and lifestyle. The changes were accomplished gradually as she got to know and understand the new person she was becoming. It is only after we are able to handle the shock of death and the terrible disruption of our lives that we can even begin to think about making significant changes.

Chapter Seventeen
FACING THE WORLD WITHOUT A PARENT

Sue

The whole structure of our family changed after my mother died. She was the central force and then everything spun away after that and we all ended up planets in separate orbits. Most of the communication had been through my mother. My father didn't write letters very often. I don't see my youngest brothers; I hardly know them. They hardly have anything to do with the rest of the family. They left home as soon as they could after my father remarried. The pattern in my family for handling any big issue was instead of coming together and talking about it openly, we would just retreat into silence.

It was a very lonely and isolated period for me that year. I was living in a basement in exchange for child care and housework and I was also writing. It was my garret year. I wondered at times if I was too wallowing, too self indulgent. It's hard to know. There are no guidelines saying this is how much you should mourn, this long for a friend, this long for your mother. I read at some point the Elizabeth Kübler-Ross book, but there's no timetable for those stages, and different people feel different things. I don't think I went through a denial stage. It hit me like a sledgehammer immediately, and I knew she was gone. I didn't want her to be gone. There were times when I couldn't believe she was, but I wasn't suppressing it or denying it. For me it was just something raw and open for a very long time. I just walked around in a general state of vulnerability. I would see maybe a bicycle and car coming very close. Everything seemed death-filled, a hair's breadth away from death.

By the summer after that November I was in much better shape to do things. But for the first six months I was in very bad shape. Then in summer I was able to work in an art gallery. In the next fall I went to graduate school. I was writing in my journal all during this period, but I couldn't write poems about it. It was the next year after that that I started shaping them into poems.

I remember I had an incredibly strong anniversary reaction that November. Every Thanksgiving since has been hard. It's not so much the date but Thanksgiving and the day after. It's a very difficult time for me; for one thing, it's a family time. I just always associate it with her death. November is kind of a bleak month anyway. On her birthday I always feel bad. Her birthday is June 21, which seems so appropriate for her. She was such a warm and generous and loving person, just so very open. There's the two poles of the year, her birthday and then six months later the death date. I think of the year as having those strong moments for me ten years later.

Part of dealing with my mother's death is just a sense of not having any family. She was such a link for everyone in the family. My father moved to Arizona a few years ago, and that makes things even more difficult. That means I have my three brothers living in Seattle, my sister living in Oregon, my grandfather and aunt living in Salt Lake City. The logistical problem of trying to visit everyone is so hard.

I saw my father in September. We had a small family reunion at my sister's. That was the most we've been together in several years. My father has made an effort in the past years to be more open and establish more contact with each of us. Because of getting married and getting involved with a new family, things had kind of dissipated. He'll be sixty and I think he's feeling that he doesn't want to get older and have the family be this separated. He's a very private man, and my mother was a much more open, public kind of person. He didn't express his feelings in the same way my mother did.

Jeremy

I think that the way I deal with it is just to deny my own grief, just to put it aside. Right now I'm working two jobs, and I think one of the reasons I'm working my second job is just to have more time away from my house. At my own house my mother is mostly always unhappy. I want to comfort her, but at the same time I want to be as far away from her grief. The other day I was sitting in the living room and she just broke down and started crying. I was correcting papers for my students, and I just went on correcting. I didn't even look up to comfort her, because that would have been too much pain for myself.

I have one brother and he's older. He's married and his second kid is coming. He took it very hard. He's not a talkative person. We don't talk about it. The things we talk about are like, "Wow, it would have been nice to call him and tell him about this," about things that happen. We really haven't talked about how much each of us feels about the loss. I've talked to his wife. Sometimes I'll stop by after work and she tells me how he feels and tells me that he feels sad about it. It's just not something that Michael and I could easily talk about. I've talked to my two younger sisters about it, but I haven't talked to my older sister about it or to my brothers. I definitely think it's a gender thing. I think guys feel a lot that they have to play the roles that society sets for them.

It's not true that I haven't cried. I just cried the other night. It's always been hard for me to cry. I sort of feel sorry that I'm feeling sorry for myself when I'm crying. You see, I get a very nervous stomach. It's the same with my father. I was weighing 137 when my father died, and now I'm down to 127. I know everyone's giving me shit about it. My mother's constantly giving me nonsense. I think by not eating I was trying to punish myself. And I've decided that it's enough and I've got to put it beside me. Not behind me, beside me. I think if I tried to put my grief behind me I would be more negative and it would block me more. Instead I should just try to acknowledge it.

Oh yeah, I was furious at my father for dying. I was really, really pissed at him. I felt that he abandoned my mother and that he really made her life a lot harder by dying when he did. I felt very sorry for my father. I think he had a hard time. He had a really bad drinking problem when he was younger. I had a lot of anger toward my father when I was young, but over the last two years our relationship had changed a lot, became more positive. Last January I spent every weekend with my father. This was the first time that we were really together alone. He was the most intelligent man I ever met in my whole life, and we would go to museums and we'd talk about history and about politics. Talking about it right now, this is hard. My father had a big problem with his weight. Before he died he was very skinny, very fragile. I think that actually because I wear his clothes and drive his car and that now I'm now the only man in the house, I think that subconsciously I've been trying to become him, that I've actually become him and that my weight problem is just part of the whole thing.

Did you ever see A Christmas Carol? *When Scrooge dies, people rifle through his clothing. My sisters and brothers were arguing with each other over his things. When I went through my father's clothes, that's exactly how I felt. My father was a very private person. I had to go down with my brother two weeks after he died to close his apartment. I felt that I was violating my father. Every time I go through his study at home, through his own room, I feel like I am violating him. I remember a couple of times when I was younger—my father and I, we have the same body shape—and everyone would say, "You know, you guys, you look exactly alike. Jeremy, look at your father. That's how you're going to be."*

I dream a lot. I dreamed about my father being alive again. I was sitting in a tree with my sister and he was with us. He was happy and we were talking about how he had fooled death. My mother was on the ground looking up at us, and she was worried. She was upset at Susan and myself for talking about death and my father in such a humorous fashion. We asked him how he was going to live and whether he would have a heart attack again. He denied that anything was wrong. The week after my father died, I kept having these dreams.

I can't talk with my mother because her grief is so overwhelming. A parent is one of the most important things in your life, part of your birth, your past, your heritage. It's not the same thing for a wife. He was part of her life plan. The plans I have don't really deal with my parents. If I tried to express my grief to my mother, she would be very angry. She would think, "Your anger is great, but my anger is greater." I don't have the right to expect any compassion from my mom about my grief because her grief is so great that I don't think I can turn to her for sympathy or compassion or understanding. If I wanted to show my grief to my mother, I think she would welcome me and we could both grieve together. But I don't think I'm ready for it. I don't think I can deal with it. I have just too many other things. My job is new. I've never taught before. I don't think I could take the time off to grieve really properly. I would lose a lot of my control of what's going on around me.

I got a letter from a friend the other day and she's really enjoying herself and doing a lot of things and I thought, "I really should be enjoying life and not having such a hard time." I can see grieving but I can't see being mad. I was mad at God for a while, but it was just half a day. I don't think that even if there is a God that he really would bother himself with making my life difficult.

I really have tried my hardest to reject what happened, because when my mom talks about it I shut her off. Thanksgiving we had some people over and I tried not to think about this being a holiday and how holidays are for family.

The death of a parent has a far-reaching impact on our family lives. Many of us who lose a parent have to face the world with a host of new responsibilities without the protection we have been accustomed to. For some of us, our deceased mother or father was the focus of our family life, and now our siblings go their own ways without that unifying force. Or perhaps our surviving parent remarries, and that either draws us together or creates dissension among us. Living with a single parent has its particular problems, as Jeremy's narrative points out. When a parent dies, we are faced not only with our own broken lives but with the issues of our family members and the survival of the family itself.

The father of one of my students was left with a large family and remarried a year after his wife's death. His new wife was a woman of great tact and understanding. From the very beginning she assured Lisa that she had no intention of replacing her mother and that she wanted to be friends with her. She went to the cemetery with Lisa and helped her plant flowers at her mother's grave. Although she had a daughter of her own who was Lisa's age, she showed no preference for her own daughter and gave them equal and loving attention. Lisa was pleased to see the change in her father after the marriage. He had been moody and withdrawn after her mother died, and she welcomed his new sense of contentment.

For every success story like that of Lisa's family, there are families who experience great difficulty when a widowed parent remarries. Often we resent the person who moves in with our father or mother and feel left out as they focus on their new life together. We feel as if we no longer matter to our parent and that his or her new partner is trying to take our deceased parent's place. It can be difficult to say these things to our parent or even to admit them to ourselves, and sometimes it feels easier to withdraw into our own lives at school and spend more and more time with our friends. But our parent's new husband or wife may be feeling the same resentment and insecurity that we are, and our mutually hostile attitudes may be hiding our discomfort at the new situation.

Facing our own grief is a tremendous burden and leaves us with little energy or inclination to face the long and hard work of forging a relationship with a stepparent. It's not always possible to deal with such demanding issues simultaneously. Our anger over our parent's death is often mingled with anger over a new situation which we neither expected nor wanted. We feel that we must compete for our parent's attention just when we need him or her the most, and our resentment at the new situation might distance us from that parent. It's difficult enough to communicate with a new family member, but when we are so sad and angry, it's that much more trying.

This is the time to turn to a counselor for help. When the demands of school, work, and family press in on us, we must be especially careful with ourselves and remember that we are entitled to our sadness. Sometimes we wonder whether we really deserve to devote attention to our own needs, given the pressures of our lives. We don't want to burden our friends with our troubles and worry that people might shy away from us if we express our pain. However, we don't have to wait for others to give us permission to grieve. We are entitled to pay attention to our feelings, to think about the parent we lost and our own needs.

Some people lose both parents and must face a life of great loneliness and uncertainty. We move in with grandparents or an aunt and uncle or live with only our brothers and sisters. Some sisters and brothers draw closer together, but others drift apart and experience two crushing losses at once, the death of the parent and the end of family life.

In families that manage to stay together, the older brother or sister often takes responsibility for the younger siblings and is propelled into the role of parenting at an early age. The older sister of one of my students had to care for her four younger siblings while she was trying to finish school and handle her own grief. In taking up this responsibility, she found herself in a very lonely position. Once she had taken up guardianship for her siblings, she felt that she had lost her sibling relationship with her brothers and sisters.

Such new demands lead us to postpone or minimize our own grief. And while we feel very strongly about the importance of keeping the family together and feel proud of what we are doing, we still resent the heavy burden we have to bear. We must make a special effort to remember the importance of our own lives. Perhaps we are trying to finish school or are in the midst of a relationship that might lead to marriage. It is difficult to arrange our priorities, but it's helpful to remember that we can't care for others if our own lives need attention.

Even if we have no responsibility for our siblings, our lives often seem less important after the death of our parents. We have lost the emotional support and motivation of our parents and have to devote extra effort to finish college or to find a job which really challenges us. One of my students who had lost both parents attended her classes only sporadically and eventually left school, although she had great promise and knew that facing the working world without an education would make her life more difficult. Losing parents leaves us with a diminished self-esteem and it is only too easy to settle for choices that are much less than we deserve.

Being left with a single parent has its own particular problems. One of my students was faced with caring for her teenage siblings after her mother died. She resented that they rebelled against her efforts, and even though her father was a loving presence, the demands of his job left her with too much responsibility for her age.

If we were closer to the parent who died than to our surviving parent, or if the parent who died smoothed over the differences we had with our other parent, we are now faced with conflict and difficult competition. Our surviving parent may want to interpret our deceased parent's wishes for us, and we disagree. The discord which had been softened by our father's or mother's presence now comes to the fore, strengthened by the pain of the death. We resent our surviving parent and feel guilty about this resentment. It's helpful to turn to outside support in such a complex situation.

It's not unusual for the surviving parent to turn to us for support and comfort. We find ourselves taking care of our parent and neglecting our own needs. Like Jeremy, we believe that our parent's grief is greater than our own. Even if our parent does not turn to us for comfort, we still feel obliged to help make up for our parent's loss. "I try to call as often as possible and visit often, but my mother seems so lost," a young woman confided. When I told her that while her mother appreciated her efforts, no one expected her to try to replace her father, she was relieved. Sometimes we can't fix things, and that's all right.

Acknowledging Sorrow and Grief

Our emotions often overwhelm us, and we try to push them away. We are angry at the disruption of our lives and our abrupt passage into the responsibilities of adulthood. We are angry at our friends for having parents, for being able just to have a good time while we are struggling with our own sorrow and a difficult home situation. We are even angry at the parent who died and left us. Sometimes we just have a more diffuse resentment surfacing in a general irritability.

As Sue points out in her narrative, what is the most trying is that there are no guidelines for the sorrow we feel. We don't know how long or how intensely we should grieve because of our limited experience with death. Perhaps we remember grieving for the death of a grandparent when we were young, but nothing has prepared us for the storm of emotions we feel when a parent dies.

At our age we are concerned with our image, with what others think of us as we try to make a place for ourselves in the world. Too often we are afraid of being self-pitying in our grief. Jeremy was afraid that his own sadness would not be manly. He was also afraid of losing control.

We often confuse sadness with self-pity and try to deny these feelings or think that our own sadness is less significant than that of our surviving parent. While this is normal, it's helpful to remember that everyone's sadness is unique and equally valid. We are entitled to our feelings and to express them in a way that is comfortable for us. Perhaps we withdraw to the privacy of our own room to shed those tears or get in the car and drive or take a long walk by ourselves.

Parents give us a sense of rootedness and emotional support during key moments of our lives. Their love strengthens us daily even if we are only dimly aware of that love. Even if our relationship with our parent or parents was troubled, they were still the source of our identity and gave us a sense of belonging. When we lose a parent we are filled with loneliness and a sense of isolation. We are now facing the world without a buffer or protector and are very unsure of ourselves as we confront life.

This loneliness is often invisible to others. We may think that our friends who still have both parents take their good fortune and security for granted. This loneliness and longing for our parents surfaces when we least expect it. We might be out with friends having a good time when something reminds us of our loss, bringing a fresh surge of grief.

Perhaps we missed our parent intensely the first year and then were able to put that loneliness aside, but many times the sadness overwhelms us at important events such as graduations and weddings. Although the depth of our feelings after so much time has passed can be a surprise; it is not unusual to have these profound reactions at the key moments of our passage.

Some, like Sue, have strong anniversary reactions on the date of our parent's death or on their birthday many years later. It's as if a wound re-opened and we were faced with all the sadness and pain we thought we had put behind us. This is a reaction many people continue to have as time passes.

The Importance of Support

While there are support groups for many different kinds of loss, groups for those who have lost their parents are much rarer. On the other hand, as young adults we are apt to have close friends we can turn to who will support us and listen to us when we need to talk. With the high rate of divorce, many of us have friends who have lost parents through a divorce and who understand the pain of our loss. For those of us who are com-fortable talking, it's helpful to air our feelings with a trusted friend. Those who are more reserved sometimes look for a shared activity, such as a sport, rather than conversation. A good friend who accepts us regardless of our moods can relieve our sadness.

Making contact with other members of our family, whether a cousin or a great aunt, can give us the sense of belonging that our parent or par-ents used to give us. No one can ever replace our parents, but it is com-forting to have a member of our parents' generation to turn to, whether to exchange letters or to visit from time to time.

Few of our friends can understand our sense of isolation. Because we have been through so much, we know more about life than they do, and our experience has set us apart from our peers. Some of our friends' par-ents may go out of their way to be helpful to us, but we don't always feel comfortable with this. It can be hard to explain to people that a parent is irreplaceable and that while we appreciate their attention, we want to keep our distance. We can tell others that we are grateful for their kind-ness but have our own ways of doing things. Those who really care for us will understand and accept these feelings.

In time we will be proud of the distance we have covered. We dis-cover a new strength and self-reliance that we have acquired through the long and painful months and years. This is a hard-won quality, but it is one that will serve us throughout our lives.

Chapter Eighteen
LOST IN A WORLD
OF COUPLES

Anne

You've got to come off it. You can't just be grief, grief, grief. There were a lot of people around, and that was good. The kids cried, but I would go off to be by myself if I were really going to let down. You're physically hit as if you had had a terrible disease and it's over, but you're weakened. I would go out for an hour and then I would have to come back. I would go to the office for a little and then I would have to rest. I didn't eat. Other people would probably eat too much. The dead person is still alive in your mind at that time. You're constantly saying, "But you're not here." You're constantly saying, "This is the first time it's spring without him, the first time you go to a party." You say, "this shouldn't be."

That first year I was interior. It's a protective thing, like the outside of pineapple to keep the sweetness. I had that sense of for me and my children, "Keep it good and keep it nice. Act as if we are doing all okay. Let's not lie to ourselves." Getting through that first year was a very delicate feeling, like you have to take care of yourself, kind of what you feel like when you're pregnant. "Can't people see?" I said to myself when I was walking in an airport.

Other people say the wrong things. I'm not a mean person. I accept that. I understand. I think that probably a lot of people aren't very nice. The main thing I noticed was the feeling, "I won and you lost, Anne." They are taking a tally. "I still have my husband." It's there. It's there in kind of a funny way, in the things they want to give you and do for you. That this happened to you means that it passed them by. That's why they avoid you in the store. You go to buy bacon and they turn away. They are ill at ease because it's such a big bad thing to have to talk about death when someone is buying bacon. They say, "How are you doing, Anne?" They want to hear the soap-opera effect, they want to revel in this.

Pity is a poisoned sweetness. Pity is one guy is up on the pedestal and the other is laying on the floor and the one on the pedestal says, "Here, poor thing, have a raisin, have a grape." When you stand up and are even with everyone else it's like you have won the Battle of the Bulge, and that scares everyone. They act weird. Many people have written me off.

I met someone I had known long ago. Death takes someone you love away from you, and then society says, "Don't you dare do it, and you can't have anymore or you're bad." You need someone you're at ease with. It was something for me to think about, and I was very surprised at how adolescent I was about it. It kept my mind, that loving part of me, busy. It didn't compensate. It's okay to use your right hand if your left hand isn't working. Of course, he's a good friend. That time everything was at high sensibilities, like playing the violin.

There's a great deal of interest in the sexual situation of a woman like me. There are men that want to take care of the fact that you need to have that because you don't have that anymore. I could have married that childhood friend. It wouldn't have been a choice that would have been [made] with all of my marbles intact, though he was a love. There's the "Who's going to marry her and take care of her?" stuff, especially toward a feminine woman. I'm not the gym-teacher type, so people do want to take care of me. I like the taking care. It's very nice. But it's nicer than the real fact of letting them take care of your physical needs. You go from being a married woman to a time warp, to the day before you got married, adolescence. You're back there in your status between the men and women thing. There was certainly nothing else in between. I was a neophyte. If someone had said to me, "How is your love life?" I wouldn't know how to talk that way. I was brought right back to my graduation at 1962, as a girlish woman. Right now, I'm probably running at about twenty-eight years old.

With the kids it was letting them see that the rest of their lives wasn't gone. No way were we going to have Bobby the man of the family. I think we've done good by letting every other fact of our lives stay the same. They think maybe Mom will be gone, the house will be gone. We did move a year and a half later, but it was our joint decision. The house was too big, and it made sense.

For generations women have been taught, they take care of people who are really outside the action. I've learned to come out of that. All the skills that women learn to be indirect could be put to straightforward use. They have not taken a risk. They're in a safe place. You must risk loss to gain. Widowed women are perceived as children. That weakens someone. If you help someone over every bump, then that person cannot grow. It is a time that you should buy all the help you can and you take the help that's healthy that you can get. The woman-child thing is very heavy when it's given with love. I would like to please other people, but I need to take care of myself first, and when I forget to do that it's wrong. Unfortunately, the most difficult road that you see ahead of yourself in the first year is the one that you should follow. It's easier to go to Grandma's and cry, but it's not quite as good for your mental health. I'm a much better person than I was.

Eric

When the shock and numbness wears off, then the real grief and sadness come. It's been two years and a few months, and it's just getting better. It feels like a long time. The changes are almost impossible at first.

It took me a month to cry. After that, it's all I did. It would be very hard for me to believe that men don't cry. I guess people do repress their emotions. I've never been a big crier, and I probably haven't cried at all since the age of twelve.

I started looking for a group right away, but most groups disband during the summer. It was just as well, because groups don't want people who can't objectify their experience. You're still under shock and you're still too numb to talk about it.

I'd wake up in the morning and I'd have this weight on my chest. And I'd think I have to get up despite it, and then I would think, "Why?" If I had one meeting during the day, even for a cup of coffee at four o'clock, that was what I built my day around. I cried about three times during the day.

It was something Diane had taught me to do. We had a chance to talk about that stuff. She sort of led me along toward her own death.

An elderly man who had been married for fifty-two years and was recently widowed exclaimed, "There's only one word I can think of to describe what it's like, and it's L-O-S-T. I feel lost!" Others have described widowhood as stepping on a train, getting accustomed to the ride, and then being thrown off in a place that's unrecognizable.

The loneliness that overwhelms us after the death of a spouse is one of the biggest issues we have to face as time passes. The death of our spouse ended a relationship, yet we still feel very strongly connected to that person. We still reach out for them in the middle of the night or wake up with a keen sense of their absence. However, after a year or so, the fact of that absence is very clear to us. We know that things won't change, that we can't reverse events.

As time passes we face our daily life without the familiar intimacy. When a spouse or lover dies, there is no longer anyone to share the events of our daily lives. There is no one to fix meals for or to prepare them for us, no one to comfort us and to cushion the countless irritations we encounter at work and in our other relationships. We miss being touched and held. If we were younger when we lost our spouse, we may experience sexual frustration and desire. Our home, which was once a retreat from the world, is no longer a shelter but perhaps a place to escape from.

Not all marriages involve companionship, but even those which were just a sharing of household routines and daily lives are a source of well-being and purpose. When I was young, the wife of an elderly neighbor died suddenly. Although the marriage didn't seem to be happy or close, the husband spent the months afterward as if he were adrift, taking his meals at odd hours, sleeping on the living-room couch and ultimately moving to another state to be closer to his daughter and her children.

In marriages where there is intimate sharing and strong companionship, the adjustment period is especially difficult. Losing a spouse is losing one's best and most trusted friend. We believe that we will never be able to find someone like our spouse and that we will have to spend the rest of our days in a state of longing and loneliness.

Men and women experience this loneliness in different ways. It is especially difficult for men who have had traditional marriages to return to an empty home after a day's work, and they end up taking their meals out or going out with friends after supper just to avoid the long hours of solitude. Finding new companions is a way for men to cope, while women spend more time dealing with the lonely feelings and take more time to look for new friends.

Older people suffer more acutely from loneliness and problems with health and mobility compound their sense of isolation. The stress of grief makes many people vulnerable to illness. Research has shown that many people suffer from illness during the first year of widowhood. My uncle, who lost his wife when he was seventy-five, suffered from a series of illnesses in that first year as he faced the prospect of the rest of his life without my aunt. There is no future for the elderly in which to find a new companion and no long stretch of time for the healing process.

When a homosexual person loses a partner, the loneliness and isolation can be heightened by the fact that the relationship wasn't legitimized, and his or her grieving may be unrecognized. In such a situation it is more difficult to find a support group and to find understanding in the workplace, and it is more difficult to reach out for new friends. Typically the bereaved first checks out whether it's okay to talk about the loved one when they are seeking support, and their pain is so often compounded with concern about social stigmas. Their vulnerability is heightened by the possibility of rejection.

New and Unfamiliar Tasks

Besides intimacy, marriages also involve a division of labor within the family. Survivors are faced with a whole set of new duties in addition to the accustomed ones. For instance, a man who must raise his children alone will have to face the immediate problems of finding adequate childcare while he is at work. Perhaps his wife had planned her schedule around the children's needs, and now he must make special arrangements for transportation, for the time after school before he returns from work, for the times when they are on school vacation or ill. If he has to travel for his work, this makes the adjustment especially troublesome. The demands of family leave single parents little time for attention to their own pain and sadness.

A widow may have not only the burden of raising children by herself but also the burden of supporting the family. If she used to stay home to take care of the children, she now has to face the job market when her self-esteem is low. Because of the gains of the women's movement, there are now a number of organizations which specialize in helping women enter the job market, and this is a good time to turn to one of them.

Taking care of younger children is especially trying. We feel too exhausted to get up and get them ready for school in the morning or are irritable and worn out from work when they come home. Our children will be grieving in their own ways and may act up at school and at home, trying to get our attention and reassurance. They will be greatly affected by the way we mourn. If we are open in expressing our sadness, they will be encouraged to talk and cry over their deceased father or mother. They can also be a source of great comfort. The twelve-year-old daughter of a recently widowed friend put her arms around her mother and held her while she wept as she was preparing dinner. This was the time her husband usually came home, and her daughter understood her tears and wanted to be close.

It is not always possible for us to be the kind of parent we would like to be. We may be struggling with our dual roles as nurturer and financial supporter when we are least able to. It's helpful to remember that we are doing the best that we can and that children are able to understand.

Depending on their generation, both men and women are faced with unfamiliar tasks in the management of a household. Older men may be baffled by cooking and laundry or by shopping. A friend of mine who was widowed developed a whole series of recipes that he could prepare once a week for the entire week, but not everyone is that inventive. Widowers and widows will need to confront new tasks, whether taking care of finances or managing daily household chores, at a time when we may be feeling unequal to new demands.

In the long run, we will acquire a new sense of competence and independence, but the path to these feelings is difficult. It's helpful to be as tolerant as possible with ourselves and not to take on too many new demands. Solving one problem at a time, living one day at a time is more than enough at this stage of our lives.

The Extended Family and Community

The death of a spouse affects our relationships within the extended family, not just the immediate family. For example, if we are a young widow or widower, we may have to face the well-intentioned but intrusive behavior of our parents or in-laws. Perhaps our parents will try to cheer us up when we feel like being alone with our sadness, or perhaps they will try to intervene in the decisions we make.

Our in-laws many times misunderstand our desire for companionship and disapprove when we begin to date or to go out. Although we know that we can never replace our loved one, they might interpret our renewed interest in a relationship as a betrayal. But our needs are important, and a renewed interest in friendship and dating is a sign of healing. A widowed friend of mine learned how to say, "Thank you, I love you for your thoughts," and then to go quietly forward with her own plans.

Older widows or widowers face the disapproval of adult children when making new friends and beginning a new social life. A middle-aged widower experienced friction with his adult sons when he started seeing women and going out frequently. He was able to tell them that while he did all he could while their mother was alive, he felt it was time for him to turn his attention to other things. He was convinced that someday they would understand. Some of the discomfort his sons had with their father's new lifestyle stemmed from their grief over the loss of their mother. If possible, it's best to keep the channels of communication open and give our children an opportunity to understand our feelings as well as to air their own views.

While it is easy for some widowers to begin a social life after the loss of a spouse, it may be hard for them to keep close contact with their adult children. In more traditional marriages, the mother may have been the center of the family, inviting the children and their spouses to the house for special occasions and telephoning them to keep in touch with their lives. Not all men are comfortable with this role. It may have been the wife who kept lists of birthdays and special days to remember. A widower in this situation could begin a new tradition of taking the family out for a meal or a movie from time to time. While the children will miss the old traditions, they will also learn to value these new times together.

Some older widows' adult children become involved in decisions about their lives. We might be confused and not know what would be best for ourselves, given our changed circumstances, and perhaps what our children are saying about our housing or living arrangements sounds good to us. However, it's best not to rush into any changes until we feel ready for them. Much as we may wish to please our children, in the long run, we are the only ones who can judge the timing for changing our way of life.

If we did most things together with our husband while he was alive, we will seem very self-sufficient. Our friends and families might not realize that we have very real needs. There is nothing wrong with asking for advice or help. We may not be used to turning to our children or other relatives, but the worst that can happen is that they would turn us down, and the best is that they would actually welcome a chance to help and were just waiting for us to open up that possibility.

When we lose a spouse we undergo changes in our family and in the broader community as well. We are probably feeling a diminished sense of self-worth because of our loss, which can be heightened by the way we are now perceived by society. We face the world as a changed person, and the world looks at us differently, perhaps with fear or pity, and we find ourselves on the margins of society.

Creating New Social Identities

While our spouse or partner was alive, we never gave a second thought to our leisure activity or social life. We were used to doing things with a partner, whether shopping on the weekend or just deciding to take in a movie one evening. Now we have to make plans for social outings and need to contact people well in advance if we would like to go out. We resent the effort it takes to have a social life.

Perhaps the people we were friendly with as a couple no longer invite us out, and our friends withdraw just when we need them most. We are angry at others for not inviting us over or thinking of us, and we are angry at others for still having a partner while we are alone. Like Anne, we may feel lost in a world which seems to be made just for couples.

Even if our friends continue to invite us over and want to spend time with us, we feel uncomfortable with them, like a fifth wheel or an outsider. Perhaps we are uneasy around longstanding friends but can't really pinpoint the source of our unease. There are so many changes in our lives at this time that it's normal to feel discomfort in our old situations.

If we have been left with young children to care for, we often experience a keen sense of social isolation. All of our time is taken up with our work and with childcare, leaving us little opportunity to be with other adults or to think of our own needs. Depending on our financial circumstances, this period of very real isolation may last for a number of years until the children are more self-sufficient. We feel that we owe our children our undivided attention and that we should compensate for the fact that they now have only one parent. However, chances are that our children will welcome a social opportunity that refreshes us and lifts our spirits, even if it means we are away from them for an evening or a weekend.

As time passes we will have new growth along with our pain. We are assailed by so many conflicting emotions that it is difficult to perceive our growth. Despite the loneliness and anguish, we do acquire new perspectives and new strengths. As Anne points out in chapter 23, it's helpful to think of this new period in our lives as filled not only with longing but with the opportunities of a blank page. This is a good time to make new friends and discover new interests.

A friend of mine who was widowed at an early age found her comfortable suburban setting limiting. Everyone had the same interests and lifestyles. She decided to host foreign students from a nearby college for weekends and holidays, a solution that gave her an opportunity to grow as well as an opportunity to express the giving side of her nature, which had previously been focused on her husband. For the students, it was a welcome break from dorm life and a chance to share their culture with Americans.

While we may have been hurt by being ignored by our old friends, we may also have the adventure of making new friends. As Anne points out, there is a special delight in finding that we are liked and admired in new settings. Living as part of a couple, while comfortable and secure, did not allow us the opportunity to test ourselves in a variety of social situations. It is frightening to enter a new social setting with a new identity, but it's also affirming when we receive a positive response.

Taking Time Out for Ourselves

Our life is in turmoil as we change our routines and work. We are not only coping with our sorrow, but experiencing the difficulty of learning new roles, new ways of being. Out of this seeming chaos come new affirmations, perhaps a strengthening of some friendships or a loss of others, but eventually a new life, one which we have built for ourselves, emerges.

All of this takes time. Early on we will need some hours or periods of the day when we are just by ourselves, either taking a walk or simply daydreaming in our own living room. It may seem as if we are doing nothing, but this is a good way to get in touch with ourselves, to plumb the depths of our own interests and discover our goals. For single parents, this time is very hard to find, so perhaps a long bath at the end of the day, or listening to music while the children are in bed or watching television would be a good way to make time for privacy.

Sometimes our extended families or friends pressure us to resume our activities and "get back into the swing of things." We may even pressure ourselves to return to a normal pace and schedule. In our achievement-oriented society it's easy to feel guilty about "wasting" time. However, this private time is part of the healing process. So much of the work of grieving is invisible that we are apt to ignore the toll it takes on us.

We need time to think about ourselves and where we are going. Grieving is a very self-regarding phase of our lives. It can be difficult to allow ourselves this focus on self, but it is necessary to help us move to a new place. It is not unusual to experience periods of depression in the year or years after the death of a spouse.

It's difficult not only to go through our daily lives without our partner, but also to find a reason for living. When our spouse was alive, we had very positive reinforcement from him or her. Perhaps our spouse made us feel special or important. Now we are no longer at the center of someone's life. Our friends and family are eager for us to "cheer up," but these periods of depression are normal in the months after we are widowed, and there is nothing wrong with slowing down when these feelings assail us.

We have lost the foundation for our daily life and our family as well as our dreams and our hopes for the future. We had made plans together for the children and now face the crucial events in their growth by ourselves. We hoped to give them special opportunities for their education or looked forward to doing things together as a family. Although we can never replace our spouse, maybe we will find a close friend who would be pleased to attend the graduations, the bat mitzvah, or the confirmation of our children. We could also share these moments with another person who has experienced loss.

Perhaps we made plans for the time our children would be grown, or perhaps our spouse was a busy executive and we were looking forward to retirement in order to be together, and his death has left us with the sense that we wasted time, that we could have done things together while we still had each other. Ultimately this leads to a reexamination of our time and values. Instead of waiting for certain things to happen, we might decide to live more spontaneously.

An older couple was looking forward to retirement together, but the husband died the year before. They had planned to renovate their home and take a long vacation. His widow did eventually carry out the renovations, and this gave her a certain satisfaction, but she was still left with a sense of having been cheated.

Younger widows and widowers experience a double loss: the loss of a mate and the loss of potential children. People may try to comfort us by reminding us that we are still young and will have an opportunity to remarry and start a family, but the future we dreamed of included children with the person we loved, and we feel robbed of memories as well as of our dreams.

Widowed persons undergo profound changes in identity in the months and years after the death of a spouse. A woman changes from being a wife to being a widow to being a single woman. A man changes from being a husband to being a widower to being a single man. In this growth process we move from a perception of being half a person to being a single, whole person. Between these two states is an uncomfortable period in which we feel neither married nor single. We feel guilty about dating because we still have a strong attachment to our spouse. Perhaps we believe that we are betraying him or her if we decide to start a new relationship.

As younger widows and widowers we will be concerned with finding sexual satisfaction. We will have a strong desire to be touched and to touch, to feel a physical closeness again, or we will simply want to express that loving part of ourselves. If we experiment with new partners we might encounter some disappointments along the way.

Dating again will be difficult for us, and we will probably feel awkward. As Anne points out in this chapter, we go from being a married person through a time warp to the time before we got married. We may feel like an adolescent again, being afraid of saying the wrong thing and experiencing all the insecurities of beginning a new relationship. It's difficult to go back to the early courtship stages if we've lived with a long-standing relationship. While some of us find it challenging or exciting, others will be hesitant about beginning the long process of acceptance and compromise which precedes the attainment of mutual respect.

In the beginning we will compare our dates to our former spouse. If we had troubling patterns in our marriage, we might worry about repeating these in a new relationship. If we had a good relationship with our deceased spouse, we will feel very differently from our divorced friends who chose to end their marriages and who are eager to start a new relationship. It's not unusual to idealize our spouses in the months and years after their death. An older friend of mine who was widowed in middle age told me, "It's never the same, never as good."

There are special difficulties in being widowed when one is young and attractive. Men may consider women fair game and assume that we are looking for new experiences. One of my older students was widowed when she was only thirty-five. Despite the fact that she had small children, she was the very unwilling recipient of the attentions of the single men in her town, and found it difficult to protect herself. "People make assumptions and misunderstand my need to keep a distance," she told me.

If we were older when our spouse died, we may take more time to find a new partner and perhaps seek options other than marriage: a relationship with a younger or older person, dating a number of people at once, or simply living with someone else. It does seem to be easier for men to find new partners because there are more women than men in most age groups.

It can be quite fulfilling to live alone after many years of catering to the needs of someone else. Maybe we have acquired a new taste for making decisions about our daily lives. We may also have developed a strong friendship group. There are many paths toward contentment.

In the long period after the death of a spouse we will receive a lot of advice from well-intentioned friends and family about how to conduct our life. As time passes and we endure the difficult and lonely months without our spouse, we will make many decisions about home, work, childcare, and friendship. Our lives are chaotic, and we feel that we are reeling from one event to another without guidance. But these decisions and our profound sorrow have helped us as we grow, and from this growth comes the steadying and peaceful realization that the inspiration for our long-term goals and our more immediate decisions comes from within ourselves.

Chapter Nineteen
LIVING WITH THE
ABSENT CHILD

Phil

The fact is that you grieve in such different ways and you don't under-stand what is going on in the other person's head. You might feel a little better one day and want to try to do something else and your spouse may feel quite differently. You have a really hard time expressing your feelings. Sometimes there are feelings of bitterness, sometimes of sadness. They don't just come together, and sometimes you just try to deal with it pri-vately. I think there's a real danger there: You're so caught up in your own self and dealing with your own emotions that you have a tendency not to look around you. The children miss her and they need your help and they're looking at you and your wife to see if everything's going to be all right, and they need to see that it's going to be all right. Sometimes we had a hard time talking about it. Our little boy drew us out by asking about it a lot.

It had a really strong effect on my younger son, who was only three at the time. He still talks about it a lot. It also had an effect on my older daughter, who was only a year and a half older and was Jenny's best friend. She didn't talk about it, but she manifested it. She was very fearful about things.

The first year or so you just basically try to survive, to get through the day. You experience a lot of different things. A lot of things, symbolic things mean a lot to us, holidays, the change of seasons. A day like the first day of spring means a warm day, a feeling that there's something happening to all of us. After that it feels exasperating. You feel worse. I can remember driving home one day in early March and having a very awful feeling about it. It's a nice day but it's really an awful day. It just heightens it, like Christmas. You're upset and you're bitter. You're out of control. The feeling of not being in control is not something that we're used to. You always face life with a certain amount of hope. No matter what happens to you and your family, there's always a way of overcoming, but this there's no way of overcoming. The idea of hope isn't there. You can spin your wheels and try different things, but they don't make any difference.

I'm more of an activist and I tend to resolve issues by going out and doing something about it, but I couldn't do anything about this. It was much bigger than we were. We do think about it every day, but we do have some perspective maybe now. We have recognized that we are going to survive. You think about things in the beginning and you wonder if you are ever going to be able to teach. You wonder if you are going to be able to interact and function in a professional way. You really have doubts about that. It's like learning to walk all over again.

You have a sensitivity to injustices, to inappropriate behavior, a lot more understanding, but not tolerance. Within a year or so afterward I was in situations at work where I thought people's ethical behavior was inappropriate. You realize it if you put it in context with what's important in life. You have to deal with it. I felt stronger about things like that afterward.

I presented a film I made about the grieving process to a group of women in my network one evening. During the discussion after the film, a woman stood up and in a hushed voice told us that her eighteen-year-old daughter had drowned the previous summer. She moved like a person who had a serious illness. Her suffering was evident in her face and the way she held herself. Her body mirrored the pain she was feeling.

Losing a child is losing a part of ourselves. As bereaved parents, we believe that a child's death is the worst kind of loss that anyone can possibly endure. We are beyond comfort and beyond hope. We wonder if we will survive the tragedy of losing a child.

It will be difficult to communicate with others about our loss because of its very depth. That the woman who lost her daughter was able to stand up and speak about it was a tremendous step in her healing process. After the discussion a number of people went up to her and put their arms around her. Because she shared her story in such a personal way, the people around her were able to draw close to her and she was able to receive comfort. But afterward we all went home to our lives while she was left with her terrible burden.

After the loss of a child, our friends try to comfort us, but we know that after their visit or their phone call, they will return to an intact family or their child waiting for them, while we face what seems like an endlessly bleak and lonely future. Sometimes the only people who can really understand what it feels like to have one's very being torn apart are parents who have suffered similar tragedies.

Children are part of our own being, physically and emotionally. As our children grow up we continually see in them traits of ourselves and members of our family. It is surprising and amusing to discover traces of our own personality in our child's reaction to events. Or perhaps our child has the same physical features, eye or hair color, walks with a similar gait. When we bury that child we are burying part of ourselves.

A child is not only a part of our past, sharing our genetic makeup and certain family traits, but he or she is also the center of our hopes and dreams, especially our dreams for the future. We spend our child's growing years planning for their education, trying to arrange our lives so that his or her unique talents develop in the best possible way. We may have started to save for their college education.

If our child was already an adult when he or she died, we would have had the pride of seeing their potential begin to unfold. Perhaps he or she was just beginning a successful career or a family. A friend of mine lost her son when he was just beginning his career as a musician. He never really had a chance to develop his considerable promise. One of my colleague's sons was killed in an automobile accident as he was driving to graduate school. We will always wonder about the potential of our deceased child, the talent and personality that will never bloom.

When our young adult child dies, we have lost not only our child, but also the grandchildren we will never have. Perhaps we have lost a son or daughter who had a young child, and the spouse remarries. We find ourselves in the difficult position of arranging for visits with someone we think has replaced our deceased child, and the couple may want to keep their distance from us until they feel more comfortable with each other in order to begin their new life together with as few complications as possible. Misunderstandings develop easily in such situations and we might wish to seek professional help in communicating with each other.

Whether we already have grandchildren from our deceased child, or we will never have the opportunity of grandchildren, we still feel as if we had lost our whole future and the perpetuation of our family. Children represent our immortality. Not all of us imagine our child fulfilling dreams that we ourselves were unable to realize, but most of us think of our children as our eternity.

There are parents who have lost more than one child. A middle-aged couple I met lost both of their sons in an automobile accident. Another couple I interviewed had lost a child to illness when that child was an infant and then lost another son in an accident when he was nineteen. No words can describe the pain and suffering of multiple losses. Although both couples have managed not only to survive but to live fully, they bear the scars of their tragedy.

As we share life events with our family and friends, this feeling of a lost potential or utter waste will come up again and again. When we attend the graduation or the confirmation of a cousin or a friend's child, we think about our child and that he would be having this experience if he had lived. A friend of mine who lost a young daughter thinks of her continually as graduation approaches at the college where he works. He keeps thinking that if his daughter had lived, he would be going to her graduation. Knowing that we will never witness the development of our child is a source of renewed sorrow.

Painful Reminders

There are so many painful reminders of the child we lost. If our child was still in school when he or she died, the opening of school in September or the end of the semester in early summer awakens our grief. So much of our family schedule is involved with our children that in the months after a child's death, we feel his or her absence keenly every day. We find ourselves reaching for things our child liked when we are grocery shopping. It is painful to prepare a meal and have to scale down the portions, or face his or her favorite foods.

Our house is still full of mementos of our child, such as photographs, toys, or trophies. Deciding what to do with the deceased child's room is very difficult, especially when there are other siblings. Some neighbors of mine who lost a daughter decided to keep her room the way it was before she died. The surviving siblings felt comfortable with this. It is not always easy to make this kind of decision, however. The brother of a child who died of an illness wanted to take his brother's room and wear some of his clothes. It was difficult for his mother to negotiate with him about those things. She was torn. On the one hand, she knew she couldn't keep his things forever unused or on display, yet on the other hand, seeing them on her other son was painful. It's normal to want to keep our child's favorite things. Keeping our child's room intact is a matter of our own timing. The time to change is when we feel the need to rearrange our life and move on.

Many life events, including holidays and the changing of seasons, spark a return of our bitterness and sorrow. Holidays are a time when families gather together, a time when the memories of Christmases or Passovers we spent with our child fill us with deep pain. As Phil mentions, the return of spring after a long winter may fill us with a sense of futility and despair. The idea of hope is no longer there for him. Illness and death among our friends and acquaintances also brings out our grief. At my aunt's funeral one of her best friends mourned not only her friend's untimely death, but the son she lost in the Algerian War many years ago.

Many of us have strong anniversary reactions when we reach the time of year our child died, and these reactions may be with us for many years. Sometimes the anticipation of this period is as difficult as living through the anniversary itself. A friend of mine whose adult son died of cancer a number of years ago always has a renewed surge of grief as April approaches.

Some parents find that commemorating the anniversary of a child's death in a special way helps them through this difficult time of year. Those of us who practice religion in a more traditional way may wish to have a special service in memory of the child. If we don't participate in an organized religion, we might want to design our own anniversary commemoration. Even though our child has died, he or she is still part of us. Spending an evening or an afternoon remembering that child and talking about him or her is a source of great comfort.

If we have other children, especially teenagers, they might not want to participate in anniversary events. Children grieve in different ways, and some children don't want to talk about their feelings. They might be more comfortable with keeping their distance from these events. They might not wish to attend a service would but be perfectly willing to go to the dinner following.

Feeling Guilty and Powerless

As parents, we feel responsible for the well-being of our children. We expend so much of our energy and our lives trying to fulfill their needs and expectations that when a child dies, we are consumed with guilt. We feel as if somehow we should have been able to prevent that death, that we have failed as a parent. In the months after our child's death, we think about all the things we might have done differently, or we remember instances when we lost our temper or quarreled with our child.

If we had fought with our child, we might now place too heavy a burden of blame on ourselves. Perhaps our deceased child was a teenager and we find ourselves focusing exclusively on our memories of angry exchanges and misunderstandings. It's helpful to remember the mutual and unspoken love beneath these quarrels. Sometimes expressions of frustration are the only way to communicate our love and concern. Sometimes we have to forgive ourselves to be able to move on to a clearer view of our relationship.

A woman I interviewed was very candid about her relationship with her deceased daughter. "We were very different," she said, "and we had difficulty with each other." Then she added, "If she had lived, that would not have changed." She told me this with great peace because she had resolved that relationship and was able to distinguish between the deep love she felt for that child and the differences in personality between them.

Although they have no bearing on the death of our child, we review our own shortcomings or behavior and see a connection where there is none. As parents, we seem so powerful in our responsibility for our child's daily life that it is all too easy to believe that our child died through some fault of our own. Perhaps we prayed intensely during our child's illness or in the hours or days after an accident, but our child was not spared.

Other people may avoid us, and many people find it difficult to talk to a bereaved parent, which contributes to our loss of self-esteem and our own feelings of failure. We feel as if we have been marked or that we are being punished. In our anguish, we search for a reason for such a senseless tragedy, and because we are at the center of our child's life, it is all too easy to blame ourselves. It's important to remember that while we are able to control certain events in our lives, we have no power over matters of life and death, nor are we responsible for tragedies that strike those we love.

We are more likely to blame ourselves for a child's death through an accident than through disease. Most parents who watch a child die from an illness such as cancer or heart disease are less apt to blame themselves because they can see that illness as something over which they have no control. When our child dies because of a long illness, we, too, are victims as we suffer through that child's agony.

However, if our child died because of an accident, it's all too easy to feel as if our own decisions were the cause. A friend of mine whose son died in an automobile accident was tormented for a long time by the fact that his son was killed crossing the street after school while a babysitter was taking care of him. He thought that if he and his wife had not been at work, their son would never have died. A good friend or a counselor will remind us that we have no power to control such events and that these tragedies do not represent a judgment against us.

When our child dies, we not only feel a sense of having failed as parents, but we are overwhelmed by our powerlessness, our inability to control events. As parents, we provide the best schooling for our children, seek out ways to fill their leisure time. We believe that money and the hard work which procured it and which can buy the best medical care can also shield us from death.

We react to our helplessness by anger, rage, and despair. In our society the nuclear family has replaced the extended family as protector of children, so there is great emphasis placed on parenting. When a child dies, we feel our impotence. We may also feel angry at all those other parents whose children are still alive and who have no idea of the depth of our pain.

Men feel this sense of impotence very keenly, because many of them are accustomed to bending events in the work environment and are more apt to see their efforts bear fruit in concrete ways. Regardless of the socioeconomic level of fathers, they often see themselves as responsible for the welfare of their families, whereas mothers see themselves as responsible for a child's health and are frustrated at the inability to save their dying child, despite all their devoted efforts. Both parents suffer from losing control.

Marital Strains

If the nuclear family bears the burden of parenting alone, it is also under pressure from the high expectations our society places on marriage. Marriage is the source of so much fantasy about togetherness, about two people becoming one and sharing everything in their lives. When a tragedy such as the death of a child strikes us, people expect that we will draw strength from each other as a married couple. However, quite the opposite often happens. Studies reveal that the majority of marriages suffer serious strain after a child's death. For those marriages that are already in crisis, such a death is a strain that is often too much to bear, causing the marriage to dissolve. After the death of a child, a couple must confront the fact that grieving is a solitary process. Everyone grieves in his or her own way, and the grieving process itself is subject to abrupt shifts as we move from despair to calm and back again.

We expected support from our spouse, and now we find that we are moving through grief in different ways. This can be a devastating discovery. If our child died of a long illness, we may have been able to draw strength from each other during this trying period. After the death, we may not be able to comfort each other or live up to the expectations we placed on each other because each one of us is bowed under his own grief.

Perhaps our husband was always a tower of strength through the hard times in our lives and it is very difficult to understand his inability to be a support while he is grieving. He may resent this expectation. The reverse is true if the wife was always the steadying force through the shoals of the marriage. Perhaps as women we feel more free to express our sorrow through tears and conversation, while our husband is trying to keep himself together in order to get through his day and may resent what appears to him as an attempt to pull him down. Our up days and down days do not always coincide, causing further friction.

In our society men are expected to behave with stoicism and to be silent when confronted with disaster. Therefore, men do not always feel comfortable talking about their sorrow or weeping openly, and a wife may conclude that her husband feels less deeply than she does. The husband may be unsettled by his wife's insistence that they discuss the dead child and talk about their grief.

Sometimes, in our anger and despair, we blame our husband or wife for the death of our child. Especially in the case of an accident, both of us are tempted to point at the other for not being more careful, for letting the child cross the street or go out on a date or move to another city. Perhaps each of us had different parenting styles, one of us more easygoing and casual, the other very protective. In such a situation it is easy to slip into mutual blame and create images of each other that will be difficult to live with. In our need to find an answer to that question which can never be answered, we lash out at our spouse. This is the time to seek counseling.

It is helpful for each of us to seek separate supports or to seek counseling as a family. A woman who is more expressive and who wants to talk about her deceased child finds comfort in talking with friends or with her own counselor. A father may find he needs time to be alone with himself. Scaling down our expectations and demands on each other will help ease the burden on our marriage.

Today, many of us are in our second or third marriages, and the child we lost may be the child we had with our first husband or wife. As a bereaved mother or father, we believe that our spouse just can't understand how we feel, and we may find ourselves resenting him or her. Perhaps we were the parent who did not get custody of the child, and our grief is now overladen with guilt, which can complicate our new marriage. It's not unusual for tension to arise between spouses at a time like this. It is wise to seek the help of a counselor in order to prevent our marriage from deteriorating under such pressure.

Many of us think that while we are grieving over a dead child and trying to deal with the grief of our spouse, it is not a time for pleasure or for socializing. This is precisely the time to be especially kind to ourselves, to find a form of entertainment that both partners feel comfortable with, whether taking in a movie or spending the evening with close friends. Nor is this the time to deny ourselves the pleasures of intimacy in a way that accounts for both partners' feelings.

We may have made a new set of friends after the death of our child, people who know our situation and who are comfortable with us whom we can turn to for a quiet dinner at home or a night out. It's best to plan these moments of pleasure when both of us are ready to socialize. They may seem like small things, but over a period of time they will lighten the burden of our daily life and help us on the road to healing.

Our Other Children

Our other children need our attention and comfort just when we are least able to provide it. We may be so overwhelmed with our own sorrow that we can neither see their needs nor respond to them, or perhaps we think that we are doing a great deal for them, yet our children have a different perception.

Spouses grieve in different ways, and so do parents and children. Younger children will want to know that everything is going to be all right in the family. We should listen to their questions and answer them as best we can, even though we ourselves have no answers to matters of life and death. It's best to be as honest as possible in responding to them. For instance, if we tell a child that God wanted her sister or brother, or that death is like a long sleep, she will grow up feeling angry and distrustful of God or being afraid of falling asleep. Sometimes, as in Phil's case, our children draw us out by their questions. If they are unusually silent, it is we who must elicit their fears and anxieties.

Older children are apt to carry a special burden of guilt over a sibling's death. They remember the times they quarreled or were jealous of their brother or sister or recall feeling anger or hatred toward their sibling and somehow believe that the death of that sibling was a form of judgment upon them. We can help them through these feelings if we remind them that there is nothing wrong with normal sibling rivalry and that there is no connection between any negative thoughts they had and the death of their brother or sister.

Teenagers usually express their feelings in private or with their peers. We should respect their sense of privacy and also accept that even though they are very saddened over the loss of their brother or sister, they are young and may still want to participate in events, such as dances or ball games, with their friends.

Having lost a child, it's easy for us to feel protective of the surviving brothers or sisters. We want to spare our children any further problems and therefore we make special efforts to become involved in their lives. With the best of intentions, we may be placing a burden on them. Real as our fears are for our children, this is not a good time to change our parenting styles.

Above all, this is not the time to place extra burdens on ourselves. We should feel free to weep openly at home, even if we are afraid it will frighten our children. At the best, they will learn that grown men and women feel pain and cry. Perhaps we will even have moments when we share our sorrow. Some friends of mine who lost a daughter have times when they reminiscence about her with her brothers and sisters and times they just cry together. If we were unable to do this in the early months after the death, when our pain was just too great, we can always begin this sharing in the years to come.

One of the difficulties we face after the loss of a child is our reentry into society. People we were once friendly with will sometimes avoid us, but we will be meeting new people. How to respond when people question us about family depends upon the individual. Although in time we will learn to live with the loss of a child, our love for that person endures. Some people are comfortable with saying that they have three children who are alive and one who died. Others think that it's not necessary to share this information in a more casual social setting.

However, the friends who knew us before our child's death may be having a hard time themselves. They don't know how to communicate with us and hesitate to discuss our child for fear of causing us further pain. Although it's not easy, it's helpful to take the initiative ourselves and to talk about our child. Chances are that many of our friends have children of their own and, as most parents, their conversation and attention is focused on family matters. If we are comfortable talking about our deceased child with them, they will feel free to talk about their own children and also about our child. Since there are no social practices to deal with this sensitive situation, they were probably waiting for a cue from us.

One of the discoveries we make in the long months and years after the death of a child is that although we thought we could never move beyond the emptiness, we do survive. Our family life continues and is a source of deep satisfaction. This is a time when we might want to make some important decisions about our life. Perhaps we want to move to a new home or a new town. Perhaps we decide to have another child, or perhaps our marriage isn't working and this is the time to end it. We can continue our lives in new ways and even be helpful to each other despite the end of our marriage.

Although we still feel sorrow over our deceased child, we regain the energy we thought we would never retrieve and discover new avenues for it. A friend of mine who lost both sons and who made his living by farming joined a local theater group and found new outlets in both acting and writing. Another friend changed jobs and moved to a new town. A colleague of mine who lost her only child adopted a young boy of ten years old. Although her adopted child is very different from the brilliant child who died, he has been a source of joy to her and her husband. We can never fill the place our child had in our lives, but we can find new outlets for our emotions and our abilities. The loss of a child changes us profoundly, but as time passes, we find that it is once again possible to invest in life.

Chapter Twenty
THE CONSPIRACY OF SILENCE: LIVING WITHOUT A SIBLING

Jim

I thought that I had worked it out with the help of friends, that I had come to some kind of acceptance of the death, that I had made a place for her in my heart and that I would now be able to move on. When I first felt that was last fall, five months after she died. A student at my university had committed suicide, a young girl I didn't know. But when she died, it was clear that she had had an impact on a number of students in the community. So one afternoon I found myself writing a letter to her parents to say how much I shared in their grief even though I didn't know their daughter, because I too had a sister who died very young and suddenly. I knew how difficult it was to experience something like that. A lot of friends and people who cared about me had helped me to come to understand that you can't measure the value of a life in time, that no matter how much time a person is here, their spirit and the effect they had on people continues. They live on in us. I felt this sense of peace that I hadn't felt in six months. And I felt that maybe that would be it and I would move on from there.

But in the beginning of summer, I started finding myself thinking a lot about it. Every time I would walk into my office, I would sit down to try and work on a paper but instead I would end up going back and looking at letters I had written to her when I was in college, or at things that I had collected after her death: a letter from this guy that she ended up going around the country with, the coroner's report, just reading the hard clinical file. Then I started thinking a lot about this plant that I had in my office that a couple of my colleagues gave me when she died. When I got this plant it became very important to me to keep it alive, and I have, much to my pleasure. It has survived even though I don't know how to take care of plants. I spent most of the month of June trying to write down my feelings about this plant. When leaves would fall off I would think about fall and how we played as kids and how it was difficult to deal with my parents. I started writing a poem about it.

I couldn't write my research, but I would work on this poem. Again I thought I had reached a kind of mini-resolution, but in fact . . . this was really initiated by a note from my mother right after Mother's Day. She sent me a picture of my sister's gravestone and on it she had written, "Mother's Day, 1984." It wiped me out. And that's what she has always done, tried to make me feel so guilty, while at the same time caring about me. I don't think she realized what she was doing. That was the stimulus that brought me back to my feelings.

As July came, again I had done a lot of short-term repression and found myself thinking about my sister's viewing and just about the cold hard shock of seeing her in that casket for the first time, how difficult it was to accept and how angry and hurt I felt.

Maureen

After she died, I went down to the Cape with my cousin, just the two of us. We had a great time. We had a week with a car. My cousin was sixteen. Guys that lived in the neighborhood had come down. We had fun. I got away from everything. I just had fun that week drinking and being crazy. That was the most helpful thing I had, just getting away. I didn't have any wildness in high school, but I had it there and on the weekends when I went there.

My first day back at school I felt like everyone was feeling sorry, was looking at me even though they probably weren't. I felt like they were saying, "Hey, there's the girl whose sister died." People sort of acted like nothing had happened. I felt like, "Why does life have to go on?" That's how I felt. I didn't want to be there. Life at school had just seemed to go on. But for my sister, life was over.

I had this boyfriend. He was three years older than I was. I tried to tell him things, but he was no help whatsoever. He didn't understand, and that was the worst of it—nobody understood.

I certainly was not myself. I was insecure about a lot of things. I lost a lot of friends. At fifteen you build a lot of friendships that you are going to have for the next few years at school. I didn't build a lot of friendships. The other kids had all these common experiences that I missed out on. I was never a bad kid, and I think that was because I didn't want to upset my parents. If they said to be in at 10:00 P.M. or at midnight on Saturday night, that was fine. I wouldn't rock the boat to upset them.

My mother believes that God did it. She believes that God took my sister, that she was such a good person, he wanted to have her near him. She can justify it. I'm not sure I can. I don't know how to. My mother thinks that's how it should be, and I suppose that's what the church does, give you some way of justifying a terrible thing in your life. I'm not sure what I think about it. I think that people just die. Everybody's got their number, and when it's up, it's up. It's fate, and I don't know how to change fate. I never think about how to give it a reason. I don't think there is a reason. That day she died was awful for me. It stunk.

I talked to my parents a lot about it. We sat down a lot. We talked. We cried. It was hard. We'd sit at the table sometimes and say, "Do you remember when . . ." and we'd just start crying. That went on for a while. Then it kind of ceased till Christmas. It was a good Christmas. It was happy, but it was also very sad. Somebody wasn't there. Our family tried to talk about how we felt. But what do you say? Water fills your eyes and you just don't know what to say.

My mother asked if I wanted to see someone to talk about it, but I never even thought about talking about it with somebody else. It was like it was something that happened and everybody had to deal with it in their own way. My mother went and took two jobs and works sixty hours a week now. She hates our house but she can't leave it. She works and works and works, and that's how she deals with it. I feel bad that that's how she deals with it, just keeping her mind so busy that she can't think about it.

My father, I don't know how he dealt with it. He cried, but he would never really say anything.

When we think of the most devastating losses in our lives, we think of the loss of a spouse or child or parent. We rarely see the loss of a sibling as equally traumatic, and therefore sibling loss is not as likely to elicit as much sympathy or understanding. However, the death of a brother or sister strikes at the very heart of our identity and has an important impact on our relationship to our parents.

Sibling identities are shaped in relation to one another within the family structure. For instance, we may have been the more outgoing child, the one most likely to take risks, or the smarter child, the one who went to college. We may have been the sibling who always assumed the responsibility of caring for the younger members of the family. Or the reverse may have been true. Perhaps as the surviving brother or sister we lost a sibling who was perceived as more talented or better looking. We may feel guilty that we were spared. We always ask ourselves why our sibling died rather than us.

Not only do we develop our identities in relation to our siblings, but these relations are colored by our perceptions of parental attitudes toward us. We carry these identities with us all of our lives, so that even if we live in widely separated cities or in different countries, we still perceive ourselves in the sibling role.

Often the empathy we feel for our siblings in early life is strengthened over the years. This is, after all, potentially one of the longest relationships we will have in our lives. Even if we lose contact with each other during our adult years, we still share childhood memories and carry with us the experience of shared family life and critical life events, whether an illness, a move to a new place, or holidays and vacations.

Given that our identities are shaped in relation to each other, we are like foils for each other. We form part of a whole. Therefore, after the death of a brother or sister, we feel within us that missing self. The middle-aged woman who lost her sister when they were both children will always see herself as a sister and feel the loss not only of her sister but of the self she was toward that sister. Although no person can ever replace another, widows or widowers can eventually remarry, but we cannot seek another sibling.

Although the loss of a sibling strikes at the very heart of our identity and affects us throughout our lives, we are apt to receive very little recognition from society. One of the most common experiences of those who have lost a brother or sister is people's silence. We take our cues from that silence and bury our own sadness within it. When I began this project, a number of people came up to me of their own accord to talk about their loss. Some of them were colleagues whom I had known for years without ever being aware that they even had a sibling in their past.

Those of us who lost a sibling when we were teenagers or younger still carry our childhood understanding of that tragedy with us. We also carry our childhood feelings of guilt and responsibility. One woman I interviewed was in her fifties, yet her perception of the death and her own reactions to it were those of a twelve-year-old. She still felt all the ambivalence of her feelings toward her mother's reaction, still felt that sense of abandonment from parents who were sunk in their grief. For many of us the loss of a brother or sister continues to be an unresolved and unexplained event.

It's helpful to think and talk about this loss with our parents if they are still alive or with trusted friends, or even to seek counseling. As we mature, we need an adult understanding of loss and need to express our loss in a meaningful way. One woman I interviewed who had lost her sister fifteen years ago started a support group for people who had lost a sibling. It was a great relief for her to talk after all these years, and she was also able to bring her own experience to help those who were newly bereaved.

As siblings we spend so much of our time together, and so much of our life revolves around our family. Even if we quarreled a great deal, which is normal, we may have been allies against our parents. Perhaps we drew strength from our differences. We may have leaned on the more out-going sister or brother and relied on him or her to deal with our parents. After the death of a sibling we are very lonely. We have lost a peer and an ally and either a buffer against the world or someone we protected. We carry this loneliness for many years.

Some of us miss our sibling so much that we find ourselves taking on some of his characteristics or trying to pick up the threads of his life. A woman I interviewed described herself as the shy and retiring one and her deceased sister as the one who was adventuresome, who always moved in a swirl of friends and projects. After her sister's death, she assumed her sister's identity, taking on her personality. Another woman who had lost a sister joined the organizations her sister belonged to and kept up her sister's friendships. In their own ways, each of these women tried to keep the essence of her sister's personality. "It's been almost twenty-five years now, and I don't think of her that often," one of them admitted. Her efforts to assume some of her sister's traits were a way of resolving her grief.

Losing a brother or sister brings changes in family behavior as well as in family structure. When a sibling dies, we may become the only child and shoulder the burden of our parents' exclusive attention. We may feel that we must not only make up for the loss but be the best person we can for our parents' sake. Some of us think that we should remain geographically close to our parents, whether going to school close to home or taking a job or house in the same city.

Some of us will want to move away from what seems like burdensome parental attention. This can give us an opportunity to strengthen our own sense of self so that we can ultimately forge a better relationship with our parents. In some cases, we may want to stay close to home to help keep the family intact. A young woman who lost both her father and her brother in an airplane disaster decided to commute to college rather than live on campus. It gave her mother and her an opportunity to re-create a sense of family continuity.

The death of a child changes the patterns of coping that families develop over long periods of time. Perhaps the brother we lost was a negotiator on our behalf with either our mother or our father. He was the one who communicated more easily with our parents or who seemed to have more in common with them. Once our sibling is no longer there to mediate we may experience conflict and tension with our parent or parents. For some of us this conflict is so burdensome that we seek relief through an early marriage or by leaving home.

If the sibling who died had an easier relationship with our parents or was more gifted than we were we may feel distant from our parents. This distance might just be perceived, because our parents are absorbed in their sadness and have little energy or emotion left for us. But we might think that they preferred our sibling or that somehow they no longer love us as much. Many people I interviewed told me that their parents were never quite the same after the loss. It is not unusual for parents to alter their behavior over long periods of time and for family coping styles to change. We carry not only our own sorrow over the loss of a sibling, but also the strains of a new family situation.

Strains develop within the family simply because adults and children have very different ways of expressing and responding to grief. Teenagers or young adults still look forward to important events like dances, ball games, and vacations with friends. We are deeply hurt by our loss but still want to continue with our lives. It's very helpful to enjoy our peers and be able to let off steam, but this can create stress with our parents, who might interpret our behavior as forgetting the loss. Our parents might misunderstand, but it's important for us to have some happy times.

If our brother or sister died when we were adults, we are still faced with complex family issues. Jim's mother turned her anger and despair on him just when he was moving through his own grief. In addition to coping with his own sorrow, he had to carry the burden of his parents' difficulty with grieving and his younger sister's silence. If our deceased sibling was the center of the family, the one who invited everyone for holidays and for special occasions and acted as the emotional support for our parents, we may find ourselves trying to fill that role.

If our sibling was married when he or she died, we have to deal with changed relationships throughout the extended family. Our sister or brother's spouse may remarry, yet we still have deep ties with our nieces and nephews. While we welcome the remarriage, we might still resent the new partner, who seems to be replacing our deceased sibling. A whole new family structure must be learned when we have the least energy and when we are absorbed with our own sadness.

A woman who lost her married brother felt that everyone saw his widow as the primary mourner. It seemed to her as if her brother's wife expected everyone to be there for her when she herself barely had the energy to survive. "It's another way of having one's own grief ignored," she exclaimed.

Whether we face sibling's death when we are children or when we are adults, our own death suddenly becomes a possibility. When we lose parents, we lose the shelter from death that an older generation provides as we become the older generation. When we lose a sibling, we are faced with our own vulnerability.

If our sibling was older, we fear our own mortality as we reach their age. Even if we reach the age our sibling died, we are anxious about our health and mortality. A woman whose brother died the day after his forty-first birthday became very anxious as she approached her own forty-first birthday, even though it was ten years after his death. After the date passed, her uneasiness subsided. She needed to get past that point to have assurance about her own future. Remember that these feelings are widely shared by those who have suffered loss and are perfectly normal.

Part Six
HOW WE CAN
HELP OURSELVES

When the waters of loss rose
I built an ark of words,
took two of every part of speech
and rode the flood.

After long buffeting
by wind and waves,
I dangled tentative lines
but didn't touch bottom.

Now the waters have receded:
I feel solid ground under my feet.
My words multiply,
gambol like lambs.

by Ruth Feldman

Chapter Twenty-One
MAINTAINING STABILITY

Phil

It was good to move away. It also heightened our loss. All our friends, the people who were our support system weren't there. After a while you do realize that you're really all alone. You go through a lot of things, but you're just alone. In the short term, it is more painful to lose your place of comfort, the little house on the hill, your friends, and whatever else you identify with. And yet it may be good because it is really saying that you need to start again. It isn't a clean slate, but at least it's a beginning, and you reconstruct yourself with some new foundations. You have to be focused all the time on making sure that the family stays together, and at the same time, you want to be productive in your work. It doesn't ever come back like it was.

We have all heard the expression "Time heals." What really happens is that we heal over time, and since we are all unique, the length of time needed to heal will vary from person to person. For many of us, grief is a new experience. We have not been taught what to expect and how to cope with it. While we all have unique personalities and coping styles, we can help ourselves through the grieving process in a number of ways: by maintaining stability in our living situations, by expressing our feelings, by taking good physical care of ourselves, by the memorials and rituals we carry out for our loved ones, by reading, and also by seeking and receiving help from friends, support groups, and counselors. While we grieve, we need to focus on ourselves as much as possible and be very gentle with ourselves.

The period of grieving is a time of upheaval and disruption. Any major change is stressful and requires a lot of energy. When we lose a loved one, we also go through far-reaching changes in our circumstances. For instance, if we are widowed, we lose a companion, a source of income, our social status, and the friends we knew through our partner.

In order to cope with such a major loss and its accompanying circumstances, we should refrain from making any further changes in our lives. Any decision involving a major change in job, home, or significant relationships adds to the stress we are already experiencing. Even what we might consider a positive change, such as a move to a better job or a more convenient house, is still a source of stress.

When our feelings are in turmoil, we are tempted to seek relief by doing something immediately, such as getting rid of certain things in our home or moving in with an adult child. With the best of intentions, our family and close friends may want to help us change our living situation in order to alleviate our loneliness and sadness. Making decisions about jobs, living situations or mementos in the early stages of grieving can be cause for regrets. Months later we long for a reminder of our loved one or find that our old apartment had many advantages that we were unable to consider at the time.

Sometimes because of our circumstances it is not possible to avoid a major change. There are some guidelines which can help us make the best choices for ourselves: When at all possible, it's helpful to wait a least a year before making a major change. After a year or more has passed following a difficult loss, we will have gained a different perspective on our lives. By then we will have a clearer view of the choices available and the direction we want to take.

If it's necessary to make a change sooner, we can approach that change systematically. For instance, we can look over the course of a typical day or week and determine which elements in our lives such as job, coworkers, home, friendships, and family, should remain constant and which should be different. We can list these changes on a piece of paper and try to imagine what it would be like to live with them on a daily basis.

A woman I know was unhappy with her job and had been considering a change for some time. Her unhappiness increased significantly just when her mother became seriously ill. Although she had already decided to change jobs and had even given notice, she reconsidered after her mother's death. Having familiar people around her was more important than a job change as she mourned the loss of her mother, and her job became more tolerable as the months passed.

When all considerations point to the necessity for a major change, there are ways to minimize the stress involved. Look at the list again and pick out the elements that would remain the same. Then try to imagine ways to strengthen these, such as more frequent contact with supportive people, planning a trip to visit family, or scheduling time to spend at home.

The essence of this technique is to keep as much stability as possible, allowing time to grieve the loss and to adapt to new situations with intact resources.

Home

It is common for a newly widowed person to consider selling a house in favor of a smaller one or to move in with other family members. Some make this decision hastily and without considering the need for stable surroundings. Often it is adult children who press parents into such a move with the best of intentions for our welfare, but often without considering the difficulty of adjusting to such dramatic changes.

Such a move should be carefully considered over a period of time. Even if our home is too large or too far away from the rest of the family, it contains all the memories of the life we lived with our spouse. Moving to another city or neighborhood entails leaving well-established friendships and routines, and getting rid of our furniture and personal possessions. We will have to face the additional difficulties of adjusting to a new family situation and unfamiliar surroundings when we are still torn by grief. Because we all are in different circumstances, we should carefully consider our attachment to our home and the meaning of that attachment.

Adult sons or daughters wishing to take in a widowed parent should also carefully consider the changes involved. The addition of another family member can create stresses as we face the reworking of our daily routine, living arrangements, family relationships, and workload. We might find ourselves in a role reversal as we take care of a dependent, elderly parent.

After all is considered, moving in with our son or daughter might still seem the best. In that case, all the family members involved should talk about such a move and prepare for the new family situation. If we talk about it over a period of time, we can come up with creative ideas of how to live together while allowing each family member to consider his or her own needs.

There are a number of other choices to be explored. Perhaps we would prefer to remain in our own home and arrange for home services or either daily or live-in help. Perhaps we can find housing close to our children, which would allow them to look in on us, leaving us both with a measure of independence. Some widowed persons have opted for shared home arrangements in their towns, group living, or senior citizen housing. Staying in the same town allows us to keep in contact with old friends and former neighbors.

If we are a widowed parent, our children will want reassurance about their lives. Any changes in their daily routines, their living arrangements, or the school they attend will be very difficult for them. Keeping the same friends and the same playtime activities will comfort them. They already feel that their lives are in turmoil, and any additional change can cause them to be fearful or withdrawn. Stability also means trying to keep our parenting style as consistent as we are able. It is as disorienting to children to suddenly become the focus of a great deal of attention and protectiveness as it is to be neglected.

There are some things we can do to give ourselves and our families a sense of continuity and stability, even if we have to move to another home or apartment. We can keep even a small thing that reminds us of our home, whether a picture, an object, or a daily routine. For instance, the widowed father of a three-year-old decided to keep his wife's car in the driveway for a number of months after her death because it was a source of comfort to his daughter. Perhaps we used to have a family outing on Sunday afternoons; continuing family practices such as this gives us a comforting sense that our lives together will remain as they were in the past. What may seem like very small things can actually help us through difficult periods.

There are other reasons beyond financial considerations to prompt a move from our home. After losing a child, we may feel that there are too many painful reminders around the house and neighborhood. If we lost someone through murder or vehicular homicide, we may want to change our home or even move to another town because of the painful memories.

For some of us, leaving behind old friends is the price we pay for continuing our lives. Phil's family found it so difficult to pass the street where their daughter was killed that they gave up their friends and memories of happier times to start over again in another state. However, they wisely made this decision only after many months of deliberation.

If our loved one committed suicide in the house, we might not be able to live there comfortably again. In these situations, too, time is needed to determine what the best decision is. Living anywhere is painful when we hurt so much. Many people have had a suicide in the family and have remained in the same home, finding a way to transform the space as they healed inside. Only time will show what is best in our own case.

Schools and Jobs

Besides keeping our living arrangements as constant as possible, it is wise to keep stability in our jobs. For some of us, the loss of a loved one suddenly brings to the fore an unsatisfactory working situation. However, because we are under stress and feeling deep grief, we should consider the timing of any change we might want to make very carefully. We can use the same technique of appraisal that we used to decide about our living arrangements, listing on a piece of paper what elements would remain constant and what elements would change with a new job. We should consider the nature of our work, the surroundings, our coworkers, and our boss and decide how important each factor is and how much energy we have to make the necessary adjustment.

Allowing enough time to pass is important in making the right decision. Sometimes it's possible to take time off from our jobs to work through our grief and to consider what kind of change we would like. Eric had been unhappy in his job and therefore decided to use the insurance money to take off a few months. He ultimately found new and fulfilling work in filmmaking. However, that decision came only after many months had gone by. A recently widowed woman found that she no longer identified with the values of her career. She realized that she wanted a change but decided to postpone that move for another year until she had sorted out her personal life.

Many of us are satisfied with our working situations and have no thought of change. However, we all need time not only for change, but also for the work of grieving. Often we return to work a few days after the funeral having very little energy and difficulty concentrating. Some people arrange to take a few months off after the death of a loved one. This is not always possible, but it may be possible to negotiate a reduced work week until we feel less fatigued. In chapter 13, Merryl describes how she took time off from her job and then returned on a part-time basis until she felt ready to take on a full-time workload. Anne describes her very gradual return to a full working day. Our fatigue may surprise us, but we shouldn't be impatient with ourselves or try to force ourselves into a full schedule. The profound emotions associated with grieving take up a great deal of energy.

If we are a college student or about to become a college student when a loved one dies, we might consider taking off a semester or delaying our entry for a year until we adjust to our new family situation. If we were an incoming freshman when our parent or sibling died, it might be very difficult to adapt to our new surroundings and new living situation.

Even when we go back to a familiar college setting after the death of a loved one, just keeping up the pace of our courses and our social life is hard. Also, we might find very little support for and understanding of grief in the college atmosphere.

It's helpful to realize that there are many choices we can make, and we can discuss these with a counselor or a family member. It has become a common practice to defer going to college for a year after one has already been admitted, and taking time off might help us to do the best we can when we eventually return to our studies.

If we have lost a loved one when we are adults, chances are that we have responsibility for other members of our family in addition to our workplace responsibilities. We might consider reducing our workload at home as well as at work. If we lost a spouse, we might feel that we have to take over our spouse's chores and responsibilities right away. Anne suggests calling repair people rather than trying to do everything alone. We should make as few demands on ourselves as possible and get as much help as we can in the household. If we lost our wife, we can buy precooked meals or frozen dinners. We can also let our family and friends know if they can help us in any way. Most people who really care for us will welcome a chance to express their concern in a concrete way.

Personal Effects and Possessions

When a loved one has died, sorting out his or her personal possessions can be an unpleasant chore, and we may want to finish this task as soon as possible. We are usually not immediately aware of what these things will mean to us later on. Also, the things that will matter the most to us as time passes may not be immediately obvious. For instance, we might want to quickly dispose of our loved one's favorite chair that is in poor condition. Yet in the months to come that chair might be a comforting memory of that person.

It's best to take plenty of time to make decisions about clothing, furniture, and personal effects. Sometimes the most insignificant objects can be a source of comfort. A young woman whose father died kept his pillow to sleep on. A older woman who lost her mother kept her sewing box in her study.

If circumstances necessitate our disposal of belongings soon after the death of our loved one, the following method is helpful. Make three piles of things. Label one pile *yes,* definitely keep, label one pile *no,* definitely dispose of, and label one pile *maybe.* Store the *maybe* pile in a suitable place and let time pass. After six months, take out those things and reexamine them. By then we will have a clearer perspective on our attachments and needs, and it will be easier to decide what to keep.

Sometimes the advice of a trusted friend or even a friend of the deceased is helpful. When my mother died, I was under great pressure to sort out her things because of the high rent on her apartment. Her best friend helped me with this and gave me some good advice both on where to dispose of furniture and on what things to keep. It was a great comfort to donate some cherished pieces to charitable organizations, because I knew that would have pleased my mother.

Unfortunately, the sorting of personal effects can create conflict within a family. Disagreement over things like a piece of jewelry or a rug actually reflect more deep-seated disagreements among family members. However, there is a way of handling this type of conflict that is simple and effective. Have each family member take a piece of paper and make a list of things he or she would like to have. The list can be rated like this: the first level is things we would really like to have, the second level is things we would like but which are less important, and the third level itemizes things we would like but could do without. The list can also include an explanation of why each thing is important to us. Then have the family meet together and discuss each member's list. Perhaps it's possible to agree on some things but not others. The personal effects that cannot be agreed on should be put aside for six months or so until the family can meet again for further discussion. Bear in mind that decisions about cherished possessions do not need to be made on a permanent basis. For instance, a prized ring could be shared among the daughters of a family for a year at a time. Other possessions could circulate among family members for months or even years.

If, after drawing up lists and meeting together, we still disagree over the disposition of our loved one's possessions, we can call on an outsider—a trusted family friend, for instance—to moderate our discussions. Think of this kind of decision as a process that takes place over months. Both the time spent and the frequent communication regarding these decisions can help us minimize the conflict and arrive at a solution that, while not ideal, at least satisfies some of our wishes.

Relationships with Family and Friends

When we are torn by the powerful feelings of grief, we should avoid making any decisions about our relationships with family or friends. During this time we are extremely sensitive to other people's behavior toward us. For instance, people we considered good friends might disappoint us by staying away from us while we are grieving. Although we might be tempted to break off such a relationship, it's best to give ourselves time. As the months pass we will have a clearer view of the role that person plays in our life. Or perhaps we disagreed with a family member over the disposition of our loved one's possessions. We might be tempted to sever our relations with that person, but we should bear in mind that we often regret decisions made on the spot and at a time when we are in great pain.

The death of a loved one overwhelms us with loneliness, and therefore we begin looking for new relationships that we might want to make permanent. If we have been widowed or lost a partner, it's normal to want to go out again and express the loving, affectionate sides of our nature. If we have been left a single parent, we miss the support of our spouse in bringing up the children. It's helpful to remember that the relationship we had with our spouse or lover was the result of years of mutual adjustment and compromise, and that any relationship needs time and hard work to become fulfilling.

When considering what to do about our personal relations, we can use the same guidelines that we used in making decisions about home and job. It's always a good idea to give ourselves time and to ride through the strains as well as we can. We can enjoy new people, but it's best to leave decisions that will create permanent changes until later.

Chapter Twenty-Two
EXPRESSING OUR FEELINGS

Jim

I cried a lot just after. Sometimes it was by myself, and sometimes it was with a close friend. I remember one of the most important things was to have people be there and willing to listen and not telling me that I shouldn't feel this way, but just listening and accepting that I felt these things. That was very helpful.

I wrote poems in the year after her death. I carry these poems around with me, and at least once every two weeks I take them out and reread them. I've since written other poems, more about my family. It's opened up a way of dealing with my feelings that I didn't have available before.

It's been a year and five months. I still am moved to write. This fall a student died at my university, and I wrote to her parents, as much for me as for them. I just know that having people with whom to share this thing was immensely important.

The way my parents are avoiding her death makes it much more difficult for me. On the one hand, it has forced me to realize that I can no longer avoid certain things in my family. So I've begun to try and express things to them.

I have been able to communicate a little bit more with my younger sister, although she doesn't like to talk about it. I've begun to talk directly to her.

Bill

A year later, after I had met a new lady, the two of us went up to the ceme-tery together. We took a potted plant to plant. We had to dig the hole with our fingers because we forgot the trowel. We planted the plant, and I still didn't cry, because men don't cry. We started down out of the cemetery and Mildred said, "Go ahead and cry." I did. That was probably the hardest cry I ever had.

Anne

By the second year, I was keeping copious journals and that helped me a lot because I was in this private time. I was writing down my observations, lists of alternative actions. I was also working, but this was my personal life. I was like Sherlock Holmes: I knew I had a big case and that I had to pay attention. I wanted to pay attention. It wasn't meant for a woman to be alone and have four kids. Once you've said that you can go on.

Eric

I did start trying to write things. I kept a journal all along. Then I tried to write short stories and then an article. That just didn't come. It felt so forced, so removed. I really couldn't express what I felt. I was quite bitter that no one had ever told me somewhere along the way how powerful grief was, what grief was. If someone had asked what the major emotions are in life, I would have answered, "Oh, well, love, hate, anger." I don't think I would have mentioned grief. I don't think people are taught about that in this culture. I felt I have been a little cheated.

When we grieve we feel many things, including sadness, guilt, anger, fear, hate, frustration, and despair. These feelings are either fleeting or prolonged. We may live with them on a daily basis, or they may arise spontaneously under the most unexpected or seemingly inap-propriate circumstance. Experiencing these emotions feels like riding a roller coaster or living at the bottom of a dark pit.

One of the most important things we can do to heal ourselves is express these emotions in ways that are comfortable for us. Living with these feelings is extremely difficult. Anyone who has suffered loss can attest to this. But when we face them head on, we can move through them. When we try to push them away, they surface later on. When we express our feelings, we allow them space outside ourselves and their power inside us is diminished.

We all have our own ways of expressing feelings. Some of us are highly verbal. Others may prefer a more physical means of expression, such as becoming absorbed in a project like carpentry or in a sport. Some of us are more private and are less comfortable sharing our feelings with others. We can choose a means of expression that is consistent with our own personal style.

Talking

Talking is the most obvious way of expressing our feelings. We can describe them in all their fullness and detail, can give examples, bring up shades of meaning, color, intensity, and nuance. We can even use metaphors for the subtle feelings that are not so easily defined.

Talking about how much we miss our loved one and sharing our memories about that person or the circumstances leading to his or her death can be healing. We need to repeat our story many times, and it will seem as if we are repeating things. Yet over time, what we say and how we say it changes. The circumstances of our loved one's death don't change, but our perception of these events does change as we work through the grieving process.

Some of us are comfortable talking with whomever is available, while others of us prefer talking to a trusted friend. Often someone who is just an acquaintance or even a stranger but who has had a similar experience can listen to us with sensitivity. If there is no one readily available, we can turn to a counselor or a support group sponsored by one of the many grief programs listed in appendix A.

The pain of loss is like an open wound. Sometimes it feels as if no one could possibly understand what that pain is like, and therefore it is risky to let someone know. Choosing someone we trust to talk to is important, but most people who have really lived have experienced pain. It may not have been the same as our own, but those who have suffered generally have compassion and understanding. Talking about our grief helps us feel less isolated and we learn what others have experienced. It's no coincidence that many of us who are grieving learn about the sadness that others around us feel.

Some of us are very private about our thoughts. A widowed friend of mine rented a cottage by the ocean for occasional weekends during the first months after her husband's death. She poured out her anguish and despair into a tape recorder. When we talk into a recorder we express our feelings as if there were someone listening. We can play it back at another time and even have a conversation with ourselves.

Those of us who aren't able to take time away from home can always talk out loud within the privacy of our apartment or house. We can talk to the person who died, to the presence we feel near us, to the picture, or to the grave at the cemetery. Our behavior may seem bizarre to us, but this is not the time to censor or judge ourselves.

Writing Letters

Another way to express our feelings is to write letters. We can address our letters to the loved one who died, telling him how much we miss him, how much we loved him, or how angry we are at him for leaving us. We may not have had the opportunity to say good-bye to our loved one, and even if we did, there are always things we wished we had said. This is a good way to deal with the unfinished business of a relationship.

Perhaps we lost someone with whom we had a troubled and unsatisfactory relationship. We can write a letter saying what we had hoped for and expressing our anger at the failure we endured. Unresolved relationships can haunt us for years. It is never too late to express our sorrow and frustration about our unmet hopes.

We can also write letters to a mythical or real friend, to a family member, or to God. If the letter is addressed to someone who is alive, it would be wise to set it aside for a few days after writing it and reread it before deciding to mail it. Such a letter really doesn't have to be mailed. Its most important purpose is allowing us to pour out our feelings.

Keeping a Journal

Many people keep journals in the months and years after the death of a loved one. A journal can be a daily companion and an impartial listener. In chapter 14, Margaret describes how she kept a journal during the first year after her son's murder. It enabled her to express her agony in an uncensored way. Anne describes the use of her journal as a problem-solver and as an aid in getting through the long and lonely days.

Keeping a journal allows us to record the dreams we have about our loved one and to note all the discoveries and difficulties of living without him or her. These are all significant episodes in our healing. When we reread past entries, we gain a sense of where we have come from, or how we are doing at a certain period of time. This is very helpful since we usually have few ways to measure our progress through the long months of grieving.

It's not unusual for people who have never written creatively to begin writing poetry after the death of a loved one. Jim wrote a number of poems about his sister during the first year after her death. It was a way of expressing his sadness and of exploring the mystery of her death and the depth of his feelings for her. Eric wrote both poems and short stories about his wife. He wrote a story about an unusual and joyous day he had with her when she was already very ill. And Marilyn ultimately wrote a book about her experience with loss. Writing poems, stories, and essays is a good way of giving free reign to our feelings and of trying to express the significance of the relationship we had with the deceased. It's also a way of holding on to the memory of our loved one. We don't have to be professional writers to enjoy the relief and fulfillment of expressing our feelings in this way.

Expressing Anger

Anger is a difficult feeling for many to express appropriately. We may have been taught that it is wrong to show anger, and being mad may conflict with the images we have of ourselves. But after a loss, we often react angrily to irritations at home or work, or to frustrations and conflicts with a partner, spouse, family members, or friends.

Sometimes we are angry at a specific target, such as the doctor, the police officer who informed us of the accident, or even God. Other times we experience a more diffuse anger and simply feel rage at the situation we are in. Each of these different types of anger calls for different expressions.

In the early weeks and months after a death, our anger may be directed at the nurses, clergy, paramedics, or anyone involved in or present at the time of death. Though we can help ourselves by expressing these feelings to someone who will listen or by writing a letter, it isn't always helpful to confront those who are the targets of our rage. If we are considering action, such as writing a letter of complaint, we should allow some time to elapse before doing it. If we are considering serious action, such as a lawsuit, it is very important to give ourselves enough time to heal. A lawsuit will serve to refresh all the circumstances of the death and the accompanying pain. One must feel strong enough to go through with sustained action of that kind.

We are also angry at the person who died and abandoned us. A woman whose lover died went to his grave and screamed at him for leaving her. If God is the target of our wrath, we can express that feeling by talking out loud or in letters or in a journal. No matter how much we loved the deceased, it's normal to be angry at him or her. And no matter how religious we are, it's also normal to be angry at God for allowing our loved one to die.

Anger is not always expressed satisfactorily by just talking or writing. Often our rage requires a stronger expression. Instead of talking, we can scream or yell. Many people find it helpful to scream in their cars, especially on long trips home from work or in a traffic jam.

Exercise is a good release for our wrath. A friend of mine who was widowed went to an aerobics class every morning when the children had left for school, just to work off her anger. We can clean the house, clean out a desk or a closet, wash the walls, or rake leaves. Sometimes it takes very vigorous activity to get at our rage. It can be helpful to pound a pillow or even use a bat or a tennis racket to hit a mattress. We can do so and yell at the same time. Often after doing this the tension of pent-up anger is released and we are relaxed. We may also find the sadness that was held back by our anger.

When we are angry at someone close to us, whether a family member or a friend, we should carefully consider how to deal with this feeling. Often this wrath is aroused by some circumstance around the death or disagreements around the funeral arrangements, wills, or estate. Maybe we are angry that the person did not fulfill our expectations for help or empathy. We may be so distressed that we are inclined to do something that will sever the relationship. Such a situation merits extra consideration.

Though we may feel hurt by and upset at our family or friends, we cannot be aware of how important a relationship will be to us when we have reached the other side of grief. Our perspective will be quite different then. Meanwhile, we can relieve our pain by talking with a trusted person. Perhaps we will decide that we need some distance in a particular relationship for a time. However, severing a relationship may cut us off from a nurturing resource for the future.

Expressing Sadness and Guilt

The most obvious way to express sadness is through tears. Tears well up when we remember our loved one, or hear a song, or see something our loved one liked, or for no apparent reason. Tears come at what seems like the most inappropriate time.

We may have been taught that adults don't cry or that men don't cry. But we should allow plenty of space for our tears. Men are just as entitled to shed tears as women and suffer the loss of a spouse, child, or sibling as keenly. Tears are cleansing. Some of us prefer to go to the cemetery and cry, or to read old letters, or to cry in the privacy of our rooms or during our daily commute. Some of us prefer to cry with a close and trusted friend. Although Bill had some strong ideas about male behavior, the fact that he was able to cry at his wife's grave and in the presence of his new friend was a turning point for him. He was then able to go on to new interests and a new life. Eric and Jim and Christian found crying a great relief, whether they were with friends or by themselves.

Some men consider weeping as a sign of weakness or as shameful and men are urged to "be strong." Yet tears are not a sign of weakness. On the contrary, they are the source of our strength and the wellspring of our joy. If we are able to cry, then we are also capable of laughter.

We may think that weeping is appropriate only in the early months after our loved one's death; however, many of us will be caught by surprise and find that the tears well up months or even years down the line when an event or a familiar landscape suddenly reminds us of our loved one. Someone else's tragedy may even remind us of our own.

A widowed friend of mine was attending a skating party for fathers and daughters at the local rink. When she saw the fathers glide out onto the ice holding their daughters' hands, she had to leave the bleachers so she could go out and cry. Afterward, she felt relieved. Trying to push away our sadness doesn't mean that we get rid of it. Our unexpressed sadness haunts us and will surface when we least expect it.

Guilt is a very difficult emotion to deal with. Our guilt is especially strong if we are parents who lost a child, if we lost a young sibling, or if we lost a loved one through suicide. We feel guilty for having done things or not having done things, for having been there or not having been there, for actions done or not done years ago.

Maybe we spent months by the bedside of a very sick child, parent, or friend and were out of the room just when that person died. We feel guilty that we were not present at the time of death, even though we gave ourselves wholeheartedly to that person. We feel guilty if a parent or child died when he or she was in another city. We feel responsible if our relationship with our loved one was troubled.

If we express our guilt to friends and acquaintances, they often reply, "Oh, don't feel guilty." But that doesn't take the feeling away. A woman whose husband committed suicide reflected a year and a half after the death that the best resources she had were those few close friends who listened to her say, "If only . . ." over and over without judging her. When she did finish, her friend reminded her of all the ways she did care for her husband and how she could not have been responsible for what he did. Her friends heard her out before they responded, and they let her repeat her guilt feelings without admonishing her.

If we do not have such supportive friends, we can turn to a counselor or find a support group, where it's all right to express feelings of guilt. If these are not available, we can write about our anguish. We can list all the things we feel guilty about, all the things we didn't do and that we wished we had done. Then we should be sure to make a list of all the things that we did do that were caring or helpful or loving toward the person who died. Referring to these lists from time to time gives us a sense of perspective.

It's not very useful to think of guilt as being justified or unjustified. Guilt is a feeling. It keeps us attached to the person we lost, and we need to feel it for a period of time. Once we have expressed it for as long as we need to, we can let it go. We can live for a long time with a sense of responsibility for an action, but that does not necessarily mean feeling guilty about it. There will come a time when we will be able to gain a more objective view of our loved one's death.

Expressing Despair

Some of us find our religious beliefs strengthened by the death of a loved one, but others view the death as a challenge to our faith. We think we were abandoned because our prayers were not answered, or we may question the existence of a benevolent God, and our whole structure of meaning is called into question. Even the most devout followers of religious faiths experience hopelessness after the death of a loved one. Those of us who have lost someone through murder are especially apt to feel that things will never be all right again. But this is a normal feeling and we will move through it.

These thoughts are very difficult to hear, and our friends may not be able to listen to us. We can talk to a counselor or turn to a support group where we will find others who have had similar experiences and who will not be threatened by our feelings.

One way we help ourselves during the weeks and months of anguish is to create positive visual images through relaxation techniques. To do this, we will need a place where we can have solitude and quiet. This can be our car, if we live with a number of people, or the privacy of our bedroom. Relaxation begins by sitting quietly with our eyes closed and paying careful attention to our breathing. As we breathe, we can tense and relax each muscle in our body from our toes to our neck. Once we begin to feel our tension ease, we start counting as we hold our breath. For instance, we count to five for each time we inhale and exhale.

As we become more and more relaxed, we can think of positive images. Some call up the image swimming past an obstacle, or swimming across a pond. Others see themselves skiing or walking or even sailing past that obstacle. Still others imagine climbing up a fireman's pole, reaching above difficulty. Each one will be comforted by a certain type of image. As we relax, images appear in our mind spontaneously, and we may feel as if we are being lifted out of ourselves. Both the breathing exercises and the conjuring up of images are relaxing. It's helpful to do these exercises for at least ten minutes and once a day if possible.

Throughout the day, we can call up those images whenever we feel despondent. Gradually, we may gain a sense that we can move through the tunnel of our pain.

Many people find it helpful to record feelings of despair in letters or a journal. In chapter 14, Margaret recounts how she recorded the painful weeks and months after her son's death and her deep sense of hopelessness. Three years after his death she reread those journals and charted the distance she had covered. From feeling utterly without hope she had regained the energy and confidence to begin a new project of victim rights advocacy.

The loss of hope is frightening for those of us who have lived with the view of an orderly universe. However, those who face this feeling and allow themselves to experience it come through with a new sense of life's meaning.

Chapter Twenty-Three
COPING WITH DAILY LIVING

Anne

Have everything taken care of. Take that time of your life and realize only once is this big thing going to happen to you. Take every cent you have and have things done for you. Have someone clean your house and do your garden. Don't take the offers of your friends to fix your pipes and do that stuff because it involves you in a whole thing that holds you down. I called the plumber and paid retail and made sure that the driveway was shoveled. Spend the money. I don't care if you only have $10,000 left, take care of everything so it's smooth. What you have to deal with is this big thing. That's big enough. I don't say don't take from other people because it's bad, but because you won't know if you're gaining in strength. You won't know if you can handle your house. You won't know until you try and it's working and your kids see that it's not done by everyone else's fathers. When they say they want to do something, make a list and tell them what it is. The ones that would really help, will. Pay the lawyers, pay everyone, and then you'll be taken care of. You're not being taken care of anymore, and you'd better well take care of yourself, because you might not find out that you can.

Do everything for yourself that you can. Buy yourself presents, personal, lovely things. I think going on a trip is good.

Don't look at the whole picture. Look at the next thing you're going to do. Don't say, "My husband is dead. I have four kids, and how am I going to pay for college?" You can't do ten things at once. Do one thing. That's all you can do. It's brought me into a whole new place.

Widows should know this, look forward to certain things. Value in a special way people you meet for the first time after your husband dies. Don't have this view of you as being part of a past. You're you because you're you. Seek something new, not widows of the world unite, but take sailing lessons. Mrs. Widow, you won't believe how special you feel when you strike up a friendship at the office. You don't have that much self-confidence at first because such a big bad thing has happened to you that you might think of yourself as diminished. It isn't true. It's nice to look forward to meeting someone new. Even if you don't try to, you do as time goes by. It's a blank notebook, like the beginning of school in September. Don't say, "Oh, I shouldn't think that; oh, I wonder if a man will like me; I shouldn't think of going to Paris." There are some changes from death that are not negative. Now you can do damn well what you please. Ask yourself, What can I do that's new, Who can I meet who's new?

Eric

I went to the Boston Film and Video Foundation after Diane died. I took a workshop there. I took the summer off because I had Diane's insurance money. I was fortunate not to have to work. I thought, "What I am really interested in is grief, and that's what I know something about." I also thought, "People are going to think this is morbid, but I'm going to propose it to the Newton Television Foundation anyway." I did a year later when I saw a notice for a competition. I called them, and they said, "It sounds good, When do you want to start?"

The documentary felt good. I thought, "Here's something new that I can learn." It is a kind of compensation. It's the only thing I have done that's valid since Diane died. Her death took a great toll on my self-esteem. It takes a lot to crawl back. The documentary made me realize that there is something I can do.

It was broadcast May 1, 1985, two years after Diane died. You become a believer after these kinds of things.

After a loss, it is very difficult to manage the routines of our daily lives and to muster up the energy for all the things we are used to doing. But remember that we don't have to keep up the same pace or shoulder the same burdens after the death of a loved one.

We can let go of some of our responsibilities while we are grieving in such a way as to avoid a loss of self-esteem. Many of us see ourselves in relation to our jobs or our roles within the home. We think we are less worthy if we are unable to be as active as usual. But we cannot be the person we would like to be if we are fatigued and overwrought. It's all right to focus on ourselves while we are grieving.

Following are some suggestions that many people have found useful, but don't forget that each one of us is unique, and it's important to find ways of coping that are comfortable for us.

Eating and Sleeping

Many of us change our eating habits when we are under great stress. We eat less than usual, more than usual, or turn to different kinds of food. Minor changes won't have much effect on our health or require special attention, but if we have been unable to eat as much as we need over a period of time, there are a number of things we can do to still get the proper nutrition. We can try eating small amounts more frequently, perhaps six times a day. We can ask our pharmacist for a good nutritional supplement, usually a powder to mix with milk or other liquid, and we can get a good stress-formula vitamin as a supplement. If we still aren't nourishing ourselves properly, we should see a physician.

If we begin eating too much junk food, we can also benefit from the nutritional supplements mentioned above. If we overeat to a great extent, we must vary our activities so that eating doesn't become a major focus of our day. However, if we gain weight, we shouldn't berate ourselves for the gain. That won't help our self-esteem. We can live with it for now.

Our sleeping patterns are frequently disrupted when we are grieving. Some of us can't sleep during the night, sleep very little, or awake several hours earlier than usual. Lack of sleep or diminished sleep leads to fatigue, stress, and a low tolerance for the irritations of work and home.

There are a few techniques that will bring us relief when our sleep patterns are disturbed for a period of time. We can take naps whenever possible during the day or in the early evening when we feel tired. We can also take extra periods of rest from our activities and responsibilities. Even if we are unable to sleep, leisurely rest can be restorative and can help us relax enough to be able to sleep. Sometimes a nature walk or simply curling up and listening to music has the same effect as sleep.

Sometimes we have difficulty falling asleep at night, or wake up during the night and are unable to go back to sleep. If this disruption is caused by anxiety or tension, we can use some simple relaxation techniques. We can progressively tense and relax each muscle in our body from our toes to our neck until we feel totally relaxed, or we can try some simple breathing exercises such as focusing on our breathing and counting to a certain number each time we exhale and inhale. We can also play music that comforts and relaxes us. If sleep just won't come, it's best not to fight it. Pick up a favorite book and plan for a rest period during the day.

It's not unusual to dream about our loved one, especially in the early weeks and months after the death. If our loved one had a painful death, we often replay these events in our dreams. In the solitude and darkness of the night, our fears are heightened. One way to cope with a dream is to have a notebook handy. Describe the dream and the feelings that the dream aroused. By writing it down, we place it outside ourselves and can relax. Our dreams will change over time. In the early months we may have more troubling dreams about our loved one's illness or well-being. As time passes, our dreams change and tend to become more comforting.

Care of Our Health

Because grieving is so stressful, it's important to take good care of our health. If we develop any symptoms which concern us, we should see a physician without delay. Even if we are feeling all right, it is helpful to have a check-up just to give ourselves peace of mind.

It's not unusual to experience symptoms which are similar to the disease that our loved one had. Many of us worry that we have or will develop the same disease. When my mother died of a heart attack, I was certain that I would develop heart disease, even though I had no rational basis for my feelings. Our physician happened to be an older and very understanding person. He looked at me and said, "Just because your mother died of a heart attack doesn't mean that you are going to have a heart condition."

Many physical symptoms are associated with grieving, including chest pains, shortness of breath, tightness in the throat or chest, dizziness, and disorientation. These are probably the effects of stress, but, we should do our best to take good care of ourselves and see a physician if we are at all concerned.

Exercise is an important way to assure our physical well-being, especially when we are under great strain. However, there may be times when we just don't feel like exerting ourselves. If that is the case, it might be better to try some mild form of exercise every day, like walking, or join a more structured program, which many health clubs offer. A structured program doesn't have to be strenuous and it will provide us with motivation and put us around other people.

While we are grieving we need to be especially cautious about the use of alcohol or drugs. Our doctor may prescribe antidepressants or tranquilizers, and these help the symptoms for a time. But they will not be helpful when we are ready to face the feelings of grief and cope with them. These drugs should not be prescribed only for grief. If our doctor does prescribe them, we should ask the reasons for the prescription or seek a second opinion. If we use drugs to help ourselves fall asleep or to feel calmer, we should limit their use to a certain period. We can monitor their use and regularly question our need to continue them.

Turning to alcohol as a way of numbing pain can also develop into a habit that might become difficult to break. Just like using antidepressants or tranquilizers, using alcohol will prevent us from facing the feelings of grief and dealing with them. Like drugs, alcohol covers up feelings. The resolution of grief can happen only when we allow ourselves to experience those difficult feelings as fully as possible.

Caring for Ourselves

Besides paying careful attention to patterns of eating and sleeping and to our health, there are many other ways we can care for ourselves. Grieving takes up lots of our energy and is very fatiguing. Losing a loved one diminishes our self-esteem. We need to be good friends with ourselves.

When we grieve, we have both good and bad days. On a relatively good day we can do this simple exercise that will help shore us up over the weeks and months: We can make a list of twenty things we like to do or twenty things we can do to be good to ourselves. These can be hobbies, special interests, or projects we have wanted to do but have postponed.

They can be simple treats like buying flowers or going to a ball game. Several items should be simple and should require little planning and energy. For instance, many of us find that being in a natural setting is a restful, healing experience, whether walking by the ocean or in the woods, or simply lying on the grass.

Each day, we can choose at least one item from our list. We can select whatever feels right for that day. It's important not to judge or censor ourselves for what we decide to do with our time. Reading a favorite book for an hour or listening to music is a good way of taking care of ourselves.

This is also a time to think of doing the things we have always wanted to do but postponed because of other responsibilities. Perhaps we have always wanted to take a trip to another state or another country. We might not be able to fly to California or to Paris, but we could arrange a weekend with a friend or by ourselves. We might have dreamed of learning a new language or acquiring a new skill. As Anne suggests, this might be the time to take sailing lessons or look for a new pastime.

This can be a good time to meet someone new. Often when we lose a loved one, we receive sympathy and support from people we knew only slightly, whether from the office or from the neighborhood. In chapter 13, Merryl describes a new friend at the office who reached out to her and who was a very important support to her. Anne suggests meeting someone new. Some of us have a tough time meeting new people casually and would prefer more structured opportunities through organizations or church socials. Everyone has his or her own timing for moving through grief. We alone know when it's time to resume social activities. As Anne points out, these things not only help us through our grief, they help us look forward to the future.

Maintaining a Schedule

It's a good idea to maintain a regular daily schedule or routine after we have lost a loved one. This won't be an issue if we continue working or if we have the same responsibilities at home, but, if our lives are greatly changed after the death, we may feel more secure with a regular schedule of duties or activities.

If our lives at home or at work are largely unstructured, we may want to take time either by ourselves or with someone's help and write out a schedule for ourselves. Even one major activity during the day can focus our energies. Meeting someone for coffee in the afternoon or taking a walk to the library can help get us through the day, as Eric describes in chapter 18.

Making a list of activities for the day gives us a place to refer to and to check off accomplishments. It's best to avoid crowding our schedule. Grief is extremely tiring and we will most likely be able to do much less than we are accustomed to. Even a simple outing might tire us.

Balancing Solitude and Activity

Generations ago it was customary for the bereaved to withdraw from society for a period of time. It was widely felt that people who had suffered loss needed time to heal before reentering society. When a loved one dies today, we are relatively free to arrange our periods of privacy and sociability. We might find periods when we feel like spending our time alone and periods when we wish to do things with friends or family. We can examine our daily or weekly routines and see if our schedule allows for a comfortable balance.

If we have a great deal of responsibility at home or at the office, or both, we will need to structure both the space and the time to be alone. We can look for ways to incorporate that private time in our daily or weekly schedule. It can be as simple as extending our commute on the way home from work so we can be alone in the car to cry or think. A widowed friend of mine scheduled a weekend away for herself without the children once a month.

After the death of a loved one we may not feel at ease at social gatherings. There are a number of ways of dealing with our new sensitivity to social situations. A widow who felt uncomfortable going to parties by herself began her reentry into social life by attending some events with her best friend's husband. A widower who disliked attending weddings and large social gatherings alone found a friend in his bereavement support group who was willing to accompany him.

Some of us would rather not attend social functions. When it is a matter of obligation such as a wedding or graduation, it's always possible to make a brief appearance and then to leave quietly. Often we feel uncomfortable with large family gatherings during the holidays or at special events. Some people have found it easier to go away during the holidays in order to have a quieter celebration. These occasions can make the pain of our loss more difficult, so we should feel free to make a decision that feels appropriate for us.

Just the opposite may be true for others of us. We might have too much time alone. There are a number of ways to be among people: We can go to a park, read in the main reading room of the library, or attend a lecture or concert, take a course, or we can join a club or a support group.

Manageable Pieces

When we are grieving, we sometimes tend to take on difficult problems. We ask ourselves, "How will I ever manage the house alone?" or "How will I ever love someone again?" or "How can I bring up three children alone?" These kinds of questions loom very large and cause us to become discouraged. As Anne suggests, it's better to do one thing at a time and to concentrate on manageable problems, such as arranging transportation for the children, for instance. Big questions do not and probably cannot have ready answers today. It is more helpful to focus on the present or on this very moment and let go of six months from now or a year or five years from today. It's enough to face each situation as it comes and to do the best we can to take care of ourselves. When we do focus on ourselves and let go of our worry, we usually find that those big problems fall into place.

Chapter Twenty-Four
SUPPORTS

Eric

It takes a while before you can be part of a social process. I did find a group, and some of us still see each other. I had been with myself during the summer. When I found the group it was a great relief.

Marilyn

Some limited reading was helpful. Books that helped me were those that talked more philosophically about how we deal with tragedy and loss; that gave me some clues as to how other people met their tragedy, lived through it, and fended off the assaults of people who were not understanding and sympathetic.

One of the things I found helpful was reading about other people's reactions to those around them, so I knew that some of the anger I felt toward people who were not understanding was a normal thing to feel. I have gained some ways of dealing with people that say such things as "It's all for the best. You don't know that now, but you will someday." I think I would say now, "I just don't feel that way."

Two kinds of reading helped me immediately after my first loss when I was sick and actually bedridden for a while. One was just imaginative literature that took me out of myself. I thought at first that I wouldn't be able to turn my mind to anything. The other was books that talked about loss in general. I didn't want to read things that talked about specifics of other people's losses, because at that point, I wanted to have hope that I would succeed eventually. Reading about other people who had all different kinds of pregnancy problems made me feel more overwhelmed and made me think, "Well, maybe I'll run into that wall next time."

I did go through counseling immediately after the loss, and we are continuing now so that the counselor is ready to deal with our adoption issue. That was tremendously helpful. The counselor was also very helpful in teaching us to accept our responses and to communicate them to people so we could fend off unhelpful comments.

Phil

One of the things that helped was that we met a psychologist who met with us hours before Jenny died and told us what was going to happen. He invited us to come and see him, and we did, and continued to see him for months. Even after we moved we did. We went as a family a couple of times and as a couple most of the time. That was important because you never grieve at the same time. You bump up against each other, and one of the things he was trying to do is to make sure that we came out of this together.

It wasn't just professional help. This man really had sensitivity and experience. I occasionally still call him. I value him as a person.

We don't have to be isolated with our grief. In fact, the more support we have, the better we are able to express our grief and heal ourselves. Support allows us to be ourselves without being judged or admonished. It lets us express who we are and what we feel no matter how difficult those feelings arc. It lets us know that we are not alone and that others have or are experiencing pain.

Support comes in many different forms. It comes from people close to us such as a spouse or partner, a family member, or a friend. We can also receive support from coworkers, neighbors, and acquaintances, and from our hobbies and interests. Most importantly, we can support ourselves in caring for ourselves and making room for our needs.

Supportive People

Some of us have a supportive spouse or family member who listens to us and understands our grief. However, chances are that our family members are also grieving the same loss. Since we all grieve in different ways and since we all expect support from each other, we might experience great strains in our relationships.

In these circumstances outside supports are of great help. Also, if we have only one supportive person or someone we see only infrequently, other supports are very welcome. Surprisingly, it is often the casual acquaintance or even a stranger who has been through a similar experience who is the most helpful. When my mother died, some of my closest colleagues withdrew, yet someone I knew only in passing wrote the most helpful letters and called me from time to time. She had suffered a great deal in her life and knew how to respond to someone else's pain.

We are looking for just that, someone who affirms our experience and serves as a model for us. One of the best places to find such people is in a support group.

Support Groups

There are many bereavement support groups around the country. Some are independent groups formed by concerned people and others are part of national or international networks. Some are focused on a specific population group, such as widowed persons, bereaved parents, or those who have lost loved ones through suicide. Some groups are general bereavement groups. Appendix A lists some major bereavement support groups and gives a brief explanation of how to contact them. We may find more than one group in an area. It's all right to explore and try out different groups. It's also best to attend more than one meeting to see if we feel comfortable in that setting.

While there are variations from one support group to another, they all have common elements. These are self-help groups, a place for people to come together and talk about their issues, feelings, and concerns, and to receive support from one another. It is comforting simply to know that there are others who are going through the same things as we are.

Some of us are used to groups and find it easy to turn to a support group when we are grieving. Others have never been to a support group and wonder what to expect. Usually support groups meet weekly or twice monthly, or sometimes they meet for a series of sessions, such as eight or ten weekly meetings. A meeting commonly lasts from one and a half to two hours.

Meetings at a local bereavement center, for example, are usually run by trained facilitators. They open with a prefacing statement which speaks of the atmosphere of the meeting, acknowledging the pain and sorrow that people bring, emphasizing that talking, silence, and crying is allowed, and requesting that participants give each other space to explore feelings and refrain from giving each other advice. The facilitator asks each person to offer his or her support, to keep everything in confidence, and to leave with the belief that each person can pick up his or her life enriched by the other members of the group.

The group is a safe place for some people, maybe the only place to express feelings of grief and to talk about ways of coping. Participants talk, weep, tell each other about their dreams, and discuss difficulties with loved ones and with marking anniversaries. The participants listen to each other without making judgments.

Sometimes a parent whose child has committed suicide searches for clues to that child's motives, and a participant whose parent committed suicide responds, and they speak to each other almost as if they were speaking with their loved one. Each one of them gains a little more understanding through this exchange.

Perhaps a participant speaks of his struggles and expresses his anxiety and fear. Another participant who has had similar feelings shares her past experience and urges him to be easy on himself. The first speaker's anxiety diminishes and the whole group experiences a sense of comfort. Sometimes a person is totally silent during the whole meeting, yet speaks animatedly with one person right after the meeting has ended. Each member of the group determines his or her own level of participation.

After the weeks and months pass, there are many changes in the participants' feelings. Some members have become calmer and are less anxious and tense. Others speak less of sadness and more of learning to cope with being alone. Another person still feels guilty but is able to tell herself that she is not responsible for her son's death. Yet another finds some good memories beyond those of illness and can even laugh at them. Someone who expressed a lot of pain for the first time can tell a newcomer just how valuable these meetings are and urge him to continue attending.

Members of support groups learn to trust the process, to trust that at each meeting people will be there for each other and that they are helping themselves in ways they may not even be aware of. Each is there for the other in quite a unique way. Such groups have demonstrated the resources we all have to heal ourselves and show that we all have the resilience, the strength, and the ability to reach out to each other and to give something of value.

A support group is not a permanent solution to our grief; it is a help along the way. As we move through our grief, we will come to a time when it feels natural to move away from the group. Some people continue to attend a support group meeting at difficult times, such as the anniversary of the death. This kind of occasional attendance can help us through a slump, even though we are getting on with our lives.

Reading

Some of us are less comfortable with a group and want to have intervals of private time for our grief. Reading about other people's experience can be a very comforting, as Marilyn attests. There are many types of reading that we can turn to: books dealing with loss, personal accounts of loss, and novels. Appendix B suggests some further reading on the topic of grief.

Novels often deal with the most difficult human problems, with issues that many people generally shy away from. A good novel lifts us out of ourselves, as Marilyn describes in her narrative, and we may also identify with a character's experience or discover that a character's expression of feeling matches our own. We come away from novels feeling less isolated, knowing that ours is a common human experience.

Poetry can be a source of comfort while we are grieving. Poetry deals with our deepest feelings and contains images and metaphors expressing emotions we cannot describe. We can carry poems with us and take them out when we need comfort. In chapter 29, Anne tells us how she memorized poems and repeated them to herself when she wanted solace.

Professional Help and Therapy

The stresses created by grief are greater for some of us than for others. In especially difficult circumstances we might want the help of a professional therapist.

Sometimes our relationship with a spouse or partner after the death of a child is riddled with tension. We judge each other's behavior surrounding the death or have expectations that neither can fulfill. Relationships within our family might be strained if we lost a key member, such as a parent. It is not unusual for children to become estranged after the death of a parent. Often in tragic deaths resulting from suicide or an accident, we blame each other. With the help of a therapist, we learn that each one of us is experiencing his or her own pain, and we learn how to interact with each other in more caring ways.

Some of us are isolated because we just moved to a new town or because we are estranged from our families or because we live at a great distance from both family and friends. We may have very few close friends, or perhaps our friends and acquaintances are unable to meet our needs as we are grieving. When we are without regular supports, is a good idea to find a therapist who can be an ongoing presence for us.

A local woman found herself very isolated after her twenty-year-old son committed suicide. She had been divorced for many years, and her two other sons had chosen to live with their father, leaving her with her twenty-year-old. Linda had no one to talk to about this painful death. Her former husband and her sons lived one hundred miles away. Her parents were unable to talk about her son and wanted all the pictures of him cleared away. It was too difficult for her best friend to listen to her.

When Linda first attended a support group, it was clear that she needed a great deal of help, more than the group could give. Linda was very verbal, very expressive, and needed many outlets for her feelings. She was extremely anxious simply because she was so alone. She very wisely knew that she needed a number of supports.

Linda began to attend two different support groups, one for bereaved parents and one for suicide survivors. She requested a volunteer counselor for one-to-one support and sought out a therapist. She continued to use all of these supports on a regular basis throughout the first year after her son's death. Because of this effort, she had people around her who cared about her and she learned new ways to cope with being alone. From her therapist she learned more about the feelings she was experiencing and became able to express them in a safe environment.

The death of a loved one often brings up the pain and anxiety of past events, perhaps the death of someone many years ago. These old wounds are now as fresh and painful as when they first occurred, yet our friends may not be as sympathetic because the event took place so long ago. The death of a friend can spark the pain we felt at the death of a parent or a younger sibling years ago. In these cases, a therapist can help us face the pain and deal with it now.

Sometimes the death of a loved one propels us toward a new identity. When our parents die, we are no longer children. When our spouse dies, as Anne so aptly points out in chapter 18, we are no longer part of a couple and begin to see ourselves as a single person. These changes in identity are profound, but can create burdensome new responsibilities and cause great inner turmoil. In any of these situations, we should seek a therapist to help us move through our struggles toward a new identity and new roles.

Some of us see therapists as only for people who are "crazy" or mentally ill, but most people are becoming aware that professional help is intended for all of us who go through difficult periods in our lives. A therapist is a listener, someone who cares, someone who adds a perspective that we don't have, someone we can lean on. However, even with the help of a therapist, we are still the ones who do the work of grieving and coping. We simply turn to the therapist for help along the way.

When seeking a therapist, it is important to select someone who is appropriate and comfortable for us. This is very much a matter of individual taste. A therapist can be a psychiatrist, a psychologist, or a social worker. A psychiatrist is a doctor and is only necessary if we require medication. In other cases a psychologist, social worker, or other counselor can usually meet our needs.

When we are looking for help while we are grieving, it is important to engage a therapist who is both sensitive to the issues of grieving and experienced in dealing with the grief process. We can ask for a referral from a physician or trusted friends, or we can call a local bereavement counseling center or support group and ask for the names of therapists. In all cases, it is important to interview a therapist either over the phone or in person to determine whether we feel comfortable with this person.

We should feel completely at ease in a good therapist-client relationship, and should feel that we can be totally honest. The therapist should genuinely care for us and desire to further our well-being and growth. Even if painful issues come up in therapy, the therapist should be supportive and caring. If we have any doubts or concerns about a therapist and about what is occurring during our sessions, we should feel free to say what we think. If we are not satisfied, it is best to seek someone else.

Building Support Structures

One of grief's many lessons is making us aware of the need for regular and varied supports in our lives. Many people who have suffered loss experience a change in their scale of values and come to appreciate just how important personal relationships are. Our careers or our material well-being might have been of primary importance, but after the death of a loved one we often consider creating supportive relationships to be more important.

We can begin by trying new activities. Eric turned his creative talents in journalism and writing to filmmaking. He started by taking courses at the Boston Film and Video Foundation. We can learn new things by taking courses at a school, an adult education center, or at any number of university extension programs. We could also join a club, a church group, or a group focused on a particular project, whether service- or entertainment-oriented.

One of the most common discoveries of the grieving process is our desire for more or closer friends. Yet friends do not just appear nor do friendships grow in a short time. Often the longing we have for friends cannot be fulfilled when we are most in need. But we can meet new people gradually as we take part in activities, courses, groups, or local events. When we take care of ourselves and develop new interests, we will find that people will be attracted to us and we will discover new friends. Many of us who have lost a loved one have found close friends in a support group.

Building supports is not an easy task, especially after a loss. We have to go through some trial and error and some disappointments along the way, yet when we find an activity or a group of people that we can relate to, it usually leads to others. The possibility of networking is endless.

Chapter Twenty-Five
REMINDERS, MEMORIALS, AND RITUALS

Eric

I wrote Linda's obituary, and it ran in the Boston Herald *and the* Boston Globe. *Apparently because of the BBC film Linda had participated in, the wire services picked it up. It ran in San Francisco, which is really bizarre because it's Linda's favorite city and it's where her siblings live.*

Anne

There are certain things I still do. I have to keep pictures of him above my eye level. I still keep them in the house, and I will look when I want to. I know another widow that had a huge portrait of her husband made. Do not conduct your life as if your husband was alive. You'd never have to think again if you're one of those widows. Don't set up a shrine.

The first Christmas afterward I took the kids to Disneyland, because everywhere we went our family and friends would go into states, crying and everything. I knew we had to get out of there. Get out the next Christmas if you've got this problem.

Sue

There are quite a few of her clothes I still have. There's an old friend of mine who said to me when I had on this sweater that my mother had made, "It's just like having her arms around you." It was true. I have her china, which means a lot to me, and I have her wedding ring. If my father had died there wouldn't have been that same connection with the clothes. Sometimes I'll see myself in the mirror or I'll say something that makes me think of my mother.

Reminders

A young woman whose father died keeps his sweater to wrap around her shoulders when she has a hard day. A widower keeps a picture of his wife in his living room. He feels her presence whenever he looks at it. A husband and wife visit their son's grave every Sunday after church. There are so many reminders of our loved ones: pictures, clothing, personal possessions, places. Sometimes a gesture suddenly brings up the memory of our loved one. We can use these reminders to awaken our memories, which can comfort us. They help us to feel less alone and to remember what the deceased meant to us and all the good times we had together.

Pictures are especially comforting reminders of our loved one's features, expressions, gifts, and energy. By looking through albums or even at one picture, we remember our love and understanding for that person. If our loved one died after a long illness, we can use pictures to bring up memories of the happier times.

A woman whose husband committed suicide periodically takes out the album that has pictures of her husband and the family. She gathers her children together to look at the album and to talk about their father. Because she is concerned about the young children's reaction to their father's suicide, she uses the pictures as a way of stimulating conversation about him.

We may also have various objects that remind us of our loved one. Perhaps a gift we once received from them has special significance. After her mother died, a woman rescued an almost-dead purple passion plant from her house and took it home. Within a few days it showed new life.

Although she moved several times and kept neglecting the plant, twelve years after her mother's death the plant is still alive. It symbolizes, for her, an ongoing source of life and a connection with her mother. Jim had a plant that someone gave him when his sister died. He kept the plant in his study as a reminder of his sister and as a comforting presence. The plant even inspired him to write a poem about her.

Many of us keep some piece of clothing or some article belonging to a loved one, such as a watch, a robe, a Christmas tree ornament, or a sweater. Sometimes we keep letters or tapes of our loved one's voice and take them out whenever we feel the need to be with our loved one's memory. My grandmother's cane leans against my study wall. Whenever I look at it, I see her setting off on one of her long walks. It's both a reminder and an inspiration. She never stopped walking, even when her health and vision failed.

A room or a place we associated with our loved one is special. Our loved one's bedroom or a corner of the living room with his or her favorite chair may be a place of comfort. Some of us keep our loved one's room unchanged for a while as we sense his or her presence, and as time passes we rearrange that space as we make changes in our own lives.

We sometimes visit places we shared with our loved one, whether a favorite vacation spot or a place close to home where we walked or picnicked together. Going to these places helps us feel connected to our loved one. But some places make us uncomfortable and awaken painful memories. We might avoid places that remind us of the circumstances of our loved one's death or of how much we miss that person. There is no need to confront that pain. We can take plenty of time to choose the reminders and the places that help us feel connected and comforted.

Rituals and Memorials

There are many rituals that express meaning, celebrate events, and give external expression to a particular reality. Rituals are not only religious, but they can be as simple and ordinary as a birthday party, a Thanksgiving dinner, or lighting a candle with a special intention or memory. Some rituals are common to our whole society and others are shared by a particular culture or ethnic group. These rituals are there for us. All we need to do is to participate and give that ritual our own particular expression.

Some of us visit the grave of our loved one at regular intervals and plant flowers around it. Tending a gravesite is a family ritual in most Latin countries. It gives family members a sense of continuity and connection with the deceased. Some of us like to spend quiet moments alone by the grave of our loved one. We can talk to that person, read a poem, or say a prayer. Others prefer to keep an urn or container for the ashes and put it in a special place. Tending that place with flowers or other decorations can be a comforting ritual.

Some people plant a tree in memory of their loved one. They make this into a ceremony and invite family or friends and have readings. Others plant a garden or create a special spot around their homes. When Maureen's sister died, her parents planted a tree and a flower garden behind their house as a memorial. When the flowers appear each spring, that spot is a source of great comfort to them.

Special days or events are appropriate occasions for a ritual. A birthday, a wedding anniversary, or the anniversary of our loved one's death can be spent in a special way. Because there are no prescribed rituals for these events, we may wonder how to mark that day. Some of us might become anxious as the day approaches.

It's a good idea to plan how to spend that day. If we want to spend the day with others, we should decide whom we want to share it with. We can go to a special place, read an appropriate poem or passage, or share memories. We may simply decide to go out to lunch or dinner with friends.

Some of us choose to spend such a day alone. In chapter 13, Merryl describes spending the first anniversary of her husband's death reflecting while sitting on the beach. Being alone with the memories of our loved one in a beautiful setting can be healing. We may want to have a number of rituals over a few days, spending some of our time alone with our letters and pictures, and some time with trusted friends.

Linda wanted to commemorate the anniversary of her son's suicide. She planned to have her ex-husband and her two sons come to her home for dinner and afterward to join her at the cemetery and share a piece she had written in memory of her son. Her family did not feel comfortable going to the cemetery, but they did come for the dinner. Linda then decided to share what she had written with her support group.

One woman wanted to mark the anniversary of her husband's death in a way that would involve the youngest child. She and her sister and brothers and all their children wrote messages or drew pictures expressing their love. They placed each one inside a balloon and blew up all the balloons. Then they walked to the top of a nearby hill and released the balloons into the air.

A ritual doesn't have to be elaborate or require a lot of planning. Some of us will simply want to light a candle, read a poem, or listen to a favorite piece of music.

A local bereavement counseling center holds a yearly memorial service in a church for all those who have been members of its support groups. The service is held just before the holidays, in early or mid-November. Participants contribute by sharing poems, readings, or passages that have special significance for them. The readings are followed by prayers and songs that are read and sung by everyone. The service is not directed by clergy; rather, the readers are introduced by group facilitators and staff. At the end of the service, the participants light a taper candle from a light passed on from a central candle. As each person lights the candle, he or she says the loved one's name. The church is filled with light as they say a final prayer and sing. After the service is a small reception prepared by the participants. Such services are a comforting way to express the importance of our memories and the relationship we had with our loved one.

Holidays

The holidays can be a tough time, and we might be very anxious as we decide how to celebrate them, especially in the first year after a death. For instance, Thanksgiving usually means a family gathering, but this time such a gathering heightens the fact that a key member of our family is missing. Christmas and Hanukkah are joyful times, yet we may not feel like being joyful or buying gifts.

We can decide how to participate in these events and choose a way that is most comfortable. For instance, we can talk with our family about where and how to celebrate Thanksgiving. Some members may want to keep as much of the family tradition as possible, while others may not want to participate at all. This is a time to respect everyone's feelings and to make it as easy as possible for each other. Perhaps we can lessen the strain on ourselves by buying prepared food instead of spending long hours in the kitchen, or even go out for dinner.

Conversation around the table may be strained, with each one of us wanting to protect the others by not mentioning the deceased. We wonder who will sit in Dad's chair at the end of the table and who will carve the turkey. We can ease these awkward moments by taking the risk of mentioning the deceased and what he used to do. We can talk about who will sit where and who will serve the food or say the blessing. It's difficult to talk about the changes taking place in the family, but once the ice is broken, the conversation will flow with greater ease.

It's important to take plenty of time to plan how we can best be at ease during Christmas or Hanukkah celebrations, knowing that total comfort is not possible. Some of us won't want to decorate a tree or give gifts. Others of us will want to keep these traditions for the children, but not for ourselves. Still others find it helpful to keep everything the same. It's best to talk among ourselves and listen to each other's needs. Then we can set those plans aside for a while and discuss them again as the holiday approaches.

Some of us prefer to take a trip during the holidays either to be alone with our feelings or because we don't feel up to a family celebration. Anne planned a trip to Disneyland with her children over Christmas. Another young widow planned a ski trip with her children. Holidays can heighten our sadness, so it's important to be easy on ourselves and each other.

It's best not to project the first year of holidays onto future holidays. If we are disappointed by an overly simple celebration, we can remind ourselves that each year will be different as time passes. We will have new choices and new perspectives to help us make those choices.

Part Seven
HOW FRIENDS AND COWORKERS CAN HELP

The Funeral

When you need them most, to ask
where to go from here, your hair
growing sparse as February grass,
they've gone, singly or united
under stone in the safest place
where the stranger who cares for them,
pulling a mower behind his International Harvester
to trim the grass they vivify,
setting poison out for mice and squirrels
that mate nearby, for weeds,
knows them better than you, seasons
laboring by like old city buses against the wind
but too far away to disturb
a parent's rest, their reward for teaching you
that being their child's the same
as being no one else, that mourning them's
the final thing you have to learn.

by David Citino

Chapter Twenty-Six
HELPING A FRIEND

Bill

It's helpful to have someone that understands. My new lady knows all about my wife. We talk about it now and then. I don't overdo it. She's been good to me.

Eric

My friends were as helpful as they could be, but if you haven't been through the experience it's difficult. People were scared to talk, to ask anything. I remember being at the beach with a friend and I started to cry, and that really frightened her. People do their best, and I think actually all my friends learned a lot. I did too because I didn't know how to help people in those situations. You give some sign that you care and that you're really willing to listen to them talk.

Phil

Men do have a hard time with this. Some people in general were trying to be helpful and did say the wrong things. "Oh, I know how you felt, I did have my daughter fall and hurt herself." Before long you realize you're role reversing with them. They don't need to say that, just to say they're sorry and just be there sometimes. There were a couple of people like that. There was a friend of mine who was highly sensitive. He always knew. We were friends since undergraduate days. There was another friend who has experienced certain kinds of setbacks and who really tried to draw me out, to get me into sports, going to events with him. I knew it was just a strategy, but I knew I needed it. I knew I needed him to be able to carry the ball for me, whereas maybe I was carrying it for him before. You have some help from family, some professional help, and your friends.

Marilyn

One of the big things we learned was that when it's a pregnancy loss, people neglect to think about the loss to the husband. One of Tim's big difficulties after our first loss particularly was that people would say things to him about their regrets on my loss. It wouldn't occur to them that he had had a loss too. This hurt him tremendously. We even had good friends who would send me cards. He was crying and grieving too.

I think it's been one of my and my husband's greatest difficulties, that so many people do not understand this kind of a loss. Many people who have been through this type of a loss have gone on to have children, and a much smaller number have had repeated losses like we have and finally given up. You find yourself picking out people you want to be near because it's so painful to be with people who don't understand. Sometimes it's all right to be around people who don't know what you've been through but who are generally sensitive people, and you know if the subject came up they would be okay. But some people who know everything about what happened are so insensitive to what it really means to you that it just hurts to be around them.

Sue

For a while my grandmother's sister started writing to me quite a bit, incorporating me in her family, becoming a surrogate figure. Her presence was very important. She and then my mother's sister became very close to me, although I hadn't been in touch with her for a long time. Only the female members of the family gave me that sense of family feeling.

I never heard my mother's father speak about my mother's death. He's eighty-seven years old and never talks about her. It's very strange to go and visit him and not have it be a topic of conversation.

Understanding the Grieving Person

Often we are uncertain about how to act when a friend suffers the death of a loved one. We are torn by conflicting feelings, by deep sympathy for our friend's loss and also by the fear of our own vulnerability to loss. It's normal to worry that it might happen to us and to want to withdraw. We want to see our friend bounce back to his or her former state, because we truly wish our friend to be happy, and also because all of us tend to be uncomfortable with someone who is in deep pain. Finally, we may be so baffled by how to treat the bereaved that we avoid mentioning the death or simply keep our distance, believing our friend needs the privacy to work out her feelings.

Perhaps we think that any mention of the deceased would only cause her pain. We may be afraid of making things worse or uncertain how to respond to such a tragedy. An important thing to remember is that we cannot cause our friend or relative to feel pain by mentioning the deceased; the pain is already there, and it is a heavy burden to carry. By visiting our friends and talking to them about their loss we can actually help relieve that burden.

Helping a grieving friend is not as difficult as we might imagine. We can give solace to our friends and family in a number of simple ways. The most important way we can help is to understand and accept what our friends or relatives are feeling. This may mean accepting that a friend or relative who was formerly a source of great support for us can no longer play this role while they are mourning. It may mean understanding that a grieving person is often torn by the very strong emotions of anger, guilt, and sadness. It may mean taking time to see just what a particular loss means to our friend.

Someone who is in great pain doesn't behave as they usually do. If our friend or relative is a man, we may be surprised at his tears and his expression of emotion. Men have a right to grieve too, even though society expects them to show a stiff upper lip. Perhaps a friend or family member is unusually silent, irritable, or withdrawn. We might think that this behavior is directed at us, but it's only a reflection of his inner turmoil. Our quiet and accepting regard for the grieving person will actually help him to move through his suffering.

Accepting the strong emotions a bereaved person feels means also accepting the time it takes to work through these emotions. A person who has suffered loss cannot return to her previous behavior in a matter of days or weeks. Although we all want to see our friends and relatives happy, there are times when we can help them more by understanding that they need to feel their sadness or their guilt. They want to be accepted as grieving persons.

We may grieve for a friend or a lover as deeply as we grieve for a parent or other member of our family. It's best not to make judgments about whether our friends are justified in grieving for someone whom we think was not close enough. A young adult who has lost a close friend will undergo all of the pain and turmoil of grief and will need the same acceptance and consideration as someone who has lost a relative. Perhaps someone we know had a miscarriage. Because that child was invisible to us, we may not think such a loss is truly a tragedy, but a only mishap. But such a loss is as searing and painful as other types of losses and the parents feel as great an emptiness and despair. Although as a society we tend to overlook the importance of a pregnancy loss or the loss of a friend, coworker, or lover, we can be helpful if we understand that these kinds of losses are deeply distressing.

The narratives have been telling us that one of the most important supports a grieving person needs is to have his or her pain acknowledged and accepted. This means not trying to coax our friends out of their pain, as well as not ignoring that pain. There are a number of ways in which we can do this. One important point to keep in mind is to be ourselves and to act naturally around the grieving person.

What We Can Do for the Grieving Person

One of the most important things we can do for someone is stay in touch and let that person know we care. This can be as simple as a phone call to let that person know that we are thinking of them. People who have lost a loved one appreciate it when friends stop by for a visit in the weeks and months after the funeral. We may be uncomfortable about making such a visit, but we don't have to say anything terribly wise during our stay. Usually a few words expressing our sympathy suffice. Just pressing someone's hand or giving them a hug conveys our concern.

After all the activities associated with a funeral have ended, the survivors begin to feel the full impact of their loss. That is the time a visit or a phone call is the most welcome. When the services are over, we all go home to our normal lives, but the bereaved returns to an empty apartment or to a house with an empty room.

We may also want to say a few words about the deceased. For instance, we might say, "Your mother was a wonderful person. It's so hard to lose a person like that." Even though our friend or family member buried a loved one, that person is still very much alive in her thoughts. She will be pleased to know that others are thinking of the deceased and that others also cared about him. Generally, if we speak just briefly about the deceased, that will give our friend the permission to talk, and that conversation may be a great relief.

Maybe our friend is not verbal and would rather not mention her memories and feelings. We can sit in silence with her. We don't always need words to comfort. Our presence alone is a sign that we care. We may think our friend has expectations about what we should do or say when we visit, so it's best to be open and to take our cues from our friend.

Sometimes just giving someone a hug or holding someone's hand is a great comfort. A close friend of mine who lost her mother broke down and wept while we were sitting in the living room after dinner. She held out her hand so I could hold it while she was crying. She needed to know that someone was with her while those tears were flowing.

However, not all of us are comfortable with someone else's tears. It's best to know our own limits, and if we have a low tolerance for weeping we might do something practical and more active to show our friend that we care. Our friend will respond more to our attitude and concern than to any specific gesture we make.

We can help the bereaved in a number of practical ways too. We can lighten the burden of everyday chores by driving the children to school, picking up the laundry, or preparing a meal. When my mother died, my relatives came from Europe for the funeral and suddenly I had a full house. A close friend of mine made up the beds and left some casseroles in the kitchen. Another friend arranged for a light meal after the funeral. These were simple gestures, but they meant so much to me both because of their thoughtfulness and because such small tasks seemed too much to handle in my grief.

The recently widowed appreciate practical help in the months and weeks after the death of a spouse. We can help a widow with legal matters or with organizing childcare. We can help an older widow reregister the car, get Social Security, or put in insurance claims. If our friend or relative is a widower, we can help with managing the household and with finding childcare. Our friend may have to juggle a demanding job and get his children to school or arrange for their care after school before he returns from work. Sometimes we can just be there to discuss issues concerning children or the household. A widowed person misses not only the companionship of a spouse but also the opportunity to discuss the small problems of work and home.

There are some simple but thoughtful things we can do for bereaved friends, such as bringing a few flowers or a plant, or bringing over something we baked. After a loss people experience dips in self-esteem, and this kind of attention will help them feel better about themselves.

There are a number of less obvious things we can do for someone who has suffered loss. If our friend is a mature adult who lost a cherished parent, just talking about that parent and the place that parent had in our friend's life is helpful. And although we can never replace a person, we can do some of the nice things a parent would do for our friend, whether inviting her out to lunch or to a movie.

We can also help our friend clear out her parent's clothing and personal effects. This is not only a very painful task for our friend, but a difficult one too because she might not be able to think clearly about keeping mementos that might be a source of comfort later on.

If we happen to have a picture of the deceased, we could have it enlarged and give it to our friend as a gift. Or perhaps we have a memento of the deceased that we know will please our friend. When my neighbor's daughter died of cancer, one of her friends had some pictures of the daughter from a wedding party. She had them enlarged and mailed them to my neighbor.

A young adult who has lost a parent will appreciate our interest in their studies or in their job. After the loss of a parent a young person feels invisible or less important. A phone call inquiring about life at school or courses will be very welcome.

Staying in touch may mean calling or visiting on a regular basis. A person who has suffered a loss will feel terribly isolated. Since most of us have very busy lives, it might not be possible to give as much time as we would like, but we can encourage other friends to get in touch. If we are too busy to even make a phone call, we can always send a card or a brief note. Any expression of concern is always deeply appreciated by someone who is grieving.

People will have strong reactions to their loss during holidays, on the anniversary of the death, or on the birthday of the deceased. Sending a note or card on Mother's or Father's Day to a parent who has lost a child is a way of letting that person know that you share the memory of that child and their sense of loss. We can send a note to mark the anniversary of a death or the birthday of the deceased. We can acknowledge our friend's loss as the years pass. While our friend or relative may not want this loss to be in the forefront of her life, as time passes and she heals, there are times when she would like to remember that the deceased and her own pain have not been forgotten.

Holidays especially are times when survivors feel not only a fresh surge of pain but also the contrast between the good fortune of intact families and partnerships and their own situation. It may be a period when we are absorbed in preparations for our own families and partners, but a few minutes of our time can bring great solace to friends.

As the weeks pass after the death, we can very gently draw the bereaved person toward outside activity. A bereaved person won't have the energy, the initiative, or the self-esteem to take part in social events. We can invite them out for coffee or dinner or a movie, some activity our friend would feel comfortable with. For instance, a recently widowed person will not feel at ease at a large party attended mainly by couples. We need to be sensitive to the changed circumstances of our friend and to the fact that the social settings she was accustomed to now emphasize her sense of loss. Phil's friend helped him renew his interest in sports at a time when he was unable to seek out diversion. He knew the kinds of things that Phil liked and used them to draw him out.

When our bereaved friend begins to take part in social activities, we should avoid treating him with pity or dwell on his loss. Pity diminishes a person's self-esteem. It's better to just simply acknowledge the loss and the change in our friend's life and leave it at that. A good guideline both for us and for our behavior is to be ourselves and to treat our friend as a normal person.

We must be sensitive to the grieving person's need for a balance of solitude and socialization. Sometimes our grieving friend longs for someone to talk to, but there are other times when he prefers just being alone. Being in tune with our friend's different needs means letting him know that we understand his need for some private time, but that we are available when he wants to be with us. A friend's need to be alone with his pain does not mean that he is rejecting us. Sometimes we all desire to be alone with our tears and our memories.

Not only do bereaved people undergo great emotional upheavals, they also experience change in their lives beyond the change of circumstances that a death leaves. After the death of a loved one, a person begins a long process of self-discovery that leads to changes in activities and even in lifestyle. As our friend goes through these changes we should be supportive and understanding. For instance, we may be surprised that our widowed friend has begun to see other people in the months after the death. This socializing is not a betrayal of our friend's deceased spouse or partner. Sometimes bereaved friends go through a period of experimentation in both relationships and lifestyle. It's best not to make judgments about our friend's or social efforts. It's part of the grieving person's journey toward a new sense of self.

Being supportive means allowing our friend to change and encouraging new activities and new identities when she is ready. Change is not only stressful but can also cause the person making changes to feel lonely. If we are supportive we can help our friend reach a new and fulfilling life. Being supportive means very simply being available to our friend and accepting her for who she is at any phase of her life.

In chapter 29, Anne describes her decision to sell her house in the suburbs and move to a condominium in the city. This new living arrangement reflected the person she had become, a businesswoman with children who were almost grown up. She was terribly disappointed when her mother questioned the move and treated it as an act of betrayal. A widower decided to move in with a woman he had begun seeing a year after his wife's death. His sons were so upset that they stayed away from their father. It may be very painful for us to see our friends and family change. No one really likes to experience change, but if we understand that a friend or a relative is the best judge of his own happiness, and that the old ways might be uncomfortable, it will be easier for us to face that change.

How to Talk to the Grieving Person

Faced with the enormity and finality of death, we are often at a loss for words. We don't know what to say to a grieving friend. Often we think that we must say something that will "make things all right." But one of the best ways of communicating with someone who has suffered loss is simply to listen and to be a sympathetic and responsive presence.

To communicate effectively with a person who is suffering, we have to know our own feelings. We have to know whether we feel uncomfortable with sadness and tears, whether we feel uneasy if someone expresses anger or bitterness. This will help us avoid projecting our feelings on others, such as telling a grieving person that we don't want them to feel sad or angry. We need to know ourselves so we can be helpful without exceeding our own limits. We don't have to change our personalities in order to be helpful. There is always a choice in how we handle both our communication and our actions.

But what do we say to someone immediately after the funeral or the first time we meet them after a death in that friend's family? The simplest comments are always the best. We can say what we feel: "I'm so sorry." The way we speak means as much as what we say. If we talk with feeling and with sincerity, if we act naturally, we will communicate effectively.

In the first days and weeks after a death, it's best to say little when we visit our friends. They may not feel like talking much but will welcome our presence. A simple hug may be just what they need for comfort. This may mean that we sit with our friends' silence. In our culture we often place negative interpretations on silence; however, it is often not possible to be articulate when feelings are in turmoil. We shouldn't feel that we have to force conversation, nor should we press for details about the death. The best practice is to let the grieving person take the lead.

When talking to the mourner, we must avoid clichés and pat statements such as "It's all for the best," "She had a good life," "He's out of pain now," or "Aren't you lucky that. . . ." We might be tempted to make these kinds of remarks when someone has died after a long illness or in old age. We must remember that when a person had a long life, his friends and family have had that much more time to love him and to build the relationship, and therefore it's very difficult to lose such a person. We must also remember that even if someone died after a long illness, her friends and relatives had still hoped that she would survive. They won't think that "It was all for the best." Such comments cut off communication about the deceased and deny the powerful feelings of grief.

It's especially important to avoid minimizing a miscarriage with such comments as "It's all right, you can try again," or "It wasn't really a baby." The man and woman who lost a child in this way were parents, and they need to have their loss and their pain acknowledged.

We must also not encourage denial about the death. Our friend might desperately want the details of his loved one's death. This is part of the grieving process and is not at all morbid. Jim was very anxious about the real causes of his sister's death beyond her fall and was restless until he had the results of the autopsy. Our friend might go over and over the story of his loved one's death. We should listen quietly without comment and without saying, "It doesn't matter now that she's gone." Our friend is trying to understand the death and is also trying to hold on to the memory of his loved one. It's perfectly normal to dwell on the death, and he will move on to other topics of conversation as time passes.

Comments about God, such as "It was God's will," may anger the grieving person if she does not share our religious beliefs. This type of comment also tends to minimize loss and to break off conversation. A grieving person feels that the world is unjust and may direct her anger at God.

As time passes, one of the best ways of communicating with a grieving friend is to listen without contradicting. We should not tell the mourner, "I know how you feel." We can ask how a friend is feeling, but it is presumptuous to tell someone how she is feeling. It's best to inquire gently and then to listen without either rebuking or comparing. Everyone's experience with grief is unique. To try to compare is to belittle or deny that person's experience. Telling our friend, "Don't feel guilty," or "Don't feel sad," is a way of both projecting our own feelings on our friend and denying her feelings.

This means allowing friends to express such difficult feelings as guilt, anger, and even suicidal feelings. Many survivors of a death express the wish to die themselves after such a tragic event. It is very hard to listen to comments like this, but they are valid feelings. When our friends express these feelings, they are literally putting them outside themselves. Saying them out loud is a way of getting rid of them, while holding them in may cause these feelings to grow.

Guilt is always a very strong element in the grieving process, and our friends should be able to express their feelings of guilt without being contradicted. In the case of a suicide, guilt is especially powerful. The survivors of a suicide go over and over their behavior in a search for understanding and also ultimately to be able to let go of guilt. Sudden deaths other than suicide also cause survivors to feel guilt. They think of all the things they wished they had said or done. We should not deny these feelings and not say, "Don't feel bad," or "Don't worry." As time passes, we can gently remind them of all the good things they did for their loved one, but in the early weeks and months after a death, mourners need to feel their guilt.

Because grieving is a self-reflective process, we may be surprised that our friend, who was always so interested in others, is now talking exclusively about himself. It's helpful to understand that this is necessary and temporary. The grieving person is exploring his new situation, and talking is a way of thinking out loud, of examining those new circumstances.

We shouldn't talk about our own troubles and pain in front of a grieving person. His feelings are so raw that he is very susceptible to other people's distress. What seems like a complaint about a trivial matter at work may feel like an intolerable burden to our friend.

We can help our friends by listening actively, not only by nodding our heads, but by the things we say. We can tell them that their feelings are valid, or we can draw them out by gently asking them questions about what they are feeling. As time passes we can tell them that the directions they are moving in and their decisions are sound. Chances are that they are a bit unsure, and such support will give them the courage to make tough decisions.

Listening has its unexpected rewards. Over a period of many months, I had a number of long lunches and dinners with a close friend who had been widowed. As I listened to her, I responded not only to her feelings but also to her search for new goals and a new lifestyle. Over the months my friend moved from anger, bitterness, and chaos toward the discovery of a new set of goals and a brand-new sense of herself. I felt that I had participated in her unfolding and had shared her triumphs as she journeyed through the dark period of the early months after the death to a new excitement about her life.

Sometimes our friends feel they need permission to talk about the loved one who died, and if we mention that person, it is a great relief. The unspoken looms very large when we are with someone who is grieving. A young woman in my neighborhood lost her mother shortly after she had given birth to her first child. When I met her as she was walking her baby in the stroller, I said, "Your mother would have loved being a grandmother." "There's not a day I don't think about it," she replied. And then we went on to speak of her child and her new home. Acknowledging loss is very helpful to grieving people. They may feel that their pain is invisible if those around them don't mention it.

After those first weeks and months, we should take our cues from our friend. If we have made her feel comfortable and she is secure about our concern, she will take the lead in conversation. As our friend begins to talk about her loss we should avoid pressing her about the future. She is in such emotional turmoil that it's hard enough to handle the present. The months after a death are much too soon to think about the demands of the future.

Some days our friend may want to talk about the one who died, and other days she may want to talk of other things. Grief is unpredictable. A person has a string of good days and then plunges back into a renewed sense of sadness, but this doesn't mean a sliding back or a lack of progress. Frequent ups and downs are a normal part of bereavement.

Helping a friend who has suffered loss can be very simple. What is required are not superhuman efforts, but a quality of sensitivity and caring, listening with concern and allowing our friend to express whatever he or she is feeling. It's also a matter of admitting that in our society, where every illness seems to have a cure and every problem seems to have a solution, there are limits. There is no cure for sadness. However, if we allow friends to express that sadness, to shed those tears, we are actually helping them move through the sorrow. We will not only have helped our friend, but we will also have learned something about ourselves and how to cope when we are faced with similar circumstances.

Chapter Twenty-Seven
HOW TO WRITE A
LETTER OF SYMPATHY

Perhaps one of the most difficult things for us to do after a death is to write a letter of condolence. We might not be able to think of things to say in the face of such an event. Following are some sample letters which you can adapt for your own use. There are a few things to keep in mind when writing such a letter. Keep it simple. Let your friend or coworker know that you care about him and his loss. Make a reference to that loss, and express your own sorrow about the death.

Writing a letter is a way of acknowledging our friend or relative's pain. People often keep such letters for years after the death and reread them from time to time. After a loss we are extremely sensitive to other people's reaction toward us because we are in such pain. A letter may bring more solace than we might imagine.

When a Mature Adult Loses a Parent

Dear Andrea,

I just learned from Doug that your mother died. What a terrible blow for you. I remember feeling that the bottom had dropped out of my world when my mother died. No one ever loves us or knows us like a mother. You spoke of your mother so often and with such love that although I never met her I gained the impression of a wonderful and understanding woman.

I want you to know that your friends are with you during this difficult time. I know just how busy you are, but I hope you will be able to have some time to be with your feelings. I will be thinking of you in the weeks and months to come.

Please accept my sympathy and my deepest concern.

Fondly,
Marianne

When Parents Lose a Child

Dear Joan and Ray,
We were shocked and saddened to hear of the death of your Elizabeth. It seems against nature to lose a child, especially such a young and gifted little person. We know what a close and loving family you are and how tenderly you cared for Elizabeth while she was ill. What a terrible loss for you and for all of us who loved her.

We want you to know that we feel very close to you during this very difficult time and that you will be in our hearts and thoughts during the months to come.

Please accept our concern and our deepest sympathy.

Sincerely,
Julia and Richard

When a Younger Person Loses a Spouse

Dear Barry,
I was so sorry to hear of Evelyn's death. The two of you had such a good marriage and so much to look forward to. It seems terribly unfair to lose a spouse when one is so young. All of us who loved Evelyn will think of her and remember her courage and her talent.

I want you to know that we are thinking of you and of your tragic loss. You will be very much in our hearts in the long months to come.

Please accept my deepest sympathy and concern,

Yours,
Andy

When an Older Person Loses a Spouse

Dearest Emma,

I was shocked and saddened to hear about Alfred's heart attack and death. I know you had been looking forward to his retirement and to some travel together after all those years of hard work. Even though the two of you were very different, you complemented each other so well. We always thought of you as one. What a terrible loss for you.

I want you to know how much Peter and I are thinking of you and that we will be there for you in the long and difficult weeks and months ahead.

Please accept our deepest sympathy.

With my love,
Susan

When Someone Loses a Sibling

Dear Craig,

I was so sad to hear about Annie's death. I know that she had been having some difficult times and just how worried you were about her. I know too that the two of you had had a lot of disagreements lately, but that you were always a loving and concerned brother. You did so much for her.

Losing a sister is a terrible blow. No matter how old we are or if we have our own families, a sister is always part of us.

I want you to know how sorry I am and that you will be very much in my thoughts in the weeks and months to come.

Yours,
Matt

When Someone Loses a
Child Through Miscarriage

Dear Karen and Allen,

I was so sorry to receive your letter telling me that you lost your baby. I wish I had been there to hug Karen and to talk to you both. It's hard for me to be so far away when you are in such pain.

Perhaps the baby wasn't visible to many people, but you were three and the two of you were a mother and a father. You made so many preparations for this baby, but it wasn't just the room and the furniture you chose. She was part of your life, your hopes, and your dreams.

Please be good to yourselves during the difficult months ahead. Take the time you need for your sadness and pain. I will stop by as soon as I return from California, and I will be with you in the time to come.

Fondly,
Martha

Chapter Twenty-Eight
HELPING THE GRIEVING WORKER

Understanding the Grief of a Fellow Worker

Coworkers, supervisors, and employers might not know how to relate to a bereaved worker. It can be hard to balance our expectations of productivity with sensitivity toward the grieving person. In too many cases, the work environment leaves little room for the strong feelings resulting from personal tragedy. Yet a little understanding and creativity can help create a more comfortable environment for everyone.

Someone who has lost a loved one wrestles with many strong emotions, and these occur any time during the day or night, even in the middle of work. The sadness, anger, guilt, depression, and fear a grieving person feels cannot be controlled at will, and while a person may find it difficult to brush these emotions aside, he may also feel guilty or embarrassed if he reveals them.

In the weeks and months after a death, the bereaved person undergoes a great deal of disruption in his personal life. Because of this disruption, he won't seem like himself and will be even less capable than before. For example, a grieving person won't be able to concentrate and may forget small things as well as large things, like showing up for appointments. Because grief affects self-esteem, someone who has suffered loss may not want to generate ideas or try new things. He will be easily irritated at small annoyances, speak harshly to coworkers, or even blow up at what seems like a small matter. A grieving person is usually depressed and therefore displays a lower level of energy and productivity. He also might be absent or sick more frequently.

289

These behavior patterns are not due to laziness or an unwillingness to work, but are a reflection of the disruption occurring in the bereaved worker's life. Chances are that the person is aware that he is not acting like himself and would welcome a chance to talk about how he feels and what could be helpful in his work.

Grief is a major source of stress and will not disappear in a matter of days or weeks. A bereaved person will have some good days and some bad days. She may even welcome work as a way of setting the grief aside for a while. Yet she will most likely still manifest the symptoms of stress in a number of ways. Grief takes many months and in some cases many years to work through.

How Employers and Coworkers Can Help

Funerals, wakes, and viewings are important rituals of leave-taking and are significant events for the bereaved. The worker should be able to participate fully in these events without pressure from the office or plant. In some workplaces this might be difficult to achieve, yet, if possible, everything should be done to assure the grieving worker adequate time off.

Many companies offer bereavement leave as part of their personnel policies and practices. For example, a worker may receive a three-day leave for the death of a family member. Often the length of leave varies with the closeness of the relationship. Many workers use other allowed days off for extending their leave from work. For example, one woman took one of her four allowed days off to attend the funeral of a close friend, telling only her supervisor the exact reason for her absence. Some employees may have their leave extended by the supervisor's discretion.

When coworkers or supervisors attend the funeral or viewing and express condolences in person, this is often a great comfort to the bereaved. During these occasions it's best not to discuss work except to assure the grieving person that she shouldn't worry about the office. For those of us who are unable to attend the funeral, sending flowers or letters expressing our support is an effective way of letting our coworker know that we care about her and her loss. The bereaved often keep letters and cards for many months and refer to them as a source of comfort. What may seem like a small gesture to us may be a source of lasting support to someone who has suffered loss.

Within the workplace, we can notify the appropriate people, our coworkers and those in personnel or managerial positions, who would want to know that our colleague has lost a loved one. Sometimes a department circular or newsletter is the place to mention personal events. Often these notices inspire people to speak to the bereaved person or to send a note. Because there are no common practices for announcing a death beyond a notice in the obituary columns of the newspaper, we might be uncertain whether we should share such news or even how we should do so, but we need to remember that a grieving person feels isolated and even invisible in her grief and will welcome any kind of acknowledgment of her loss.

Sometimes the return of the newly bereaved person to the workplace is a difficult time for everyone. The bereaved person won't know what to say, and coworkers and supervisors may also be at a loss for words. The situation is awkward, yet we can do some simple things to ease the way.

First of all, a supervisor or manager can be in touch with the person to talk about her return. We can carefully discuss the day and time, whether the first day or week will be full or part time, as well as how the person would like to return. For instance, she might want to return to a normal workload and regular schedule right away, or perhaps wants to ease back in, meeting with the supervisor first and taking on a lighter workload or fewer responsibilities. In chapter 13, Merryl describes how she worked only a few days a week when she returned to work and also how she was able to discuss her sadness and low energy with her secretary. In some circumstances, it is appropriate to arrange for a different set of responsibilities or even a different job description for a newly bereaved worker.

On the other hand, it can be just as difficult to return to work after a funeral and to have everyone come up to one's desk and express condolences as it is to have everyone act as if nothing had happened. While silence isolates the grieving person, being overwhelmed with condolences can make her feel pitied. As coworkers or managers we can be sensitive both to the person's need to feel useful in the work environment and to her need to have her loss acknowledged. In these circumstances a touch, a look of understanding, or a simple note can be comforting. When it comes to tasks, we should avoid the extremes of being overly protective or too demanding.

As the weeks and months pass, things will have returned to normal at work, and we may easily forget the bereaved's grief. Perhaps it is not evident. Yet this is often when the grieving person is feeling the disruption in his life most acutely. He may be irritable, cry in spurts, or be unable to concentrate or remember things.

When a worker displays such behavior, he might want to talk to someone on a regular basis, perhaps once a week. Some workplaces have an employee assistance program with trained counselors. Sometimes the personnel or human resource department has counselors who are able to spend time with employees. If a grieving person is able to take an hour a week to talk and express his feelings, he is often able to be much more productive.

If the bereaved worker is having difficulty with schedules, tasks, memory, or concentration, supervisors can help by assisting with schedule preparation. We can also be clear and direct about our expectations. Perhaps a particular job requires time after hours, yet the bereaved person is not willing to work overtime. This lack of interest in overtime may be due to decreased energy or to the need to spend time alone or with family. We must be sensitive to these needs and refrain from requiring long hours at such a traumatic period in a worker's life.

Some bereaved persons need additional time off either because of symptoms of stress or because of family needs. If we are sensitive to such needs and allow sufficient time off, the worker will be able to return to work with renewed energy. Accumulating stress can cause illness and result in long periods of absence from work. Allowing time off for the demands of grief is an investment in that worker's future productivity, and often such situations inspire the development of new policies for employees that are more humane and that reflect individual needs.

There are many community resources for the grieving: support groups, counseling centers, and support/education programs. Today many companies keep files on such resources for their employees. Supervisors or managers can assist the bereaved by directing them to the appropriate resources.

Taking time off from work to attend a funeral, or a gradual return to a full schedule, or time off to see a counselor or participate in a support group may seem like time lost, yet the opposite is true. A valued employee is far more productive in the long run if we allow sufficient time for the disruptions of grieving. If a worker is allowed long periods to deal with the stresses of grief, his time at work will be more concentrated and energetic. In addition, employees tend to be more productive when they are happier at work. When we address the disruptions caused by grieving and try to meet the needs of the bereaved, we are creating the conditions for greater productivity and greater satisfaction in the workplace.

Part Eight
REACHING THE OTHER SIDE OF GRIEF

Flood

Grief opened the sluice-gate:
words flooded forth
faster than I could set them down.

Something sweet
washed up on this salt shore.

by Ruth Feldman

Chapter Twenty-Nine
THE PATH TO A NEW LIFE

Sue

I don't feel like I walk around with the heaviness of it every day. I have incorporated that. As I've grown up I've come to terms with myself in many ways. Even though I was in my early twenties and on my own, it would have been great to have more of a family than I had at that time. Now I feel like I have a lot of long-term friendships in the community. It's very, very different from when I was just a year out of college and not having many connections to places or people. Sometimes I wonder if her death and my grieving didn't prevent me from relating to other people. I had so many things to work out I couldn't give as much energy to someone outside. It affected my relationships with men and women. And then I was trying to figure out how I was going to make a living, doing all kinds of odd jobs and trying to write.

Jeremy

I am just sad that he had to die. He was only fifty-one years old. I think if he had lived longer we would have had a really nice relationship. I see a lot of people with a lot of worse things than I have had. I see a lot of kids at work who never had a father. I'm just happy that I had twenty-two years of my father and a good last year with him.

There's grief in life, and life isn't easy. But if you can't live with grief, it's much harder to live your life. I can't see myself stopping to live be-

297

cause of what happened. I can't see myself stopping everything so I can wallow in my grief. I don't think I want to do that. I don't think my father would want me to do that.

Anne

I decided to buy a condominium in the city. It was just right for me. It was surprising, my decision to sell the house and move into the city. It was a question of timing. There were the children before, and I had to prove to the world and to the kids that we could keep the house, that we'd have two cats, a mom, and four kids. The apartment in the city is more for who I am these days. I'm not the mother with little children drooling all over me. I'm dressed up more. I think I will like this elegant new situation.

There are still some difficulties. When the children are in a play or at graduation, I find myself wishing there were someone with me that I could be proud with. But when I find myself feeling that way, I use mental exercises. I memorize poems like I did when I was a kid in school. You can make yourself learn from that.

Bill

Every time I see my daughter's new baby, I think, "Wouldn't Ginny have loved to have this baby to play with?" That always reminds me of her. There are a lot of things that will remind me, and I have a moment of grief. But there are a lot of other things in my life, and I don't dwell on it. I could never forget someone I'd been living with for over thirty years any more than I could believe she was dead in the first few days after she died.

I have always liked to talk about this. I'm not so sure the kids want to talk about it. They don't want to be reminded. The most I say is, "Oh, your mother really would have liked that," or "She wouldn't have liked that."

Eric

It's been two years. It is still hard, although I feel much better. If I feel better it's because of that film project. I also met a woman, and even though that relationship fell apart, it did because of its own problems, not because of Diane, and that actually felt good.

The sadness is still there, but now I can control it. I know where it is. I can live with it. I feel better about being in this apartment. Diane and I were happy here.

The last two winters were very hard. I never could figure out if it was because that was the time when Diane was dying or the bad weather. I used to dread winter. Now I that this winter is not going to be bad. I think a lot of it is just the passage of time. I knew it would happen, but I thought it would happen sooner.

It doesn't ever go away. There will be other relationships, and I will probably get married, but I will be thinking every day of Diane. It means that there's always that sad place inside you. You wish it weren't like that. Even though things are getting better, I wish I could let go of that. You always wonder what it would have been like if she had lived.

Marilyn

You invest the child, whom you actually never knew, with the ideas of what you would like the child to be, the things that all people invest their child with during a pregnancy. When a pregnancy is suddenly brought up short, those ideas never take form, and you never see the real person, yet you still carry those ideas with you. The problem is that there actually was a physical being there, and because you never got to know that person, you've lost not only the idea but the specific individual which you can't possibly ever know. You often look at other children and wonder what yours would have been, blond or dark, cute or ugly. You just wonder. I think that's one reason you actually find yourself not wanting to be around children.

Writing has always been an outlet for me. I found myself automatically writing some poems that dealt with the experience. I also found myself writing down a lot of the details that I was going through because it was the deepest experience of my life and it seemed important that I remember. I think part of that was for the child I couldn't get to know. This is really the only existence she had. Gradually I began to see that I really wanted to write a book that narrates my experience and explores some of the ideas that I invested this child with. When I started writing this I was very hopeful that I would have a child, and I envisioned a book that would end with my succeeding in bearing a child. I know now that it will end with my coming to terms with the fact that I am not going to have a child through birth. Questions of adoption are really separate from all this. I see it now as a book about coming to terms with this kind of loss, finally saying no to pregnancy. The doctors may be saying you still can succeed, but you see yourself as being so battered in the process that you have to say no. It's an act of will. It's very difficult to do.

Another aspect of coming to terms with this type of a loss is dealing with the question of whether to adopt a child. We have had a moratorium on talking about that for several months. Now we are just beginning to deal with looking ahead to that type of answer.

Phil

We had a fund started in her name, and we sometimes put on a little children's program anonymously. Sometimes we take our kids to it. My wife has had a real good feeling about being able to do that as an outlet for herself. It's a small thing, to give annually to help children in that area educationally. I think you have to do those things. That keeps her alive.

Our son is now two and a half. He's full of life. It brings us some dimension of hope and expectation. I go through life in a different way, a lot different. My memories are different.

I have four children, and one of them is not with me. It depends on who asks me that question, whether it's someone that you are going to get to know or it's more formal. Most of the people where I live don't know that, and they don't need to. It's not something you stop and dwell on. It's somewhat private. I feel like I have four children.

It's been three and a half years. I still feel very sad, and I feel unfortunately at times that there are little pieces that ebb away. I try to keep memories fresh in my mind. But you just know that the human faculties are such that you're going to lose little pieces now and then. Other things and experiences are coming in, and they're fresher. Our life is so different now after three and a half years. Our life seemed so different then. We were living in a small town and our children were small and life seemed so tightly knit. You can feel the void that has transpired since then. You try to hang on. I try to hang on to what she represented. When I have difficult decisions to make or issues that are highly moral, I try to think about my daughter, because I think that helps. She's a part of maintaining what religion is to me. If I didn't have that connection, even though the way she died is hard, or if I didn't adhere to Christian beliefs, it would be hard.

I don't try to set many long-term goals, but I try to make sure that what I'm doing is as fulfilling as possible, particularly the depth of my relationships with my students. Some of the students, I get to know them well. I could see what it would have been like for Jenny if she were nineteen or twenty. I'd want someone to help her in her education. The students give me a lot. I can see how some of the students are growing here. I feel good by being a participant observer and seeing them prosper. And then I see them leave, and I can cherish that. They represent a lot.

I'm an achievement-oriented person, and I've got a lot of drive, but I'm not so sure that's important anymore. When you get knocked down, you get to look at the world from a whole different angle. You're looking up instead of looking down. That humbling experience gives you another perspective.

I was out running around the track and I got to talking to this elderly man that I had always seen there. He was probably in his late seventies. I walked around the track with him when I wasn't running and discovered that we both went to the same college and that he lost his son when his son was in his early twenties. He was his pride. That was really interesting, and I asked him how he dealt with that. He said that was really hard but you have to be really tough. It increases your sensitivity. You can't let it all overwhelm you. You can get help and have friends reach out, but you have to have inner toughness. It is a word that is important to me. I understand now what he meant when he said that. He gave me a lot of hope because I saw him going about his life and putting things in place. I said I could do it too.

Maureen

A few years later, my friend called me when her grandfather, whom she was really close to, was dying. The first thing she did was call me and say, "I really want to talk to you about death, and how you dealt with it and where we go from here." It made me feel so good that she turned around and said, "I need your help now. I know you've been through it and you can tell me how it's going to feel." You can have all the compassion in the world, but until you've been through it, you don't know what someone is feeling after a death. I knew what she was feeling. I didn't know if what I was saying was going to help her, but I said what I would have liked to have heard. She asked me, "Did you feel lost, this emptiness that you couldn't fill?" I said, "Yeah, that's how I felt, and no one can tell you that you'll feel better or how to feel." I felt so needed. I felt that the death gave me something that I could give to somebody else.

I still feel she's so close to me. For Mother's Day my mother and I went up to the cemetery. I've introduced my husband to her, and my best friend has been up there with me. I know she won't slip away from me.

There are plenty of older people that have died in my life, a lot of great aunts. When they died, I don't think I ever really cried a lot. They were old people, I loved them. They had a good life and they're gone. But I think of my sister, how much life she missed, how I miss her, how much life we could have shared. All I have now are memories.

When I got married, it was Maureen getting married, rather than Joan. I could see a lot of things that my mother and father were going through. I had my best friend as my maid of honor, but I missed having my sister there. It was Mary Beth and me, but it just wasn't the same as being close with Joan, sharing the looks I know we would share, jokes that we would have shared. I had her favorite flowers on the altar. I had a bouquet of daisies right next to me, because that's where she would have stood.

When I see someone that's handicapped or anyone that is suffering, I just feel for them. Little things don't bother me anymore. When my husband leaves the house every morning, I have to tell him that I love him, because God knows what can happen to him. I say, "I love you," every time I hang up the phone with my mother, my grandmother, my father. I never knew when I was fifteen that my sister was going to die.

There's this man at work. He never goes to funerals or says good-bye to anyone. If you can't say good-bye, you can't feel right about that relationship later. After living through what I have, I'd never want to give that cop-out to somebody. I find that the best things I can do for people now is to send them cards, or call them out of the blue, or just be aware of their thoughts and their feelings. Someone I hadn't seen for years just had a baby, and I sent her a card. She called me up and was so pleased. That made me feel great. And I won't say now I won't do things or think I won't go out of my way for someone. I do go out of my way.

When I hear something about someone else, I get upset, and it brings back all the feelings I have for Joan, and that is good. Sometimes I need those to bring me back, because sometimes I put her out of my head for a while. Sometimes she'll pop into my thoughts for no reason, and those are the best times.

Jim

It is always there. I expect that I will again get back into periods where I will be able to think of nothing else. I still feel very angry at my parents and I feel angry at myself, partly for not seeing the light sooner. It will be there for a long time. I'm struck by how powerful the emotional part of our life is, and at the same time how mysterious.

Two weeks ago my university wanted me to talk to a newspaper reporter about how to prevent alcoholism and drug abuse in teenagers. So I did the interview. I emphasized things like communication in the family. I did all of this interview without ever once thinking about my sister or myself. That was the strangest and most amazing thing, that I could do that without thinking about her. Yet the things that I said apply to her situation and my own.

I feel that I will continue to struggle with it, but it has made me pay more attention to what the important things are. There used to be a time when I thought my job was so important. Since this happened, well, it's not so important. What's important now is my own family, my wife and son, but also accepting the things in my family that aren't helpful, and not being afraid to tell my parents that we're not healthy. I've only begun. It's so much easier to just not rock the boat and just not say anything. Easier in the short run, that is.

Living Again

One morning we wake up and suddenly notice that the trees are in bloom or the leaves are beginning to turn color. A student of mine told me how months after her father's death she walked out her front door one morning and noticed the apple trees bursting into flower. We find our-selves looking at the sky again or noticing the people around us. There does come a time when we accept our loved one as lost and begin to take pleasure in new things. We know that we are going to live again.

This means different things for each of us. For some it means that we are beginning to experience more good days than bad days. For others of us it means that a day went by without our thinking of our loss or perhaps when we think of that loss, the pain is not as sharp or overwhelming. It is no longer the center of our lives. We find ourselves investing our emotion and energy in new things rather than in our grief. We begin to think about spending time and passion on new projects.

If we are a young adult who lost a parent or sibling, we begin to see ourselves as young again and start going out with our friends or putting our energy in our studies or job. We may be out at a movie with our friends one evening and realize that we are enjoying ourselves and that it's possible to have fun. Sue describes the long-term friendships that she began to build after a long period in which she was unable to give herself to relationships.

If we lost a husband or a wife, we begin to see ourselves as a whole person again. One day we look in the mirror and are pleased with ourselves. We may begin seeing other people again and invest in new relationships for their own sake rather than as an antidote to our loneliness. A widower friend of mine spent a great deal of time playing tennis after his wife died. It was a release from tension, a way of lessening his pain. Months later he met someone he could care about and started going out for enjoyment. He was believing in life again and began experiencing ease and contentment.

These changes occur almost imperceptibly. They are extremely subtle and gradual. This does not mean that we no longer think of our loved one or that we no longer feel the pain of our loss. It simply means that our pain has become manageable, that the energy we spend on living is increasing and the emotion we spend on our loss diminishes. In his narrative, Eric talks of his new film project and new friends. He also speaks of the place his wife will always have inside him. In chapter 13, Merryl tells us that although she has a new relationship and plans to marry, she still thinks of her husband at times during the day. We learn to carry our loss around with us and still invest in our lives, or, as Eric so aptly puts it, the sadness is there, but we know how to live with it.

When we reach the other side of grief, we find that we have undergone tremendous growth. We have learned to incorporate loss and sadness into our lives without being overwhelmed by them, and also learned that we can go on living in new ways. It isn't necessarily what we expected before the grieving began. We may have thought that our lives would be the same and that we would forget. But it's not a question of forgetting or getting over our loss, but rather of finding that our life is significantly different now and we are not the same person we were before.

We create a new relationship with the loved one who died. This is one of our most surprising discoveries. As time passes we continue to see our loved one in different ways and to understand his or her personality with greater depth and perspective. If we lost a parent, we begin to develop an appreciation of our parent as a person rather than just as our parent. We come to understand what they experienced in their lives and learn from that experience. When thinking about my mother, I gain understanding of the aging process and of what she might have gone though. I feel that I will continue to learn from her throughout my life.

If we lost a child, we develop a greater understanding of the place that child had in our lives. In his narrative, Phil speaks of how memories of his daughter serve as a reference for his decisions. He also describes the depth of his relationship with his students. It's as if he were reaching out to his own daughter and helping her through her college years. The relationship we have with our loved one continues to be dynamic. It reflects our own age and our accumulating experience as well as our changing perspectives of the deceased.

Those of us who have dealt with suicide or homicide gain a greater understanding of ourselves and our ties with the deceased. If our loved one took his or her own life, we learn a lot about personal responsibility in relationships. We learn what we have control over in our lives and what escapes our control, that we cannot be responsible for someone else's life. Letting go of that belief in our ability to control our loved one's destiny helps us move beyond grief.

If our loved one was murdered, living again simply means making the best of a very painful situation. We may have to live for years with the fact that the murderer is out on the street, that our sense of justice has been violated by the judicial process, and that the world continues to be a frightening place. Living again means simply that we have more good days than bad days and that we can continue our lives at work and at home.

It is not unusual for families to experience estrangement and divorce after a death. We go through a whole series of losses in addition to the loss of our loved one. In these cases, reaching the other side of grief means that we gain perspective on our relationships, that we cease to blame ourselves for a failed marriage or the inability to keep the family together after the death of a parent. We learn to develop a more positive view of ourselves despite our losses, and this self-regard will help us continue our lives in the best way possible under the circumstances.

All of us who experience the suffering of loss undergo great changes. We are healed in different ways by these changes, and we eventually reconstruct our lives. Resolving sorrow means being able to express it and putting it into a place inside us, weaving it in our lives as a thread in a complex and rich tapestry.

Building a New Life for Ourselves

As we move beyond grief, we begin to focus on ourselves again and find that our view of ourselves has changed. Because of what we have been through, we see ourselves as more capable. While our loss may have dealt a heavy blow to our self-esteem, we drew on our inner resources and coped with that loss, perhaps without being aware of our growth. The disruption of our lives can actually open up new vistas for us, and we begin to ask ourselves what we want to explore. We begin to dream again and to see ourselves as people with possibilities. Musing on the passage of time, a famous author commented that the development of new energy and new interests and the discovery of new truths happen not just in our youth, but over and over again as we progress through life.

Although we thought that the building phase of our lives had come and gone, we find ourselves in the process of creating a life once again. If we lost a parent we were pushed toward independence, and we now begin to express it the way Sue did, by making new friends and finding ways to support herself. If we are a widow or widower, we also begin to express our independence in more positive ways, whether deciding to remain single or to marry or to live with someone. But this time, we are the ones doing the planning and selecting the alternatives that will best suit the people we have become.

After such a searing experience as the death of a loved one many of us develop not only a sense of the fragility of life, but also a desire to make the most out of the life we have. In a sense we are more demanding.

After we have gone through the grieving process, many of us look for more satisfying jobs or a more fulfilling way of life. Many of us have discovered new talents along the way.

Eric discovered a new interest and new talents as he turned his efforts to filmmaking and away from journalism. A woman I know whose husband committed suicide decided to go back to college and get a degree in fine arts. Some years later, she developed a career as a painter. An older man whose son died in an automobile accident became involved in local theater and even tried his hand at writing, although he had been a probation officer for most of his working life.

Our changes in careers may reflect not only the discovery of new talents but also a shift in values. After his daughter died, Phil left his job as superintendent of schools to become a college professor. He wanted to make sure that his work was as fulfilling as possible. Working with young women was a way of remembering his daughter and imagining the young adult she would have become. He developed a new image of himself beyond that of good provider and successful administrator. Anne too developed a new image of herself as a successful and competent businesswoman at ease in an urban setting.

Those of us who don't work outside the home can find new sources of fulfillment in traveling or in meeting new kinds of people. We may maintain the living situations we had before the death of our loved one, but with changes in outlook. A widow I know decided to stay in the same town and in the same house after the death of her husband, but she began to travel and make new friends. We may strike up a friendship with a person outside of our usual social circle or take a course in an area we are completely unfamiliar with. These are not negligible steps. What seem like small, isolated decisions represent a steady, incremental movement toward a more satisfying life.

Each one of us will experience significant growth, spiritually, psychologically, and emotionally. As we grieve we learn a great deal about ourselves and our relationships to others. We learn how to express our feelings in new ways and how to take support and help from others. Perhaps we have learned how to shed tears and still maintain self-esteem. Some of us may have learned how to face life on our own. Other of us may have had our faith strengthened. All of us, however, learn that we are able to cope and use our new strengths in different ways to enhance our lives.

Spinning Gold Out of Flax

In a well-known fairy tale, a young woman is locked in a room with a pile of flax and ordered to spin it into gold. A dwarf ultimately appears and gives her the magic formula that will help her spin the gold and thus save her life. This fairy tale can be seen a metaphor for the way we turn the experiences of our suffering and the circumstances of our loss into gold when we discover a new capacity for giving and for using our experience to help others.

We developed emotional strength and practical skills that enabled us to cope with loss, and now some of us undertake service projects or establish funds that will help others who experience tragedies. For example, most bereavement support groups, such as Compassionate Friends or Parents of Murdered Children, were started by people who experienced loss.

The people who volunteer for one-on-one support and peer counseling in hospice programs and bereavement centers are people who have suffered loss themselves and who are able to use their own experience to help the newly bereaved. Most of these volunteers receive a lot more than they give, because this kind of work gives them an opportunity to learn more about their own grief. It is a privilege and a source of richness to enter other people's lives at a time when they are vulnerable and in great need.

Chapter 14 describes how Margaret channels her anger and sorrow to help others through her work in victim rights. A woman I know whose elderly mother died began volunteering in a nursing home. She discovered that she was able to use her experience in caring for an ailing parent in new ways. Some of us who have lost loved ones to cancer or heart disease volunteer for fund-raising drives to help research in eliminating these illnesses.

Some of us who are financially able start funds to help others who suffer similar tragedies, turning our loss into positive support for others. Phil describes the fund he started in his daughter's name and the solace it provides for his family. A young couple who lost an infant during pregnancy started a fund to help bereaved parents and to upgrade a local hospital's child-care equipment. We don't have to be wealthy to make such helpful gestures. A young woman whose daughter died donated a small amount to an organization that provides for needy children throughout the world.

Some of us write books or articles about our experience which serve as guides and supports for others who are struggling with loss. Jim was able to publish a newspaper with some useful advice on the prevention of drug abuse as a result of the understanding he gained from his sister's death. Anne frequently addresses local groups to share her experiences as a young widow. In our journey through grief, we discover not only that we are not isolated in our grief, but also that our own suffering is of use.

Learning Compassion and Sensitivity

When Maureen discusses the changes in her outlook since her sister's death, she speaks of the insight she has gained into other people's pain. One of the most important things we learn when we have grieved the loss of a loved one is compassion. While the pain of our grief can be very isolating, ultimately it brings us to a deeper understanding of others. We realize how many people labor under the burden of pain not only from the loss of a loved one, but also from difficult jobs, family circumstances, or health.

We discover a new ease in relating to different kinds of people. We also recognize that for all the differences between people, the distinctions tend to fall away as we draw close to others. From this recognition flows an ability to communicate. Now we know what to say and what not to say when we go to a wake or a funeral. We know how to talk to the newly bereaved or to those who have suffered loss at any point in their lives.

We know what to do as well as what to say when tragedy strikes others. For example, if we are a supervisor, we might bend work regulations when someone is in need and be more willing to put people's needs as a priority. We will know what to do for coworkers and friends when they suffer a loss. Maureen speaks of the wonderful discovery that she was able to help her friend who needed support. We become both role models and sources of solid practical help for others.

As Maureen discovered, the compassion we gain attracts people. Maybe now someone at work stops at our desk and tells us about an illness or death in his family. A friend calls us to say she needs help with a problem. Often even strangers are drawn to us and tell us their stories. We have learned a very important skill that will serve us in many situations — how to listen.

As we reach the other side of grief, we also learn to develop compassion for ourselves and our own difficulties. We learned not to demand so much of ourselves and to be more tolerant of ourselves as we struggle with the problems in life. Because we have lived with our own need and vulnerability throughout the grieving process, we may have learned to accept and even value that side of our personality.

Developing New Outlooks

Our experience with grief changed our outlook on life and affected our scale of values. What used to be so important to us, such as our work or perhaps our material comfort, now takes second place. We emerge from the grieving process with a keen sense of both the fragility and the preciousness of life. In this future-oriented society of ours, we may have gained a new respect for the present.

Maureen speaks of enjoying the here and now and making the best of things, because "the people you love won't always be there." A student of mine whose boyfriend had a very difficult relationship with his mother advised him to tell his mother that he loved her. She wanted him to realize that what he had was precious and would not always be there. She also told him that for her, having a house before they got married was not important. After having lost both parents as a young adult, she understood that the real strength in life lies within us and not in material things.

Many of us look back on our lives and wish we could have done things a bit differently. Surviving the loss of a loved one can seem almost like a blank slate, a chance to do things in a new way. We have learned what really matters, and because time is fleeting, we need to make the most of it.

A man who lost a child commented, "For a long time, work was important to me. But work has taken second or third level. There are things in life that are important than making a buck." After his sister died, Jim found that achieving success in his work was no longer as important to him. Perhaps because of our loss, we no longer take the people we love for granted and have come to regard our personal relations in a new light. We may now care more about finding meaning than about the more fleeting satisfaction of success.

For some of us, this means taking time to do things with our loved ones. Perhaps we look for a job that will give us more time with our family, or we decide to take that vacation now rather than postponing it until we reach a certain job level or salary. My mother always worried about having enough money to retire on, so she went without taking a vacation for years in a row and postponed the travels she often dreamed of. After she died, I realized the importance of taking time for living and for one's dreams. After we struggle with loss, we develop a sense of both the limits and the possibilities of life.

The experience of grief tests many of our friendships. In chapter 24, Marilyn describes how she had to choose her friends very carefully after her loss. Some of her friends were insensitive to her tragedy, so she needed to distance herself from them. But she also discovered new friendships that evolved into close relationships. After our long struggle through grief, we may be attracted to different kinds of people. We might get real pleasure from friendships with people who are different in age or interests but who have experienced some kind of loss. Or we might find ourselves less tolerant of those who are more like us in superficial aspects but who are more concerned with values we have either rejected or placed in a low priority.

For many of us a change in outlook means a new appreciation of the simple things in life, such as taking the time to enjoy a beautiful day or walking in the woods. We might find that having a quiet conversation with a friend is just as renewing as a more elaborate social event. We have come to see what is around us with new insight and learn to take pleasure in our immediate surroundings.

Becoming Our Own Best Friend

The long and lonely months and years of grieving may have felt like a tunnel with no exit. We have lost our loved one and experienced myriad other losses as our former lives and relationships were transformed. Many of us changed our homes and livelihoods. We may have been disappointed by the reaction of our friends and developed new friendships. Even those of us who stayed in place with the same friends and the same lifestyle have experienced profound and lasting changes. We have all made an extraordinary journey not only in our external lives but also deep within ourselves. Even when we felt the most helpless and vulnerable, we were coping with our sorrow and learning that we have inner resources to draw upon.

While it may not have seemed that we were making progress during the bleak time of our sorrow, when we underwent personal crisis we moved forward in every sense of the term. We explored new interests and new relationships, but most importantly we discovered new sides of ourselves, drawing on inner resources that we never dreamed we had. While we were working so hard to build new support structures and make new friends, we were developing the best friend of all—ourselves. Though we still look for and are nourished by outside support, we now have a new and strengthened resource to draw on all our lives. We have become our own best friend.

In learning that we can be comfortable with ourselves, we discovered the difference between loneliness, which we rarely choose, and solitude, which we now cherish as an alternative. We may prefer spending the evening by ourselves either listening to music or watching TV. We are proud of the way we are able to take care of ourselves instead of resenting that we are now in charge of our own well-being. Most of all, we not only accept who we are, but we appreciate that person.

A widowed friend of mine whose children had grown up described her Thanksgiving to me. She set candles on the table, and after dinner she spent the evening in front of a wood fire with her dog and a good book. Rather than bemoaning that she was alone during a family holiday, she relished the time as an opportunity to unwind from her work and a chance to be with herself. A well-known poet wrote that the time will come when you will greet yourself "at your own door, in your own mirror" when you "will love again the stranger who was yourself."[1]

This is a time to take stock of all we have accomplished and to be proud of the way we have survived. We have gone through one of the most profound changes we will experience in our life, and even if things didn't turn out as we had hoped, we have endured. Regardless of whether our marriage or our family relationships have remained intact, we have survived as a person. As Margaret so aptly phrases it in chapter 14, "the human spirit is amazing." Because this was the most trying experience of our lives, we can face other and lesser difficulties with greater perspective. Reaching the other side of grief is a new beginning. Painful as the journey has been, it has prepared us for a lifetime of growth and change.

Note

1. Derek Walcott, "Love After Love," in *Sea Grapes* (New York: Farrar, Straus & Giroux, 1976).

Appendix A
RESOURCES

It can be difficult to find appropriate information and support about grief, because we have not needed it in the past. The following pages include a list of resources divided into several categories. Some categories overlap, so it is important to read through all of them to find the right resources. This list is not exhaustive, but it provides enough leads to find the nearest resource and information.

Education and Information Centers

AMERICAN INSTITUTE OF LIFE-THREATENING
ILLNESS AND LOSS

> 630 West 168th Street
> New York, NY 10032
> 212-928-2066

Primarily educational; cosponsors conferences on grief and death. Most material and seminars are for mental-health professionals.

CENTER FOR DEATH EDUCATION AND RESEARCH

> 1167 Social Science Building
> 267 19th Avenue South

University of Minnesota
Minneapolis, MN 55455
612-624-1895

Books, pamphlets, and articles on many topics about death for both
mental health professionals and the layperson.

CHOICE IN DYING—THE NATIONAL COUNCIL
FOR THE RIGHT TO DIE

200 Varick Street, 10th floor
New York, NY 10014-4810
212-3666-5540
800-989-WILL

Information on issues of health care and dying. Promotes the living will
and has sample documents available.

NATIONAL CENTER FOR DEATH EDUCATION

Mount Ida College
777 Dedham Street
Newton Centre, MA 02150
617-925-4649
http:/www.mountida.edu

The center has an extensive library of books and films; also sponsors
seminars and workshops for professionals.

THE ELIZABETH KÜBLER-ROSS CENTER

South Route 616
Head Waters, VA 24442
703-396-3441

Besides being a retreat for terminally ill patients, the center holds workshops and seminars and publishes a newsletter, which includes a reading
list.

How to Find a Support Group

Some support groups are mutual help groups and are informally organized; others are based within a larger agency and are professionally led. It may take a few telephone calls to find one in your area that is right for you. Besides the resources listed, there are other ways to locate a support group. The following is a list of places to contact:

- a local hospice program
- The local mental-health agency
- United Way information and referral service
- the state Self-Help Clearinghouse (see national listing below)
- the social service department of your local hospital
- the local Council of Aging (for widowed groups)
- the state Victim Assistance Organization (for death by violence)
- a local church
- your local newspaper
- the World Wide Web has national and state listings of hospices and bereavement support groups as well as a variety of bereavement programs and sites. See the GriefNet site.

National Organizations that Serve the Bereaved

AIDS NATIONAL INTERFAITH NETWORK

300 First Street NE, Suite 400
Washington, D.C. 20002
202-546-0807

Provides information about AIDS and support groups.

AMERICAN SUDDEN INFANT DEATH SYNDROME
INSTITUTE (ASIDS)

6065 Roswell Road, Suite 876
Atlanta, GA 30328

404-843-1030
800-232-SIDS

Promotes infant health through research, clinical services, education, and
support for SIDS families. Conducts seminars for health care professionals and laypeople.

AMERICAN SUICIDE FOUNDATION

1045 Park Avenue
New York, NY 10028
212-410-1111
800-531-4477

Support groups for suicide survivors.

THE COMPASSIONATE FRIENDS, INC.

P.O. Box 3696
Oak Brook, IL 60522
708-990-0100

An international organization for bereaved parents and siblings with over six
hundred chapters in the United States. Local support groups are run by volunteer bereaved parents; literature is available and often a library as well.

CONCERNS OF POLICE SURVIVORS, INC.

COPS National Office
P.O. Box 3199
S Highway 5
Camdenton, MO 65020
573-346-4911

National network of survivors; national office contacts surviving families
at least six times a year providing support and information on survivors
issues. Specialty programs for surviving parents and for children, including education, counseling, and volunteer support during trials and parole

hearings; publishes handbook of support services for surviving families of Line-of-Duty Death.

In Loving Memory

1416 Green Run Lake
Reston, VA 22090
703-435-0608

Support groups for bereaved parents with no surviving children; newsletter, annual conference.

National Association of Military Widows

4023 25th Road North
Arlington, VA 22207
703-527-4565

A referral service for the newly widowed; sponsors support groups.

National Law Enforcement Officers Memorial Fund

605 E Street NW
Washington, D.C. 20004
202-737-3400

National outreach programs to the newly widowed; group discussions, educational programs, and seminars.

National Organization of Parents of Murdered Children

100 East 8th Street, B-41
Cincinnati, OH 45202
513-721-5683

Many local chapters across the country offering support groups; provide information about the criminal justice system regarding survivors of a homicide victim. Publishes a newsletter and sponsors an annual conference.

NATIONAL SELF-HELP CLEARINGHOUSE

25 West 42nd Street
New York, N Y 10036

Clearinghouse on support groups throughout the country; provides referral. Conducts research and training and has speakers' bureau. Many states also have a clearinghouse of support groups.

NATIONAL SHARE OFFICE

St. Joseph Health Center
800 First Capitol Drive
St. Charles, MI 63301-2893
800-821-6819

Support for those grieving death of a baby through miscarriage, stillbirth, or newborn death; sponsors over one hundred chapters nationally; offers parent a state-by-state printout of perinatal bereavement support groups and resources.

RAY OF HOPE, INC.

P.O. Box 2323
Iowa City, IA 52244
319-337-9890

Suicide support groups; provides workshops and publications of suicide postvention; publishes pamphlet, book, and videotape.

THE SUDDEN INFANT DEATH SYNDROME ALLIANCE (SIDS ALLIANCE)

1314 Bedford Avenue, Suite 210
Baltimore, MD 21208
410-653-8826
800-221-SIDS

Local chapters offer support groups, one-on-one contact and/or educational guidance; referrals to local programs and up-to-date SIDS information on toll-free hotline; newsletter; annual conference.

THEY HELP EACH OTHER SPIRITUALLY (THEOS)

1301 Clark Building
717 Liberty Avenue
Pittsburgh, PA 15222
412-471-7779

Servicing the widowed, this group has chapters across the country; also publishes *Theos,* a magazine about bereavement.

TRAGEDY ASSISTANCE PROGRAM FOR SURVIVORS, INC.

2001 S Street NW, Suite 300
Washington, D.C. 20009
800-959-TAPS

Support through a national network of military survivors for parents, children, spouses, and friends; operates national toll-free crisis and information line; provides case workers to support families in tracking information and benefits following death of a military serviceperson; newsletter.

UNITE, INC.

7600 Central Avenue
Philadelphia, PA 19111-2499
215-728-3777

Sponsors local support groups following the death of a baby, including miscarriage, stillbirth, and infant death. Provides newsletter.

WIDOWED PERSONS SERVICE

American Association of Retired Persons
601 A Street NW
Washington, D.C. 20049
202-434-2260

WPS has over 470 chapters nationwide of widowed support groups as well as a directory of services. Sponsors a yearly conference for those leading support groups.

Regional and Local Groups Serving the Bereaved

AIDS ACTION COMMITTEE

131 Clarendon Street
Boston, MA 02116
617-437-6200

Comprehensive services for people with AIDS and loved ones. Groups for bereaved, also referral to other resources.

GAY MEN'S HEALTH CRISIS

129 West 20th Street
New York, NY 10011
212-807-6664

One of the largest service organizations for people with AIDS.

THE GOOD GRIEF PROGRAM

Boston Medical Center
91 East Concord Street MAT5
Boston, MA 02118
617-534-4005

Education, consultation, and services for groups of children who have experienced a death. Also helps parents and teachers to deal with children after a death.

HELPING OTHER PARENTS IN NORMAL GRIEVING (HOPING)

Sparrow Hospital
1215 East Michigan Avenue
P.O. Box 30480
Lansing, MI 48909
517-483-3873

State, regional, and local groups for parents who have experienced a miscarriage, stillbirth, or death of an infant. Speakers, educational programs, newsletter.

KARA EMOTIONAL SUPPORT SERVICE FOR THE BEREAVED

457 Kingsley Avenue
Palo Alto, CA 94301
415-321-KARA

Individual counseling for the bereaved; serves adults, children, and adolescents. Serves several counties just south of San Francisco.

OMEGA EMOTIONAL SUPPORT SERVICES, INC.

34 Heath Street
Somerville, MA 02143
617-776-6369

Support groups for people dealing with traumatic death, including homicide, sudden death, accident, disaster. Also provides individual counseling and conducts workshops for professionals. Serves the Greater Boston area.

SAFE PLACE

> The Samaritans
> 500 Commonwealth Avenue
> Boston, MA 02215
> 617-247-0220

Support groups for those bereaved through suicide. Also has chapters in other cities. The Samaritans is an international organization offering counseling to the suicidal and depressed.

SEASONS: SUICIDE BEREAVEMENT

> Tina Larsen
> P.O. Box 187
> Park City, Utah
> 801-649-8327

Support for those bereaved by suicide; chapters in various parts of the country.

UCSF AIDS HEALTH PROJECT

> Box 0884
> San Francisco, CA 94143-0884
> 415-476-6430

A consortium of service programs. Referral to appropriate resource.

VICTIM SERVICES AGENCY

> 2 Lafayette Street, 3rd floor
> New York, NY 10007
> 212-577-7700

Crisis support, counseling programs, and support groups for families of homicide victims.

Information and Services about Illness

The following organizations can provide information and/or services about a particular illness.

ALZHEIMER'S ASSOCIATION

> 919 North Michigan Avenue
> Chicago, IL 60601
> 312-335-8700
> 800-272-3900

AMERICAN CANCER SOCIETY

> 7272 Clifton Road NE
> Atlanta, GA 30329
> 404-320-3333
> 404-329-7648
> 800-ACS-2345

Your local chapter of the ACS is found in your phone book.

AMERICAN HEART ASSOCIATION, INC.

> 7272 Greenville Avenue
> Dallas, TX 75231
> 214-373-6300

See phone book for local listings.

AMERICAN LUNG ASSOCIATION

> 1740 Broadway
> New York, New York 10019
> 212-315-8700

See phone book for local listings.

CANCER INFORMATION SERVICE

Office of Cancer Information
NCI/NIH Building 31, 10A07
9000 Rockville Place
Bethesda, MD 20892
1-800-4-CANCER

This telephone number will put you in touch with your local or regional
Cancer Information Service. This service provides information on the
causes, detection, prevention, treatment, rehabilitation, and continuing
care of cancer. They also give referral to medical facilities, home health
care, and support groups.

CANDLELIGHTERS CHILDHOOD CANCER FOUNDATION

7910 Woodmont Avenue, Suite 460
Bethesda, MD 20814-3015
301-657-8401
800-366-2223

MULTIPLE SCLEROSIS NATIONAL SOCIETY

733 Third Avenue
New York, NY 10017
212-986-3240

NAMES PROJECT FOUNDATION

310 Townsend Street
San Francisco, CA 94107
415-882-5500

Promotes creation of a memorial quilt as an appropriate compassionate
response to the AIDS epidemic.

NATIONAL AIDS HOTLINE

800-342-2437

Provides nationwide and local information and resources.

NATIONAL ASSOCIATION OF PEOPLE WITH AIDS

Box 34056
Washington, D.C. 20043
202-898-0414

Provides information about AIDS and support groups.

NATIONAL HOSPICE ORGANIZATION

1901 North Moore Street, Suite 901
Arlington, VA 22209
703-243-5900

Hospice programs provide care and support for people living with a terminal illness; care includes nursing and medical care at home. You can obtain the names of your local hospice programs from the national organization.

NATIONAL KIDNEY FOUNDATION

30 East 33rd Street, Suite 1100
New York, NY 10016
212-889-2210

NATIONAL STROKE ASSOCIATION

8480 East Orchard Road, Suite 1000
Englewood, CO 80111
303-771-1700
800-STROKES
212-734-3461

Other Resources

MOTHERS AGAINST DRUNK DRIVING

> 511 East John Carpenter Freeway, No. 700
> Irving, TX 75062
> 214-744-6233

NATIONAL ORGANIZATION FOR VICTIM ASSISTANCE

> 1757 Park Road NW
> Washington, D.C. 20010
> 202-232-8560
> 800-TRY-NOVA

NOVA can help you locate resources for victim assistance in your local area.

PARENTS WITHOUT PARTNERS, INC.

> 401 North Michigan Avenue
> Chicago, IL 60611
> 312-644-6610

Appendix B
ADDITIONAL READINGS

The following list is not meant to be exhaustive. It includes a selection of books about loss and grief for those who wish to do further reading in this area. The list comprises three categories: a general list for those experiencing grief or who wish to help a grieving friend or acquaintance; a selection of works in fiction and poetry which focus on grief; and more technical works for health care providers or those who would like to do research on grief.

General

Angel, Marc. *The Orphaned Adult: Confronting the Death of a Parent.* New York: Human Sciences Press, 1987. Acknowledges the grief of adults when they lose a parent.

Ascher, Barbara. *Landscape without Gravity.* New York: Penguin, 1993. A sister's memoir of grief over her brother's death from AIDS.

Bolton, Iris. *My Son, My Son.* Atlanta: Bolton, 1983. The author's account of living through her son's suicide.

Campbell, Scott, with Phyllis Silverman. *Widower: When Men Are Left Alone.* New York: Prentice-Hall, 1987. A collection of personal experiences of widowers.

Colt, George Howe. *The Enigma of Suicide.* New York: Summit, 1991. History of suicide, stories of adolescent suicide, and stories of survivors of a loved one's suicide.

Doty, Mark. *Heaven's Coast: A Memoir.* New York: HarperCollins, 1996. An autobiographical account of living with AIDS.

Edelman, H. *Motherless Daughters: The Legacy of Loss.* Reading, Mass.: Addison-Wesley, 1994. Stories of women whose mothers died early in their lives and how the absence of a mother shapes their identity.

Ericsson, Stephanie. *Companion Through the Darkness: Inner Dialogues on Grief.* New York: HarperCollins, 1993. The author's inner journey following the death of her husband.

Gayton, R. *The Forgiving Place: Choosing Peace after Violent Trauma.* Waco, Tex.: WRS Publishing, 1995. The story of the author's wife's brutal murder and his healing.

Graves, S. *Expressions of Healing: Embracing the Process of Grief.* North Hollywood, Calif.: Newcastle, 1994. Combines expression, grief, and recovery in a workbook format; includes journal writing and art exercises.

Grollman, Earl. *Talking about Death: A Dialogue between Parent and Child.* Boston: Beacon, 1990. This book is designed for children and adults to read together; answers the questions children ask about death.

Kübler-Ross, Elizabeth. *Death: The Final Stage of Growth.* New York: Macmillan, 1981. A book of essays about the dying.

———. *Living with Death and Dying.* New York, Macmillan, 1981. Explores issues of death and dying.

Kushner, Harold J. *When Bad Things Happen to Good People.* New York: Schocken, 1981. A rabbi's approach to the question of human suffering.

Levine, Stephen. *Healing into Life and Death.* Garden City, N.Y.: Anchor, 1987. A book of meditations and exercises, including meditations on grief and death.

———. *Meetings at the Edge: Dialogues with the Grieving and the Dying, the Healing and the Healed.* Garden City, N.Y.: Anchor, 1984. Conversations with people in various phases of dying and bereavement.

Lewis, C. S. *A Grief Observed.* New York: Bantam Books, 1980. A diary of a widower's grief.

Lord, Janice H. *No Time for Goodbyes: Coping with Sorrow, Anger and Injustice after a Tragic Death.* Ventura, Calif.: Pathfinder, 1990. A helpful book about coping with a sudden, violent death. Includes how to deal with the criminal justice system.

Lukas, Christopher, and Henry Seiden. *Silent Grief: Living in the Wake of Suicide.* New York: Charles Scribner's Sons, 1987. A psychologist and a man whose mother died by suicide offer emotional and practical help for survivors of suicide.

Magee, Doug. *What Murder Leaves Behind.* New York: Dodd, Mead & Co., 1983. Stories of several people in the aftermath of a homicide.

Metrick, S. B. *Crossing the Bridge: Creating Ceremonies for Grieving and Healing from Life's Losses.* Berkeley, Calif.: Celestial Arts, 1994. Discusses ceremonies to find wholeness in the face of loss.

Myers, Edward. *When Parents Die: A Guide for Adults.* New York: Viking/Penguin, 1986. A sensitive and informative book about the loss of a parent.

Rando, Therese A. *How To Go On Living When Someone You Love Dies.* New York: Lexington, 1988. Includes suggestions for ways to deal with sudden and anticipated death.

Shiff, Harriet Sarnoff. *Living Through Mourning: Finding Comfort and Hope When a Loved One Has Died.* New York: Viking, 1987. A guide through grief with emphasis on how to set up support groups.

Sontag, Susan. *Illness as Metaphor* and *AIDS and its Metaphors.* New York: Doubleday, Anchor Books, 1989. Reflections on social myths and stigmas of illness and AIDS.

Staudacher, C. *Beyond Grief: A Guide for Recovering from the Death of a Loved One.* Oakland Calif.: New Harbinger, 1987. Information about grieving and ways to survive specific types of death; also presents guidelines for creating support groups and offering support to others.

Tatelbaum, Judy. *The Courage to Grieve.* New York: Harper & Row, 1980. A clearly written book about the resolution of grief.

Wasserman, Marion Lee. *Searching for the Stork: One Couple's Struggle to Start a Family.* New York: New American Library, 1988. A stirring personal account of a couple's struggle with still-birth, miscarriages, and genetic problems.

Wolfelt, A. D. *Understanding Grief: Helping Yourself Heal.* Muncie, Ind.: Accelerated Development, 1992. Based on the philosophy that we do not get over grief but learn to live with it. Helps the reader to become an expert on his or her experiences of grieving.

Zagaranski, D. *Stuck for Words: What to Say When Someone is Grieving.* Melbourne, Australia: Hill of Content, 1994. Gives suggestions for the ordinary person on what to do or say to someone who is grieving.

Fiction and Poetry

Berg, Elizabeth. *Talk before Sleep.* New York: Dell, 1994. A friend recollects the illness and death of her best friend from cancer.

Davies, Phyllis. *Grief: Climb toward Understanding. Self-Help When You Are Struggling.* New York: Carol Communications, 1988. A collection of poetry begun by the author when her thirteen-year-old son was killed in a plane crash. Includes helpful checklists of what to do when someone dies.

Hoffman, Alice. *At Risk.* New York: Putnam, 1990. A child's illness and death from AIDS and how it affects her family and friends.

Kenney, Susan. *In Another Country.* New York: Viking. 1984. Living with a spouse who has a life-threatening illness.

McEwan, Ian. *The Child in Time.* Boston: Houghton Mifflin, 1987. Grieving the
    kidnapping of a child.
Moffat, Mary Jane. *In the Midst of Winter: Selections from the Literature of
    Mourning.* New York: Random House, 1982. A collection of poetry and
    prose which the author gathered after her husband's death.
Ray, David. *Sam's Book.* Middletown, Conn.: Weslyan University Press, 1987. A
    father mourns his son's death and remembers their life together through
    poetry.
Shilts, R. *And the Band Played On.* New York, St. Martin's, 1987. A revealing
    book about the myths and realities of AIDS.
Ziesk, Edra. *Acceptable Losses.* Dallas: Southern Methodist University, 1996.
    Love story about a young woman who loses her mother and a man whose
    father disappears. A blending of beauty and grief.

Books for Professionals

Bertman, Sandra L. *Facing Death: Images, Insights and Interventions.* New
    York: Taylor and Francis, 1991. Discussion of how we feel and think about
    death by drawing on the arts and humanities as well as on literary works and
    pop culture images of death, loss, and suffering.
Bowlby, John. *Attachment and Loss,* Vol. III, *Loss.* New York: Basic Books,
    1980. A study of loss and bereavement by a man who is famous for his work
    on describing how infants make attachments to mothers.
Dane, Barbara O., and Samuel O. Miller. *AIDS; Intervening with Hidden
    Grievers.* Westport, Conn: Auburn House, 1992. A serious examination of
    the special issues of those who mourn deaths from AIDS.
Doka, K. J. *Disenfranchised Grief: Recognizing Hidden Sorrow.* Lexington,
    Mass.: Lexington Books, 1989. Insights into the grief of socially stigmatized
    groups.
Janoff-Bulman, Ronnie. *Shattered Assumptions: Toward a New Psychology of
    Trauma.* New York: The Free Press, 1992. Examines the impact of traumatic
    events on the lives of the victims. Explores fundamental assumptions about
    the world as safe, kind, and meaningful.
Parkes, Colin M., and Robert S. Weiss. *Recovery from Bereavement.* New York:
    Basic, 1983. A study of adult reactions in various circumstances of loss.
Rando, Therese A. *Grief, Dying and Death.* Champaign, Ill.: Research Press,
    1984. A thorough resource for persons working with the grieving and dying.
———. *Treatment of Complicated Mourning.* Champaign, Ill: Research Press,
    1993. Describes the assessment and treatment of bereavement in adults with
    special emphasis on traumatic death.

Raphael, Beverly. *The Anatomy of Bereavement.* New York: Basic Books, 1983. A classic study of bereavement.

Redmond, Lula. *Surviving When Someone You Love was Murdered: A Professional's Guide to Group Grief Therapy for Families and Friends of Murder Victims.* Clearwater, Fla.: Psychological Consultation and Education Services, 1989. Examines issues of survival after a murder and offers a program for families and friends of murder victims.

Silverman, Phyllis. *Widow to Widow.* New York: Springer, 1986. Explains the theory behind and the growth of mutual help groups for widows.

Worden, William. *Grief Counseling and Grief Therapy: A Handbook for the Mental Health Professional.* 2nd ed. New York: Springer, 1991. Describes ways to help clients accomplish tasks of mourning; outlines role plays for training; includes a chapter on grieving traumatic losses.

Appendix C
ABOUT THE AUTHOR
AND COLLABORATOR

About the author

Marguerite Bouvard was an interdisciplinary professor for over twenty-five years. She holds a doctorate from Harvard University and is the author of a number of books in psychology, politics, women's studies, and poetry. She has written articles on coping with grief and chronic illness and is a frequent speaker on these topics. She was a fellow at the Bunting Institute and at the Wellesley Center for Research on Women and is a resident scholar with the Women's Studies Program at Brandeis University.

About the collaborator

Evelyn Gladu, M.Ed., is in private practice as a psychotherapist. She facilitates groups for people who have lost a loved one to homicide. Drawing on her seventeen years of experience with bereaved persons, she conducts training for professionals and also trains people to facilitate groups on grief and loss. She is currently exploring alternative approaches to assist people in healing loss and trauma wounds.